RECONNECT

RECONNECT

Building School Culture for Meaning, Purpose, and Belonging

DOUG LEMOV
HILARY LEWIS
DARRYL WILLIAMS
DENARIUS FRAZIER

JB JOSSEY-BASS™
A Wiley Brand

Jossey-Bass
A Wiley Imprint
111 River St, Hoboken, NJ 07030
www.josseybass.com

Jossey-Bass books and products are available through most bookstores. To contact Jossey-Bass directly, call our Customer Care Department within the U.S. at 800-956-7739, outside the U.S. at +1 317 572 3986, or fax +1 317 572 4002.

Wiley also publishes its books in a variety of electronic formats and by print-on-demand. Some material included with standard print versions of this book may not be included in e-books or in print-on-demand. If this book refers to media such as a CD or DVD that is not included in the version you purchased, you may download this material at http://booksupport.wiley.com. For more information about Wiley products, visit www.wiley.com.

Library of Congress Cataloging-in-Publication Data

Names: Lemov, Doug, 1967- author. | Lewis, Hilary (Educational consultant), author. | Williams, Darryl (Educational consultant), author. | Frazier, Denarius, author.
Title: Reconnect : building school culture for meaning, purpose, and belonging / Doug Lemov, Hilary Lewis, Darryl Williams, Denarius Frazier.
Description: Hoboken, NJ : Jossey-Bass, [2023] | Includes index.
Identifiers: LCCN 2022029599 (print) | LCCN 2022029600 (ebook) | ISBN 9781119739975 (paperback) | ISBN 9781119739982 (adobe pdf) | ISBN 9781119739999 (epub)
Subjects: LCSH: School environment—United States. | Public schools—United States. | Belonging (Social psychology)—United States. | Social learning--United States. | Affective education—United States. | COVID-19 Pandemic, 2020—Influence.
Classification: LCC LC210.5 .L46 2023 (print) | LCC LC210.5 (ebook) | DDC 370.15/80973--dc23/eng/20220815
LC record available at https://lccn.loc.gov/2022029599
LC ebook record available at https://lccn.loc.gov/2022029600

COVER DESIGN: PAUL MCCARTHY
COVER IMAGES: © SHUTTERSTOCK | HOBBITART

To all of our colleagues who have given

so much on behalf of students during an unprecedented time.

Contents

Acknowledgments

In the course of writing this book we have leaned heavily on the support and wisdom of others. This includes the members of the Teach Like a Champion team and our partners around the world, who have humbly kept their schools and classrooms open to our team for learning during an unprecedented time in education. Many of our colleagues took time out of their very busy work trying to run the best schools and classrooms possible in the wake of a national crisis to discuss the experiences and challenges they were living through. They include David Adams, Jen Brimming, Eric Diamon, Samantha Eaton, Charlie Friedman, Stacey Shells Harvey, Jody Jones, Rhiannon Lewis DeFeo, Shawn Mangar, Ishani Mehta, Lagra Newman, Rebecca Olivarez, Eddie Rangel, Elisha Roberts, and Bill Spirer.

In addition, several colleagues read parts of this book in draft form and offered insightful and often invaluable feedback. They include Robert Pondiscio, Russ Roberts, Tracey Schirra, and Erica Woolway. The videos included here were edited and prepared with skill and wisdom by John Costello. We are grateful to the team at John Wiley & Sons for their flexibility as the idea for this book evolved and their knowledge throughout the process of writing it. Amy Fandrei and Pete Gaughan warrant special mention. Rafe Sagalyn did as he has done with all of the Teach Like a Champion team's books, and helped steer us steadily toward the book we needed and wanted to write.

We also wish to express some personal thanks.

Hilary wishes to thank to her family for their immeasurable love and support, and expresses her deepest gratitude to her mother, Linda Lewis, her first and most phenomenal teacher.

Darryl wishes to thank his family, particularly his children, Mia and Darryl, for their love, grace, and understanding as he travels the country directly supporting and learning from amazing educators.

Denarius wishes to thank his students, for all the countless lessons they have taught over the years; his teachers and mentors, for their patience, support, and guidance along the journey; and his family, for always believing in him and his ability to succeed.

Doug wishes to thank his wife, Lisa, and his children, Caden, Maia, and Willa, for their love, support, wisdom, and humor.

About the Authors

Doug Lemov is the founder and Chief Knowledge Officer of the Teach Like a Champion team, which designs and implements teacher training based on the study of high-performing teachers. He was formerly a managing director at Uncommon Schools.

Hilary Lewis is the senior director of Consulting and Partnerships with Teach Like a Champion. Hilary attributes her love of education to her first and best teacher—her mother.

Darryl Williams is CEO of Teach Like a Champion team. He previously served as the chief officer in the Office of School Leadership for Houston Independent School District, a regional superintendent with the Achievement First network, and a principal and teacher in Albany, New York.

Denarius Frazier is the principal of Uncommon Collegiate Charter High School in Brooklyn, New York, and serves as a senior advisor on the Teach Like a Champion Partnerships and Consulting Team.

See what the Teach Like a Champion team is up to at teachlikeachampion.org.

Introduction: What's the Problem?

After successive school years disrupted by masks, isolations, and mass experiments in remote teaching, educators at last returned to school last year to find that classrooms and students had changed.

In the first days of the return, perhaps we didn't see this fully. Yes, most of us knew that there would be yawning academic gaps. Most of us understood what the data have since clearly borne out: that despite often heroic efforts at remote instruction, the result has been a massive setback in learning and academic progress, with the costs levied most heavily on those who could least afford it,[1] and that it will take years, not months, to make up the loss. But at least we were all together again. We were on the road back.

As the days passed, though, a troubling reality emerged.

The students who came back had spent long periods away from peers, activities, and social interactions. For many young people—and their teachers—the periods of isolation had been difficult emotionally and psychologically. Some had lost loved ones, while others had to endure months in a house or apartment while everything they valued—tennis or track or drama or music, not to mention moments of sitting informally among friends and laughing—had suddenly evaporated from their lives.

Even if they had not experienced the worst of the pandemic, most were out of practice at the expectations, courtesies, and give-and-take of everyday life. Their social skills had declined. They looked the same—or at least we presumed they did behind the masks—but some seemed troubled and distant; some struggled to concentrate and follow directions. Some didn't know how to get along. They were easily frustrated and quick to give up. Not all of them, of course, but on net there was a clear trend. The media was suddenly full of stories of discipline problems, chronic disruptions, and historic levels of student absences. In schools where no one had ever had to think about how to deal with a fight, they burst into the open like brushfires.

At the time we needed good teaching the most, it was suddenly very difficult to accomplish, and young people seemed troubled and anxious. It didn't help that we were short-staffed, straining just to get classes covered. In the end it's possible that the first post-pandemic year was harder than the pandemic years themselves. The students who came back were not the students we'd had before the pandemic.

But, we argue, the story is more complex than it appeared even then. What had happened in the lives of our students wasn't just a protracted once-in-a-generation adverse event, but the combined effects of several large-scale, ground-shifting trends reshaping the fabric of students' lives. These events had begun before the pandemic, but they were often exacerbated by it. Their combined effects are significant, and probably not fully reversible. We can't turn back the clock. But they should cause us to plan and design our schools and classrooms differently going forward—not just for a year or two of "recovery" but perhaps more permanently.

In this introduction, we'll examine three unprecedented problems our young people face: 1) a crisis of mental health amid rising screen time, 2) a lack of trust in institutions, and 3) the challenge of balancing the benefits individualism with the benefits of collective endeavor in institutions that rely heavily on social contracts. We should note that this book is not all doom and gloom: the rest of it will be focused on solutions to the issues we describe. And we believe the solutions are out there. But first we have to be clear-eyed about where we stand.

A PANDEMIC WITHIN AN EPIDEMIC

Even before the pandemic, the psychologist Jean Twenge had found spiraling dosages of depression, anxiety, and isolation among teens. "I had been studying mental health and social behavior for decades and I had never seen anything like it," Twenge wrote in her 2017 book *iGen: Why Today's Super-Connected Kids Are Growing Up Less Rebellious, More Tolerant, Less Happy—and Completely Unprepared for Adulthood.*

This historic decline in the psychological well-being of young people coincided almost exactly with the precipitous rise of the smartphone and social media and more specifically with the moment when the proportion of social media users was high enough that any teenagers wishing to have normal social life no longer had an alternative but to become users themselves. It also coincided with the moment in time when the "Like" button was added to social media apps. As a result, social media use became far more compulsive and users far more dependent.

"The arrival of the smartphone has radically changed every aspect of teenagers' lives, from the nature of their social interactions to their mental health," Twenge and co-author Jonathan Haidt wrote in the *New York Times.*[2] "It's harder to strike up a casual conversation in the cafeteria or after class when everyone is staring down at a phone. It's harder to have a deep conversation when each party is interrupted randomly by buzzing, vibrating 'notifications.'" They quote the psychologist Sherry Turkle, who notes that we are, now, "forever elsewhere."

By the time Twenge published *iGen,* screen media use had doubled in ten years—across gender, race, and class—from an hour a day to two.[3]

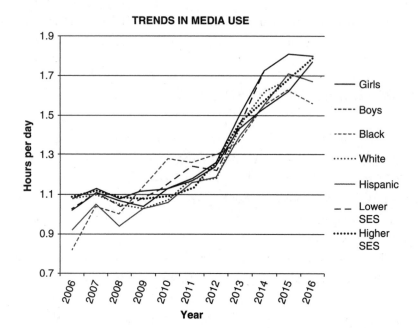

TRENDS IN MEDIA USE

Legend:
— Girls
---- Boys
---- Black
······ White
— Hispanic
– – Lower SES
······ Higher SES

Y-axis: Hours per day (0.7 to 1.9)
X-axis: Year (2006 to 2016)

By this point 97% of 12th graders (and 98% of 12th-grade girls) were then using social media. It was "about as universal an experience as you can get," Twenge noted. And these data predate the newest and most addictive social media apps, such TikTok, which was released in 2016 and whose influence is not fully reflected in it. But the results were still plenty alarming. Twenge and Haidt found that across 37 countries, teenage loneliness, which had been "relatively stable between 2000 and 2012, with fewer than 18% reporting high levels of loneliness," suddenly spiked as smartphones and social media proliferated. "In the six years after 2012, they wrote, "rates. . .roughly doubled in Europe, Latin America and the English-speaking countries."

This was already an epidemic reshaping every aspect of teen's lives. As the following chart shows, the average 12th grader in 2016 went out with friends less often than the average 8th grader ten years before, Twenge pointed out. Instead of hanging out at the shopping mall, meeting up at a McDonalds, or cruising around in cars, they were in their rooms interacting on social media (or gaming, especially if they are boys). And even when they were "out and about" they were often not fully present.

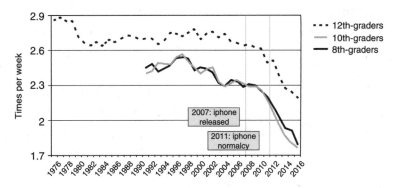

Going out without parents

The tendency of young people to socialize online and from their rooms instead of in person has had a wide variety of consequences—both good and bad, Twenge is careful to point out. Far fewer had sex, drank, or used drugs. The teenage pregnancy rate dropped to its lowest in decades. Teenagers became less likely to die in car accidents. But they didn't learn the responsibility and social skills you get from being out in public—having a job, doing volunteer work, meeting new people, learning to drive, even going to parties. (By the way, they did not spend any more time doing homework, in case you're wondering, which suggests that the common theory that school-related workload was the source of rising mental health issues is not likely true.) The number of young people who got insufficient sleep increased to unprecedented levels. And most of all, and far most importantly, rates of depression, anxiety, loneliness, and even suicide spiked suddenly to all-time highs, at rates Twenge had never seen the equal of.

Meanwhile, young people's intellectual lives were changing too. In competition with the cell phone and social media, the idea of reading a book for pleasure had all but disappeared. As recently as 1996, half of teens regularly read for pleasure; by 2017, only one teen in ten did. And reading had become a different activity. Those teens who did read mostly did so not as older generations did—via deep immersion in another world, with sustained empathy-building experiences and little interruption, for long periods of time—but as they do other activities: with their cell phones by their side interrupting them every few seconds with a "push" message. Their internal narrative, the one in which they discover why the caged bird sings, is mixed with equal amounts of reflection on what is up with the Kardashians and "Dude, where R you?? We R Over @ Byrons!"

Young people had traded social relationships for virtual ones, but at a high cost. The nature of virtual interactions conducted on social media is engineered by a third party—app creators—whose purpose is not to create true connection but dependence. As a result, even social acceptance on social media can be problematic. The Like button (first added to social media platforms in 2009) in particular is designed to manipulate our desire to connect socially to create product addiction. It creates "short-term, dopamine-driven feedback loops."[4] Getting a like communicates social approval and inclusion to us. This releases a bit of the same brain chemical (dopamine) released by other pleasurable activities. Social media algorithms ensure that the tiny chemical dividend is released on a *variable unpredictable reward schedule*: you don't know when and whether you will get the little burst of well-being that comes with a like; its schedule is unpredictable so you are socialized to constantly check for it. Such feedback loops highjack our evolutionary desire for social inclusion and translate it into digital currency. For teens, whose need for validation and affirmation is especially high, it makes their lives a constant public popularity contest.

Like buttons are catnip for brains, in other words, but the results of being unliked are worse. "It used to be that if you were bullied at school, you went home to your family. You were able to leave that negative environment. You were safe. You got a break from it. That allowed you to deal with it. Now if you are bullied online, it's in your pocket. It's in your room with you. You are never free. You are never safe," noted Cristina Fink, a Rowan University psychologist, in a recent conversation.

In 2017, Twenge had found that the most reliable antidote to the negative effects of social media and extensive screen use was sustained, in-person social interaction—away from phones and in direct engagement with others. The most powerful effect was often in the little things: smiling at one another, sharing a laugh, working together to accomplish some small, shared task like blocking stage positions for Act 3, Scene 1. Young people who played sports were far less likely to experience anxiety and depression, because they had an extended and enforced break from their phones *and* because when they were off their phones, they had connection-building social interactions to balance them.

But the numbers of kids who engaged in organized activities was declining. By 2019, a report by Common Sense Media found that the average teen spent more than seven hours per day on screens. Nearly two-thirds spent more than four hours per day on screen media.[5] For almost 30%, the average was eight hours a day.[6]

And then in 2020, the pandemic hit, and everything that might have offered such an alternative to screen time suddenly disappeared. When youth were not in school, not at practice, or not at the mall with friends, they were on their phones. Common Sense Media updated its findings in March 2022, reporting that screen and social media use had risen sharply during the pandemic, with the average teen *and pre-teen* spending more than one extra hour on screen media on top of already intense levels of exposure. Daily screen use went up among tweens (ages 8 to 12) to five and a half hours a day on average and to more than eight and a half hours per day for teens (ages 13 to 18). Low-income families were hit hardest, with parents most likely to have to work in person and fewer resources to spend on alternatives to screens.

At these levels of use, smartphones are catastrophic to the well-being of young people. "It's not an exaggeration to describe [this generation] as being on the brink of the worst mental-health crisis in decades," Twenge writes.

And the problems aren't limited to mental health. All that time on screen degrades attention and concentration skills, making it harder to focus fully on any task and to maintain that focus. This is not a small thing. Attention is central to every learning task, and the quality of attention paid by learners shapes the outcome of learning endeavors. The more rigorous the task, the more it requires what experts call directed (or sometimes selective) attention—defined as "the ability to inhibit distractions and sustain attention and to shift attention appropriately," according to Michael Manos, clinical director of the Center for Attention and Learning at Cleveland Clinic. In other words, to learn well you must be able to maintain self-discipline about what you pay attention to.

The problem with cell phones is that young people using them switch tasks every few seconds. Better put, they *practice* switching tasks every few seconds, so they become more accustomed to states of half-attention, more expectant of new stimulus every few seconds. When a sentence or a problem requires slow, focused analysis, their minds are already glancing around for something new and more entertaining.

The brain rewires itself constantly based on how it functions. This idea, known as neuroplasticity, means that the more time young people spend in constant half-attentive task switching, the harder it becomes for them to maintain the capacity for sustained periods of intense concentration. After a time, a brain habituated to impulsivity rewires to become more prone to that state. "If kids' brains become accustomed to constant changes, the brain finds it difficult to adapt to a nondigital activity where things don't move quite as fast," Manos continued.

Though all of us are at risk of this, young people are especially susceptible. Their prefrontal cortex—the region of the brain that exerts impulse control and self-discipline—isn't fully developed until age 25. In 2017, a study found that undergraduates (more cerebrally mature than our K–12 students and so with stronger impulse control) "switched to a new task on average every 19 seconds when they were online." It's a safe conjecture that younger students can sustain even less attention.

In other words, any time young people are on a screen, they are in an environment that habituates them to states of low attention and constant task switching. At first our phones fracture our attention when we use them, but after a time our minds are rewired for distraction. Soon enough our phones are within us.

LOSS OF FAITH IN INSTITUTIONS

Along with its effect on the lives of students and their social media usage, the pandemic has overlapped with and probably exacerbated another important social trend affecting students, schools, and educators: declining levels of trust in institutions. In their November 2020 report, *Democracy in Dark Times*,[7] professors James Hunter, Carl Bowman, and Kyle Puetz describe a "slowly evolving crisis of credibility for all of America's institutions." While the clearest places of declining credibility are (in this study and others) government and the media, declining faith in "the government's ability to solve problems," as the authors put it, also affects other institutions of public life, including schools.

The long-term trend, which began in the latter years of the 20th century but has accelerated since, shows citizens increasingly perceiving institutions as "incompetent" and "ethically suspect." This creates a legitimation crisis: people are far less likely to accept or support decisions from an institution they don't trust. They are less likely to contribute their time and effort to its initiatives. All this, of course, makes it harder to run those institutions effectively.

By mid-pandemic, the results of this disaffection ran deep. Half of all Americans, regardless of politics, said that there were days when they "felt like a stranger in my own country."

We should pause here to define the word "institutions." The political analyst Yuval Levin defines them as "the durable forms…of what we do together. They're clumps of people organized around a particular end, and organized around an ideal and a way of achieving that important goal."[8] The range of institutions in American life is broad. An institution can be specific (a school district) or more abstract (public education).

The decline of faith in institutions affects schools directly, since they themselves are institutions. Schools can no longer count on receiving the goodwill and trust of the parents they serve. We can see this trend clearly in the data. The Pew Research Center, for example, regularly asks a wide sample of Americans about their faith in specific authority figures in various institutions. In early 2022[9] they found that, for example, faith in journalists had declined steeply. In 2018 more than half of Americans—55%—said they trusted journalists "a great deal" or "a fair amount," while 44% said "not too much or not at all." By 2022 the number had flipped: 40% of Americans trusted journalists, 60% did not. The level of mistrust in the profession increased by 50% in four years. Faith in elected officials declined slightly from already dismal numbers (perhaps there wasn't much farther those numbers could go).

These were among the professions with the greatest erosion of trust, but notice that the data also ask specifically about public school principals. There too we see significant declines. In 2018, 80% of Americans trusted school principals a fair amount or more. Only 20% were at "not much confidence" or less. In 2022 the trust numbers had declined to 64% and the mistrust numbers were at 35%. They had almost doubled.

It's worth noting that within the general trend—declining trust— the numbers show two subtrends. The first is increasing skepticism from the majority of parents. It's going to take a little more work to make them see they can believe in their school and its capacity to get its core work of educating children done well. Then there is a separate trend of people who feel outright mistrust. These are families who may fight the school's policies if their skepticism is not effectively addressed.

This is critically important. Like the nations they are a part of, schools are institutions that rely on a social contract to do their work. Participants agree to accept relatively minor restrictions on their own actions in order to participate in the larger, more important benefits that accrue when everyone follows those rules. As a citizen, I accept that I will not steal my neighbor's possessions, no matter how much I want them. In return, I live in a society where everyone's possessions are secure, where it is worth having possessions because you are likely to keep them, and where people invent things worth having because others will value them, which they are only able to do if they can protect them. Want a vibrant entrepreneurial economy? Start with property rights.

Schools rely on a version of this social contract as well. As a student I accept that I will not shout out things in class and disrupt instruction so that others can learn; I benefit from the fact that I now have a space in which I can plausibly aspire to become what I dream of in life.

Public confidence in scientists and medical scientists has declined over the last year

% of U.S. adults who have _____ of confidence in the following groups to act in the best interests of the public

● A great deal ● A fair amount ○ Not too much/No confidence at all

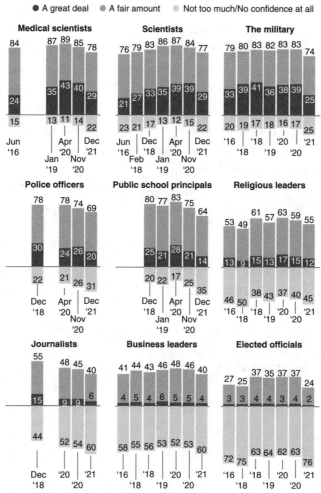

Note: Respondents who did not give an answer are not shown.
Source: Survey conducted Nov. 30–Dec. 12, 2021.
"Americans' Trust in Scientists, Other Groups Declines"
PEW RESEARCH CENTER

As a parent I accept that my child will be asked to accept this social contract. This is to say that every school lives or dies on people's willingness to accept that authority is not just different from authoritarianism but benign and in fact beneficial—necessary to the construction of a social contract. That contract only works when participants trust the leader of the school to determine the terms of the contract. It does not take a majority rejecting the terms of a social contract to erode its viability. A handful is enough.

While we are talking about trust in schools, it's worth looking at one more data point. The Pew data above are specific to principals. How do people feel about their schools overall? The polling organization Gallup has been asking Americans the following question since 1973:[10] "I am going to read you a list of institutions in American society. Please tell me how much confidence you, yourself, have in each one—a great deal, quite a lot, some or very little."

Here are the responses when respondents were asked about public schools.

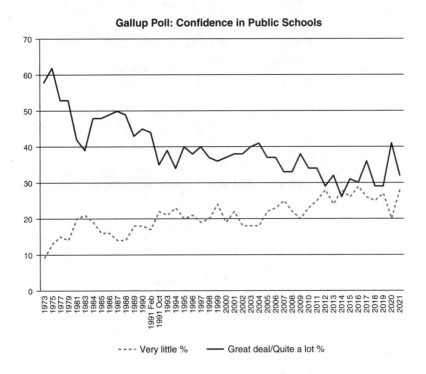

Gallup Poll: Confidence in Public Schools

- - - - Very little %　　——— Great deal/Quite a lot %

The long-term trend is clear. Over the 50 years that data have been gathered, confidence in public schools has declined steadily but pervasively. The percentage of respondents who felt "quite a lot" of confidence or more has dropped by half. Even in the first decade of the 21st century, numbers were routinely 10 points higher than they were in 2021.

This larger trend was broken by a short uptick of goodwill in 2020—our long pandemic year. Americans appeared to be grateful for the efforts of schools to respond to the crisis and were more forgiving and appreciative in their responses. But that uptick was a brief honeymoon. The data snapped back quickly.

The converse trend is also clear. The percentage of respondents who feel *very little* trust in their public schools has almost tripled in the years since the survey began. The lines now nearly touch. The average parent is just as likely to start at a point of mistrust as he or she is at a point of trust. Things are likely to stay that way or even get worse. Many parents' experience during the pandemic—their frustrations or outright anger with masking or distance learning, the historical rates at which they withdrew their children—will not soon fade from memory. Those are difficult conditions under which to hope to build and defend a new social contract. Schools face a clear challenge in the fact that the families they intend to serve feel less faith in their reliability, skill, and trustworthiness.

Meanwhile, a secondary challenge also looms. As schools struggle to operate in a climate of mistrust, the institutions composing the ecosystem schools work within—religious institutions, cultural institutions, those institutions that offer programs like sports and music and drama that connect young people throughout their community—are also struggling.

One result of the increased lack of trust in these institutions is lowered levels of participation in them. As a result, people are more and more likely to connect online instead of in person, say at a church or an activity or even a community meeting. Young people are less and less likely to infer codes of mutuality and cooperation from those institutions. In those places, they are more likely to meet with people whose beliefs and values do not mirror their own. Without them, they run the risk of living in an echo chamber where initial perceptions are easily reinforced and where people who disagree are vilified, their motives suspected.

Individuals who live in these sorts of environments rarely have cause to challenge or change their ideas and perceptions. Jonathan Haidt's research in *The Righteous Mind* makes this clear: people change their minds when people whom they trust and feel a connection to express a differing perspective. An adversary castigating you or impugning your motives almost never changes your mind or broadens your views. You change your mind or moderate your assumptions because someone whom you admire or appreciate in some other way holds a different opinion. The fact that people—particularly teenagers—are now less and less likely to meet and connect with people who are less like them in thought or background means the risk of increased cultural isolation (and probably political polarization) as well.[11] The declining trust in institutions not only makes schools' missions harder but also exacerbates the isolating effects of social media on students.

THE TENSION BETWEEN INDIVIDUALISM AND BELONGING

The final key challenge students and schools face today is how increasingly individualistic our culture is, often at the cost of communal orientation and mutual obligation.

The Dutch social psychologist Geert Hofstede defined individualism as "a preference for a loosely knit social framework in which individuals are expected to take care of only themselves and their immediate families." Its opposite, collectivism, is "a preference for a tightly knit society in which it is understood and expected that members of the group will look after each other in exchange for mutual loyalty." Hofstede ranked societies on a scale of 1 (maximum collectivism) to 100 (maximum individualism). China—a society grounded in Confucian roots that stress principles of mutual obligation—scores a 20. Brazil, also a relatively collectively inclined society, scores a 38. Western nations tend to be the most individualistic. Germany scores a 67. But the US scores the highest of any nation: a 91, with the UK not far behind.

Not only is the United States currently the most individualistic society in the world, it's also a safe bet that we are the most individualistic society in the history of humankind. As you might guess, the shift to modernity has been a shift away from a collective mentality. As Jonathan Haidt puts it, most societies historically chose the "sociocentric" answer—a belief in communal bonds—until in the 20th century, when "individual rights expanded rapidly, and consumer culture spread." An individualistic orientation replaced a "sociocentric" one. In other words, individuality is a modernist tendency.

We want to be clear: we're good with individualism. Much of its rise is a reaction to the destruction of individual rights and freedoms demonstrated by totalitarian regimes of the 20th century. It's hard to watch the erosion of individualism in Russia and China today and want to trade.

But we also think it's important to recognize the ways in which our culture's extreme emphasis on individualism, even with its upsides, might benefit from moderation—and might cause us to overlook ways of doing things that might create a stronger sense of belonging and that might be therapeutic in times of difficulty and disconnection.

After all, as highly individualistic societies, we are temperamentally resistant to many of the key tenets by which purposeful groups are formed. The social order, Jonathan Haidt writes in *The Righteous Mind*, is "built around the protection of individuals and their freedoms" and far less so our mutual obligations. "Any rule that limits personal freedom can be questioned," Haidt writes. "If it doesn't protect somebody from harm then it can't be morally justified."

Those are challenging terms on which to build community and mutual obligation. Talking to people in a highly individualistic society about sacrifice and the broader good—in society, in schools, in a pandemic—is challenging and invariably runs up against resistance. But a viable social contract in which people routinely defer and relinquish their short-term desires and impulses (I don't feel like doing what my teacher asks) to the greater common good of a shared endeavor (if I do that I keep her from teaching myself and others) is a necessary condition to schools that foster achievement and well-being.

WE'RE OPTIMISTIC, ACTUALLY

We apologize if the first part of this introduction made you anxious. It feels at times like a litany of woes. At times it was hard going, emotionally, to write it. But things get brighter from here. Now that we have framed the problem we can get down to solutions. And there *are* solutions, we believe: clear steps schools can take to respond to each of these challenges successfully. We are deep in the forest. It might seem hopeless. But there are breadcrumbs to follow. It's not going to be easy, but we humbly hope we can help schools find a path out of the woods.

Consider, for example, a meeting we recently observed—or more precisely three of us observed. The fourth, Denarius, was running it. The meeting was with a group of students at Uncommon Collegiate Charter High School in Brooklyn, where Denarius is the principal. He was soliciting his student's input on their experience regarding a series of school policies and decisions in preparation for a strategic planning session with his co-leader.

It was a case study in what something we'll discuss more extensively in Chapter 1, *process fairness*, can look like. In some cases, Denarius wanted the students' input on decisions he was actively making or thinking of revising. In other cases, he just wanted to know what students thought of things that seemed fine to him. How should morning arrival work? What should the latest tweaks to cell phone and uniform policies be? What events and activities in the school did the students value? If they had a magic wand and could change one thing about the school, what would it be and why?

In one case he had a specific purpose, and in the other he was just in the habit of constantly gathering input, of listening well as a matter of course. It's worth noting that in the first case, listening and asking students' opinions *did not imply that he would agree or give them what they wanted*. Several students argued for the convenience of scanning into school as soon as they arrived, then having space to change into full uniform and proceed to class. Denarius listened carefully. He was smiling. He explained that in a previous year, they had tried that had students scan into school as the first step in the system, but had changed it after many students had been late to classes because they'd lingered in the cafeteria (and stairs). Scanning into school last and outside of the cafeteria had resulted in higher rates of students being on time to class. "Do you want to see the data?" Denarius asked, again warmly and smiling. In his mind it was a good thing that students wanted to ask about the policies, even though he was confident he knew what the right decision was on this specific question.

Still, the fact that he valued them enough to constantly ask their opinions and to show them data about the decisions he made built process fairness. The students felt like the school valued their opinions and took them into account. It resulted in trust and appreciation *even though many, even most, of the decisions were not what students had asked for.* (Some of them were. "I always try to find at least one 'yes,'" Denarius said.) Suddenly, they saw the reasons more clearly, how they aligned to their goals and weren't arbitrary. They not only accepted the decisions; they understood and came to agree with them. In the end, many students appeared happy not to get what they asked for!

There wasn't anything rocket science-y about the meeting Denarius held. Just careful listening and taking the time to ask and explain—and being okay with constructive criticism from young people. He and a colleague were taking notes when students spoke. That small detail said: *Your words are important to me.* So did their ability to talk about values and goals without talking down to young people. Laughing occasionally helped too—laughter tells people we are connected. So did the fact that he was smiling. Students who care enough to discuss or even argue about policies are engaged students, and that's a good thing. They should feel that we listen and value that, whether or not they get their way. In fact, a good rule of thumb, we think—for running schools and possibly more broadly—is that the most important time to listen is when you think you disagree.

We bring up this example to show that it's possible to combat the effects of the pandemic, the epidemic, and the rising tide of mistrust that our students are facing, and to help them feel a sense of belonging in their schools. We will come back to the idea of belonging in this book—to the question of how we create schools that foster it in students. When schools do that, we argue, they create community—a mutual expectation of shared benefit and shared obligation. When those things happen, you have something like a village—an entity that sits within a larger society, that has a distinct culture, a social contract of reciprocity, and which prepares people to thrive as a group within it and in the larger society as a whole.

Every day, people in schools do things like what Denarius did in his meeting. Our goal in this book is to source them and describe them for you. We'll tell you about how Charlie Friedman and his staff in Nashville redesigned extracurriculars to build a greater sense of belonging at his school, Nashville Classical. We'll tell you how Sam Eaton and her colleagues at Cardiff High School in Cardiff, Wales, reengineered recess to allow students to connect and build relationships and relationship-building skills. We'll show you videos of Ben Hall teaching his students to talk to rather than past each other so they feel a sense of belonging while they learn.

It's a challenging time, but this is a hopeful book that seeks to honor and share the problem-solving already done by educators like you.

We should note that the schools whose ideas we draw on have set out to build a wide variety of cultures in a wide variety of ways. They are all inclusive and academic cultures, but there is not just one version of what a school culture characterized by such things looks like. There are variety of ways this can be built. What these school cultures have in common is that they are all *carefully designed and implemented*. There are principles to help a school do this, but no one "program," no one model of what a school that helps young people thrive must look like.

With that in mind, here's a bit more about what's ahead.

In Chapter 1, "How We're Wired Now," we'll explore more deeply the challenges we've raised in the introduction and begin pointing to some solutions. We'll try to draw on what we know about the evolutionary importance of connection and belonging to human well-being, what we know about how smartphone technology has affected young people, and what we know about rebuilding trust in schools as institutions to sketch the path forward.

In Chapter 2, "A Great Unwiring," we'll dig deeper into technology. We start with some of its benefits, but we'll also discuss its downsides and look practically at the reality: we need to restrict cell phone access during the school day. We know that won't make us popular, and that's why we spend a significant amount of time explaining the *why* behind the unwiring we think our students deserve. Doing so is going to be difficult, so we'll get practical about how schools can make such a hard decision successfully.

In Chapter 3, "Rewiring the Classroom," we'll start talking about how schools can design themselves to best serve students given where they are now, and we'll begin with the classroom. We'll show how we can "wire" classrooms to constantly send signals of belonging to students, even as teachers retain their critical focus on academics. Classrooms must ensure that students feel connected and that they learn as much as possible. We cannot allow it to become a choice between these things. Many readers will be familiar with Doug's *Teach Like a Champion* books. Chapter 3 discusses how to apply, adapt, and prioritize some of the techniques from that book, given the realities of here and now. We'll share videos too. There's a lot more to beating the current crisis than outstanding day-to-day teaching, but in the end, we can't win the struggle without it.

In Chapter 4, "Wiring the School for Socio-emotional Learning," we'll talk about rewiring the socioemotional work of schools. We'll focus on character education and the instilling of virtues that promote individual and group well-being. We'll share powerful research on the value of resilience and gratitude and how to use them to help ensure that students are happy and connected and fulfilled.

In Chapter 5, "Case Studies in the Process of Rewiring," we'll talk about the planning processes that are required to design and operate our schools more effectively in response to the current challenge and will examine a few case studies: how extracurricular activities could be redesigned, how culture could be redesigned, and in particular how we could rewire what we do when student behavior breaks down.

We close with an afterword, "How We Choose," a brief coda on the role that school choice might play in building more responsive and connected schools. Throughout the book we discuss the importance of a social contract to a viable institution—people have to accept sacrifices of personal freedoms in order to achieve shared mutual gains. Doing that is harder in a more fractured society. But a broader vision of choice where parents select schools for their purposes could help us to give more families more of what they want and massively reduce the practical difficulty of running excellent schools at the time we need them most.

Notes

1. https://emilyoster.net/wp-content/uploads/MS_Updated_Revised.pdf; https://www.nytimes.com/2022/05/05/briefing/school-closures-covid-learning-loss.html among others
2. Jean Twenge and Jonathan Haidt, "This Is Our Chance to Pull Teenagers Out of the Smartphone Trap," *New York Times,* July 31, 2021, https://www.nytimes.com/2021/07/31/opinion/smartphone-iphone-social-media-isolation.html
3. Two hours a day may not seem like much—by the end of Chapter 1 it will seem positively quaint—but 2 hours a day times 7 days a week times 52 weeks a year means 728 hours. Leave 8 hours for sleep and divide by the remaining 16 hours in a day and that's 45 days—45 days of not playing soccer, being in the school play, reading, or spending time with friends, and replacing it with something that creates anxiety, isolation, and unhappiness.
4. https://sitn.hms.harvard.edu/flash/2018/dopamine-smartphones-battle-time/
5. https://www.cnn.com/2019/10/29/health/common-sense-kids-media-use-report-wellness/index.html
https://www.nytimes.com/2022/03/24/well/family/child-social-media-use.html#:~:text=On%20average%2C%20daily%20screen%20use,(ages%2013%20to%2018)

6. It's often difficult to break out how much of that is social media use because teens are constantly switching back and forth among apps. Surely the time is fractured and almost always with social media "on the brain." It's also worth noting that these data are based on self-report. The real numbers are probably higher.

7. https://iasculture.org/research/publications/democracy-in-dark-times

8. https://www.hoover.org/research/importance-institutions-yuval-levin-1

9. https://www.pewresearch.org/science/2022/02/15/americans-trust-in-scientists-other-groups-declines/

10. https://news.gallup.com/poll/1597/confidence-institutions.aspx

11. Jonathan Haidt discusses the connection between social media and political tension and polarization here: https://www.theatlantic.com/magazine/archive/2022/05/social-media-democracy-trust-babel/629369/

Chapter 1

How We're Wired Now

The beauty and tragedy of the modern world is that it eliminates many situations that require people to demonstrate a commitment to collective good.

—Sebastian Junger

In the introduction, we laid out three major challenges facing our students and schools: our need for belonging in an age of individualism, the smart-phone induced mental health crisis, and a broader lack of trust in institutions. Those arguments will inform the solutions we outline in the rest of this book. In this chapter, we'll explain the challenges they pose in greater depth and begin to explore some ways schools can use an understanding of them to rewire the ways they design interactions with students and even with their families.

ARGUMENT ONE: THE IMPERATIVE OF BELONGING

One of the most important things to understand about human beings is that we have evolved to form ourselves into groups with mutual responsibility and shared purpose, and to crave the feelings of belonging, meaning, and community such group membership creates. This profoundly shapes our motivations and desires—even when, as is often the case, we don't realize it.

The desire for belonging comes to us via a million or so years of evolution—both human and, before that, hominid. When we glance backwards at that process, we tend to see it through the lens of our contemporary individualism. That is, we explain the processes of becoming "us" by focusing on the critical role of *individual* traits and characteristics. In the simplest possible terms, we believe that we prospered thanks to our big brains, bipedal posture, and opposable thumbs. And while that's undoubtedly true, it's only part of the story. Just as crucial to the success of our ancestors was the building of purposeful, cooperative, and mutually responsible groups.

Through eons of prehistory, to be a hominid standing alone on the grassland with a big brain and a host of exceptional attributes was nonetheless to starve to death or become something else's meal, probably very quickly. Humans alone are weak and slow and far outclassed by a host of rivals in the tools of hunting and defense. But to be standing on the grassland as part of a small group of humans capable of sustained coordination, loyalty, and cooperation—a group that could successfully pursue prey in a coordinated manner for hours at a stretch; a group that would stick together when something with claws and teeth attacked—to form such a group was to become, suddenly, an apex predator. *The* apex predator.

For the overwhelming majority of our existence, only humans who were able to form productive groups and facilitate their successful inclusion in them survived. Those who failed to join, those who made groups that splintered, those who were kicked out of groups, did not survive. We are individualists now, all of us—particularly those of us in the United States and the United Kingdom—but for most of our evolution, too much individualism was a death sentence.

Across thousands of generations of selection, the imperative of group formation was wired into us as strongly and profoundly as the instincts to mate and nurture our young. That's the way evolution works. We must be drawn to the survival imperatives without knowing it. It has to be bred in the bone.

The importance of rock throwing, described by William von Hippel in his remarkable study of evolutionary group dynamics, *The Social Leap,* is a case study. Rock throwing, or more precisely *group* rock throwing, is "the most important military invention of all time," von Hippel argues, and one of the most critical breakthroughs in the cognitive development of humankind.

We no longer think of rocks as deadly weapons, but well into the 19th century, von Hippel points out, professional soldiers bearing firearms were frequently forced to retreat with casualties in the face of indigenous peoples armed with nothing other than rocks. Even a rifle column was occasionally no match for a score of individuals who had cleverly surrounded it and were pelting away with brutal accuracy from carefully coordinated positions.

In the context of evolutionary history, von Hippel writes, cooperative rock throwing allowed a weaker species to defend itself from, and even to hunt, bigger, faster, or stronger adversaries for the first time. Suddenly humans could attack or defend from a distance—a position that allows for far greater safety. Fifteen humans might prevail over a lion in close combat but only at the likely cost of several members of the group, but fifteen humans throwing rocks at the lion offers a potential triumph at defense or even conquest, with far better odds of survival for each individual and therefore more reliably, more effectively, and more aggressively. It turns prey into predator. At last humans were not among the weakest species—if *and only if* they could achieve mutual cooperation.[1]

Individuals who learned to work cooperatively in this manner were at an enormous advantage, and, von Hippel notes, "evolution would have favored any subsequent psychological changes that supported the quality of the group's collective response. Our ancestors who could be counted on by others to be cooperative reaped a great reward as a result." Soon enough the competition was among groups within the species, and once again selection would have rewarded those groups that were most successful at cooperation and reciprocity.

The individuals who survived and thrived were those who were able to form groups that stuck together even under duress, but this only worked if the overwhelming majority of group members could be relied upon to embrace mutualism. We evolved to constantly seek groups where we feel the pull of mutual responsibility, where we see evidence that complex tasks can be achieved reliably, where trust and cooperation are understood. Once we find such a group, we continually look for confirmation that we are members in good standing or, on the other hand, signs that we may be pushed out. To our evolutionary selves, being cast out is a death sentence. To a slightly lesser degree, so is being in a group not capable of mutual defense, coordination, and loyalty. Groupishness was (and is) of the highest importance to us because it was so utterly central to our survival.

Only in the plural form were humans the winners of natural selection, in other words, and even if the importance of the group to our success now seems far less relevant to us, we are wired still to attend powerfully to group norms and to fear isolation, separation, and the possibility that we might be ostracized. "Individuals aren't really individuals," observes Sandy Pentland, director of Connection Science at MIT,[2] or at least not exclusively so. Of course, throughout evolution we also competed as individuals within groups at the same time as we competed among groups: we competed for status within the group, for the right to choose mates.[3] But better from a selection perspective to be a mid-status member of a close-knit group than the alpha in a group that could not marshal unity and cooperation.

Evidence that the social nature of evolution is wired into us isn't far beneath the surface. Social isolation is stressful to us, and people who experience sustained loneliness and social disconnection suffer in both physical and mental health. BYU psychologist Julianne Holt-Lunstad studied the relationship of social connections to mortality rates and found that having a lack of social connections was equivalent to smoking 15 cigarettes a day.[4] Similarly, UCLA professor of medicine Steven Cole found that the immune systems of socially isolated individuals were less robust and less able to fight pathogens effectively.

Our anger is often another example of our groupishness. Humans are quickly angered by "free-riders"—those who break the code of mutualism and seek to reap the benefits of group membership without doing their part to contribute. Far more cultures are permissive of theft, for example—or fail to conceive of it as a problem—than are tolerant of free riding. Its censure is nearly universal, says von Hippel. When we sense that mutualism is breaking down, our instincts tell us that the group could come apart. That's among the biggest threats we can imagine.

We feel far safer when we constantly receive signals of reciprocity and belonging and—perhaps more interesting—when we send them. Generosity—especially generosity within close-knit groups—also exists in every culture on earth. It is almost always accompanied by feelings of satisfaction and happiness. We are happy and feel safe when we reconfirm our own connection to the group. After a few thousand generations, the psychological and emotional well-being that accompanies such behaviors has become deeply encoded.

Small Moments and the Gestures of Belonging

Belonging is among the most powerful human emotions, and Daniel Coyle discusses its role in modern group formation in his book *The Culture Code: The Secrets of Highly Successful Groups*. Belonging, he notes, is often built via small moments and seemingly insignificant gestures. In fact, it is *mostly* built that way. Cohesion and trust occur when group members send and receive small, frequently occurring signals of belonging. The accrual of these signals is almost assuredly more influential than grand statements of togetherness or dramatic gestures. "Our social brains light up when we receive a steady accumulation of almost invisible cues: we are close, we are safe, we share a future," Coyle writes. But it's not a one-time thing. Belonging is "a flame that needs to be continually fed by signals of connection."

A colleague of ours described a simple example of this when we visited her school in the days after the mask mandate was lifted in her area. "I'm trying to make sure I focus on eye contact and smiling," she said. "That *we* focus on rebuilding that habit as a staff, so kids see someone smiling at them when they walk down the hall and they know: this is my place."[5]

Smiling and making eye contact are two of the most important belonging cues. They are also indicative of the nature of belonging cues more broadly; they tend to be subtle and even fleeting in nature so they are easily overlooked. Saying "thank you" and engaging in ritual forms of civility—holding a door, letting someone else go first, shaking hands—are other examples. Holding the door or letting someone go first as you enter provides little if any practical benefit; like most acts of courtesy, it's really a signal: "I am looking out for you." It reaffirms connectedness. And it affects more than just the individual to whom you show courtesy. Coyle notes that in one study,[6] "a small thank you caused people to behave far more generously to a completely different person. This is because thank yous are not only expressions of gratitude. They're crucial belonging cues that generate a contagious sense of safety, connection and motivation."

When we respond to a belonging signal not just by signaling back to the person who sent it but by sending additional signals to other people, it is an example of what the political scholar Robert Keohane calls "diffuse reciprocity." "Specific reciprocity" is the idea that if I help you, you will help me to a roughly equal degree. It is often the first step in commercial or political exchange, but it tends to engender only limited levels of trust and connection. Diffuse (or generalized) reciprocity, however, is the idea that if I help you, someone else in the group will likely help me at some future point. "Diffuse reciprocity refers to situations in which equivalence is less strictly defined and one's partners in exchanges may be viewed as a group," Keohane writes.[7] Norms are important. When participating in or initiating diffuse reciprocity, I go out of my way to show I am not keeping score and don't require equal value in every transaction. I am trying to show that I think we are part of a group, that what goes around will come around.

This is why in many cultures and settings, nothing is more insulting than insisting on paying for what was freely given. It is responding to an offer of welcome or help—diffuse reciprocity—with a signal of specific reciprocity. It suggests "transaction" rather than "connection" and downgrades the other person's gesture.

Perhaps the most interesting thing about signals of gratitude and belonging, however, is that the true beneficiary is the sender. It makes us happy to be generous and welcoming in part because it makes us feel like good members of the community and, perhaps, like more secure members of the community as a result. As the French philosopher la Rochefoucauld observed, "We are better pleased to see those on whom we confer benefits than those from whom we receive them." Summarizing his research, von Hippel writes, "Life satisfaction is achieved by being embedded in your community and by supporting community members who are in need." Note the centrality of mutuality; there's equal emphasis on the psychological benefits of giving to the group as well as receiving from it.

Gratitude too is one of the most powerful human emotions. As Shawn Achor explains in his book *The Happiness Advantage,* expressing gratitude regularly has the effect of calling your (or your students') attention to its root causes. Done regularly this results in a "cognitive afterimage": you are more likely to see the thing you look for. If you expect to be thinking about and sharing examples of things you are grateful for, you start looking for them, scanning the world for examples of good things to appreciate. And so you notice more of them.

The psychologist Martin Seligman asked participants in a study to write down three things they were grateful for each day. They were less likely to experience depression and loneliness one, three, and six months later. "The better they got at scanning the world for good things to write down, the more good things they saw, without even trying, wherever they looked," Achor writes of the study. The world became a better place for them, one that valued them and stood ready to embrace them because they made a habit of noticing the signals it was sending. "Few things in life are as integral to our well-being [as gratitude]," Achor writes. "Consistently grateful people are more energetic, emotionally intelligent, forgiving, and less likely to be depressed, anxious, or lonely."

The fact that what we look for so profoundly alters our sense of the world is just one way that the eyes are, perhaps, the most critical tool for establishing belonging. Even their physiological structure shows how critical they are. Humans are the only primate with white sclera—the part of our eyes that surrounds our pupils. This is the case, von Hippel writes, because advertising our gaze allows for cooperation and coordination, and because it communicates our status within the group—all of which are far more important to a human than to a primate that is less absolutely reliant on cooperation and mutualism for survival (as all other primates are, even those that live in groups). "If I'm competing with other members of my group, I don't want them to know what I'm thinking, which means I don't want them to know where I am looking," von Hippel says. "Whether I'm eyeing a potential mate or a tasty fig, I'll keep it a secret so others don't get there first. But if I'm cooperating with other members of my group then I will want them to know where I am directing my attention. If a tasty prey animal comes along and I spot it first I want others to notice it too so we can work together to capture it."

Humans also compete *within* their groups, we've noted, and eye gaze, advertised to others via the whites of our eyes, also communicates stature and status within the group. Anyone who has ever given or received a flirtatious glance or participated in a locked-eye challenge can attest to this. "Our scleras . . . allow us to monitor the gazes of others with considerable precision," Bill Bryson notes in *The Body: A Guide for Occupants*. "You only have to move your eyeballs slightly to get a companion to look at, let's say, someone at a neighboring table in a restaurant." More potently, glances between and among fellow group members tell us whether we are respected and safe or resented, marginalized, or scorned. "Affirming eye contact is one of the most profound signals of belonging a human can send. Conversely, the lack of it could suggest that our inclusion is at risk."[8]

How valuable is the information carried within our gazes? A "genetic sweep" is the name for a physical change that confers such immense benefit on recipients that over time only people having the change prevail. Having white sclera—in other words, being able to communicate more with a look—is an example. There is no human group in any corner of the planet where the benefits of enhanced gaze information were not evolutionarily decisive.

Consider, in light of that, this photograph, which comes from a video of one of Denarius's lessons when he was a math teacher (and which Doug wrote about in *Teach Like a Champion 3.0*).

So I want to change my answer.

The student Vanessa has just been speaking authoritatively about what she thinks is the explanation of a given solution to a math problem, but suddenly, midway through, she realizes that her explanation is not correct. She has confused reciprocal and inverse. She's been speaking confidently in front of 25 or 30 classmates—advising them "if you check your notes"—and now, with all eyes on her, she realizes she is dead wrong. She pauses and glances at her notes. "Um, I'd like to change my answer," she says playfully, without a trace of self-consciousness.

She laughs. Her classmates laugh. Laughter too communicates belonging (or exclusion) by the way, and here it clearly communicates: "We are with you." The moment is almost beautiful—it's lit by the warm glow of belonging. Students feel safe and supported in one another's company. The level of trust is profound.

Now look at the girls in the front row. Their affirming gazes—eyes turned to Vanessa encouragingly—communicate support, safety, and belonging. In fact, it's hard to put it into words just how much their glances are communicating—each one is a little different—but they are as critical to shaping the moment as Vanessa's own character and persona. They foster and protect a space in which her bravery, humor, and humility can emerge.

Moments that are the converse of this one send equally potent signals, and almost assuredly occur more often in classrooms. The lack of eye contact (or the wrong kind of it) is a signal that something is amiss even if you are told you are a member of a group, and even if someone's words tell you that you belong. When something feels amiss in the information we receive from the gaze of our peers, we become self-conscious and anxious.

Let's say you're at dinner with a handful of colleagues, all sitting around a table. An eye-roll after you speak is a devastating signal. Or if, after you've said something, no one looks at you, you start to wonder: Was what I said awkward? Tactless? Clueless? Not-so-funny or even so-not-funny? Without a confirming glance you are suddenly on edge. Even if you have not been speaking, an ambiguous eye-roll you notice out of the corner of your eye is a source of anxiety. Was that about you? Have you done something to put your belonging at risk?

Or suppose you arrive late and saunter over to the table to find that no one looks up; your mind suddenly scrolls through an anxious calculus of what that might mean. Your peers might merely be absorbed in their phones and thus not look up to greet you but your subconscious mind may not distinguish much among potential explanations. No matter the reason for the behavior, it sends a worrying signal of nonbelonging.

In too many classrooms, students often speak and no one among their peers shows they heard or cared; they struggle and no one shows support. They seek to connect and there is no one signaling a similar willingness. Think here of the loneliest and most disconnected students most of all. How many of them look up to see only disinterest or blank expressions from their classmates? This is the nonverbal environment in which we ask young people to pursue their dreams. Imagine Vanessa in a room full of averted, disinterested gazes. If she was smart—and if she was like most young people—she'd have known better than to have raised her hand in the first place.

Flow and Its Role in Belonging

It's worth observing something else Vanessa is feeling in the moment when she reads signals of belonging and support and so decides to engage in productive and positive learning behavior. A sense of efficacy and productivity pervades the room. Vanessa doesn't just feel like part of a group; she feels like part of a *successful* group, one that is moving forward and accomplishing things, one that, through an evolutionary lens, is likely to survive and thrive. The sense of belonging we get from being a part of a group is especially strong when combined with feelings of sustained dynamic progress. The psychological state of "flow" describes what happens when humans engage in a task with uninterrupted focus and engagement for a sustained period of time. To lose track of time and lose ourselves in a task is one of the most pleasurable and gratifying mental states we can experience.

Hunting is probably the classic example of a task that induced a flow state for our ancestors. Many scientists think early humans were primarily persistence hunters. That is, a group would collaborate to chase a creature, most likely one that was faster over the short run. The quarry might successfully dash away when first chased, but the hunters would track it and find it and then chase it again. Imagine an antelope. Again and again the hunters would find and chase the antelope as it rested after its initial escape. This required teamwork, persistence, absolute focus—remaining highly attuned to the tiniest clues as to the antelope's location, for example—for hours and hours until finally the prey would drop dead of exhaustion or give up and allow itself to be captured. Those who could lose themselves in a task like that and sustain focus for significant periods of time would have had a significant selection advantage over those who could not, so perhaps our preference for flow state began there. Regardless, the groups in which we achieve flow are not only the most productive but often the ones within which we are most likely to feel belonging. Ultimately, we are happiest when we belong within groups that remind us they are productive and efficient.

This is reflected in Seligman's definition of happiness, a term many people define as being roughly synonymous with "pleasure." True that happiness often includes pleasure, Seligman argues. But it also consists equally of engagement—becoming absorbed in a task, living almost entirely in the moment—and meaning—being a part of something important and valuable, often something that feels larger than yourself.

Perhaps this is why so many students' stated sense of identity comes from extracurricular activities like music, drama, and sports that are more likely to involve a state of sustained dynamic engagement for participants. A math class, say, is far too likely to be subject to constant low-level disruptions in many schools—breaks in the flow of forward movement. Momentum, the feeling of full engagement, like one is "losing oneself" in a task, is difficult or impossible to sustain under such circumstances. When a young person says, "I'm a musician" or "I'm a soccer player," it suggests that these activities have established for him or her a sense of belonging that has shaped their identity. This perhaps should tell us something. Yes, we should make sure that belonging-intensive activities are readily available to young people across a variety of interests outside the classroom. Yes, we should make sure that these are well-designed and well-taught to maximize belonging and connection. But we should also recognize that what young people love about those activities could also happen more in classrooms. Students might feel the same sense of identity about history or science as they do about drama or basketball if classrooms helped them to lose themselves in the pursuit of the former as much as other settings do the latter.

We've journeyed far and wide in our effort to look more deeply at the roots of human motivation, so let us pause to summarize the argument that we are making: human beings are profoundly social and group oriented—far more so than we often realize—and our well-being is profoundly influenced by whether we feel we are part of purposeful groups. If we want young people to thrive, be fulfilled, and maintain psychological health, schools must ensure that activities they offer—including the core activity of classroom instruction—make students feel like they belong, especially when the group to which they belong is characterized by shared purpose, meaning, and mutual responsibility.

Notably, much of what enables feelings of connection and belonging is embedded in tiny moments of interaction that are frequently overlooked. Mutual responsibility and commitment are at the core of group formation, so what you give is as important as what you get. Being ready to support other group members, demonstrating your willingness to support shared aims, even and especially when it involves small sacrifices for the greater good, is as important as what we receive from others. At a time when students have been profoundly isolated and cut off from the groups in their lives, it's critical that we engineer schools carefully to maximize these characteristics of daily interaction.[9]

Could you take this too far? Of course. There is an important balance to be struck. Belonging only works if each student feels valued and appreciated as an individual, as opposed to merely one more member of the class. But given that we are the most individualist society in history, most of us are keenly aware of our desire for individual freedom and autonomy. "Liberation from ossified community bonds is a frequent and honored theme in our culture," Robert Putnam writes in *Bowling Alone*. "Our national myths often exaggerate the role of individual heroes and understate the importance of collective effort." We are far less likely to recognize the need for more group connection, more reciprocity, more groupishness. To succeed—and to succeed now in particular—schools will have to harness the power of the group.

ARGUMENT TWO: SCHOOLS AND THE SMARTPHONE EPIDEMIC

In the introduction, we presented data on just how devastating smartphones have been to student (and probably adult) connectedness, happiness, and well-being. Here, we'll reexamine those phenomena in light of what we now know about human belonging to better understand what happens when students pay increasingly more attention to their phones than to those around them.

A Generation Both Connected and Isolated

It's especially important for the people who run places where youth gather and interact to understand that the mass adoption of smartphones has radically changed the social fabric of young people's lives, even when they are not actively using them.

As we discussed in the introduction, chronic phone usage has changed the patterns of social interactions everywhere. "I've seen my friends with their families," one student told psychologist Jean Twenge. "They don't talk to them. They're just like yeah, whatever, and then they're on their phones." Times of informal interaction, where once connection and communication between young people and their parents, extended family, or friends were built—family dinners, driving to practice in the car, just hanging out after school—are now often marked by precious little eye contact and other belonging signals. They instead involve far more swiping and scrolling. The messageis: that's what people do in each other's company. "It's non-screen activities that help teens feel less alone," writes Twenge, but such interactions and the antidote they potentially offer are degraded. You're in the room with your friends but they are just as likely looking down at their phones and only half there, smirking at something (maybe about you!) that flashed across their screen.

Even the awkward moments when we are new to a group—when, arriving, we stand for a moment and scan the room until someone realizes they might say hello (perhaps a bit of eye contact cues this)— even that is altered. Now you glance around, but everyone's eyes are down. So you take out your phone as well. Rather than connecting, you remain apart.

This affects the life and culture of institutions, too. "Sometimes I'll get to school so excited to see everyone, but then in homeroom or in the hall when I get there, my friends are all on their technology," one teenager told us. "All the way to school I was so psyched to see them and then I'm like, why am I even here? I could just remote [i.e. attend via remote classes] if you don't even want to talk." The phrase *if you don't even want to talk* is most likely a description of the feeling people get when they don't receive the acknowledgment, eye-contact, and confirmation humans expect (and hope for!) from one another. We don't say we don't want to talk; we signal it. To walk into a room and receive no discernable response is disconcerting and anxiety-inducing to anyone, whether we are fully conscious of it or not. But to adolescents, who are especially sensitive to their place in the world, it is doubly so.

"Often I'll arrive early to a lecture to find a room of 30-plus students sitting together in complete silence, absorbed in their smartphones, afraid to speak and be heard by their peers," a college student told Twenge. Does anyone think this social isolation even among peers is not also common in K–12 schools that allow phone use during the school day?

Combating the Smartphone Epidemic

Establishing limits on the amount of time young people spend on their phones is important but it is also important to note that some uses of time when away from devices appear to be more beneficial to young people's well-being than others. Ensuring experiences that are fully engaging and "connecting" when students are away from their phones is also critical to reconnecting them.

The chart here shows Twenge's data on how involvement in certain activities has a strong negative correlative to the spiraling rates of unhappiness among eighth graders.

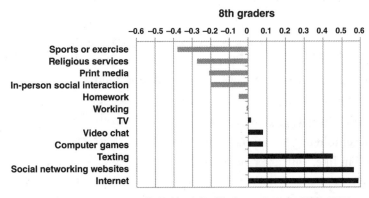

8th graders

| -0.6 | -0.5 | -0.4 | -0.3 | -0.2 | -0.1 | 0 | 0.1 | 0.2 | 0.3 | 0.4 | 0.5 | 0.6 |

Sports or exercise
Religious services
Print media
In-person social interaction
Homework
Working
TV
Video chat
Computer games
Texting
Social networking websites
Internet

Relative risk of being unhappy, 2013–2015

The two activities Twenge found with the strongest negative correlation to unhappiness—participation in sports and participation in religious services—have several things in common: they involve engaged interaction with fellow participants; they involve shared purpose; they require cooperation and interaction. Spending 90 minutes at volleyball practice means 90 minutes of attending to facial signals and subtle interpersonal cues—relearning the foundational grammar of human interaction. It means 90 minutes of group cooperation and coordination in pursuit of a goal. And it means 90 minutes when you can't be on your phone. Such interactions, Twenge's research suggests, could serve as "antidotes," in that they appear to counteract some of the adverse consequences of social media use.

This distinction between "off phones" and "off phones and in a setting that is psychologically beneficial" is important. Schools along with parents and other youth-based organizations—should consider three separate types of action to address the smartphone/social media epidemic: restriction, antidote, and intervention.

Restriction: It's unrealistic to think we'll ever go back to the time before smartphones. It's doubly unrealistic to think that schools can make a lot of headway reshaping broad societal norms.[10] That's not really our job. But it is our job, we believe, to set up environments within our institutions that ensure the learning and well-being of students. Screens degrade attention, learning, community, and mental health. Ensuring extended spans of time when students are reliably screen free—not merely not using them but with the screen actually not present—is necessary to rebuilding attention, optimizing learning, and maximizing social well-being, especially in the aftermath of a crisis that left students drastically behind academically and disconnected socially.

It's really hard work to do this. One of us has a child in a high school that set a "no phones during class" rule to great fanfare. A fraction of the teachers followed through on the rules diligently and successfully. Some lacked the will or skill to handle students who tested the rules. Others chose to ignore or scoff at them. Classrooms that adhered to the policy were soon outliers and within two weeks it became clear that the initiative would be quickly forgotten. (It's worth reflecting as well on what such a failure to follow through on an announced policy communicates to parents and students about the efficacy of the institution in an era of increasing skepticism.)

But, of course, some schools do implement restrictions successfully. In Chapter 2 we will share details of how, but we note here the importance of getting buy-in from staff and parents as the first step.

We believe that with diligence and focus, schools can create sustained space and time for students to engage each other and their learning tasks without distraction: face-to-face and pencil-to-paper—"high text, low tech" we like to say. Importantly, schools are one of the last institutions that can reasonably hope to implement the kinds of moderating effects on the universality of phones. We are just possibly the last redoubt.

Antidote: In addition to restricting smartphone access, schools can encourage antidote activities. In fact, the best antidote may just be a well-run classroom with a strong dynamic lesson that engages everyone, where students feel a strong sense of belonging because they are constantly receiving cues from their peers that their presence and efforts are valued. Schools can add to that an intentional array of activities that engage students outside the classroom, as well. These activities—clubs and sports and events—must be well-run and carefully designed, just like the classroom. It's not enough just to offer a martial arts team or a science club if no one shows up, or if people show up but half of them are on their phones, so that students are just as likely to feel alone in the room as out of it.

Ironically, fewer options can sometimes be better. A common narrative in schools is that choice motivates—if we let young people choose their activities and their books and their learning, they'll like it more. But in fact what motivates people far more is their reading of social norms. We do what we do in part because we want to connect and engage in shared endeavor with people around us. Choice might motivate sometimes but connection motivates a lot more. A hastily added debate club that's sporadically attended, run by an indifferent staff member, and where a smattering of students file in and glance at their phones—or look out at their peers swiping through their phones while they are practicing—doesn't create much value. It's often similar in the classroom, we believe, where book choice is often valorized and the result can be each child reading their own book in some corner of the room without the opportunity to discuss it or, better, benefit from the emotional connection that the shared experience of reading a story together. Far better to read the book together—maybe even aloud—and hear one another laugh and gasp as the story unfolds. Far better to ensure students spend their school days in constructive and intentionally designed environments where the culture is vibrant and supportive. If in doubt, it's far better to do fewer, highly connected things better.

Intervention: Young people today experience a slower version of adolescence than young people did even a decade or two ago. A tenth grader in 2017 has in some ways had the life experiences of an eighth grader a few decades ago. Even before the pandemic, they were less likely to have held a job, less likely to have their driver's license, and typically spent less time out in the world interacting with new people in the thousands of unexpected interactions that build mastery of social cues. The pandemic cut them off even further from this range of experiences.

A stop for an ice cream on the way home from church, mosque, or temple—the type of thing that didn't occur for most young people during lockdown—teaches the rituals and patterns of civic and communal life, such as the norms for greeting and socializing with a wide range of people. How you greet your pastor is similar to but also different from how you greet the scooper in the ice cream shop. Those experiences teach you about how to make your way in a complex world.

The young people returning to schools had been isolated from normal doses of such interactions, not just because of the two pandemic years but quite possibly because of newly risen technological norms that cause them to glance down at their phone and walk by their pastor without making eye contact or ignore the ice cream scooper because they have neglected to remove their headphones—and more likely neglected to even consider whether it would be odd not to remove their headphones while speaking to someone. When these activities did return for young people after a long hiatus, they were distorted by masks and social distancing. How do you learn to read facial expressions when you can't see faces, or to greet someone when you cannot hug or shake hands?

Some students will fill in the gaps left by this diminished experience if we present more opportunities for them to connect during the day, via the antidotes discussed above. But in some cases (for some students, and perhaps for some of the norms we want to set) mere opportunity won't be enough. We will have to be prepared to teach social norms and expectations in a deliberate way.

In many ways, the best schools we know already did this. They were keenly aware that only the most positive and productive classroom climates could encourage and foster the sort of intellectual culture that students require if excellence is truly a goal. They were used to setting and teaching social norms.

That work can take two primary forms. First, schools can set and instill broad ongoing social norms outside the classroom. Perhaps unexpectedly, a soccer club Doug works with provides an interesting model. The club is the "academy" for a professional team. The athletes there (ages 12–18) play at an elite level and train daily. Each of them has grown up as the best player from their town or neighborhood. A few will become professionals. Most will not, however. They will go on to play in college, most likely, and then move on to some other life. They can't see that clearly now because they are young and chasing their dreams. But this can also lead to counterproductive mindsets. In the world of teenagers, they are high-status individuals. It would be easy for them develop a bit too much ego. The academy spent a lot of time thinking about this. They (and the athletes' parents!) wanted to develop people of character and humility. The organization wanted them to take pride in and feel belonging within the club but also remain grounded.

As a result, whenever you show up on their campus, *every athlete who passes you,* whether they are 12 or 18, greets you with a handshake or a fist bump and a bit of eye contact. Most tell you their name and say "Welcome" or "I'm Domari." It's lovely for visitors—they feel relevant—but even better for the athletes themselves, who have practiced greeting everyone as important and an equal, who have practiced making the first step to connect, and who are skilled at being confident and welcoming.

There's no reason schools couldn't think about similar routines or rituals. In fact, in Chapter 5 we'll show you video of staff, students, and parents greeting each other on arrival at North Star Academy Downtown Middle School in Newark, New Jersey. It's a ritual that establishes belonging, builds social skills, and sets cultural norms.

The second form of intervention schools may have to plan is specific to young people who struggle with social cues, who are a little less observant about how to engage peers or make friends or say something appropriate at any of a dozen moments of their life in school. School is hard on young people like this and it's a safe bet that there will be more of them in the wake of pandemic and there will be fewer other social settings in which to learn to read cues and signals.

At one school we know, the dean of students routinely invites students to family-style lunch with him. There's a box of cookies for dessert and a basket with real salt and pepper shakers and a few bottles of hot sauce, so eating with the dean feels pretty special to middle schoolers (roughly like getting bumped up to first class in an airplane). The lunch also features grown-up-style conversations about school, family, music, or what's in the news. Among the crowd are always a few kids who are there for a reason. They need the practice. Afterwards or perhaps beforehand, they might get a bit of feedback. "Asking people questions is a great way to connect. Try to ask them what music they like instead of just telling them what you're into." This is a small but lovely example of what we'd call an intervention: a deliberate effort by the school to build social skills and understanding among a smaller group of students who require a bit of extra help.

Denarius was struck recently when interviewing his students about their experience at his school this year by how much they valued community meeting, a time when the whole school gathers for announcements, culture building, and inspiration. It's a time when Denarius deliberately teaches and reinforces norms of positive culture within the school. It's schoolwide teaching of social norms. The students, it turns out, wanted more community meetings. They valued that time even more than he knew. They liked that it meant they got to see peers across grade levels at the meetings. They liked being in large groups. They sometimes rolled their eyes just a little at some of the things the adults said or taught them there—about greeting people with eye contact, about showing gratitude, about keeping one's school uniform up to standard—but they were listening nonetheless and, as it turned out, they valued it. They appreciated the things he and his staff taught there and understood that they might be important—now or later, here or somewhere else. They wanted to be ready for all the places their life might take them. And each of them was perfectly capable of deciding what to do with that knowledge once they left the building.

To some readers the behaviors they instill might sound "paternalistic." Is socializing students to greet one another in a specific way culturally intrusive? Does it trample on students' own culture?

We don't think so, mostly because we think students are smart. We think it's beneficial for them to learn the norms of the schools they attend, especially when those norms help them connect and learn while there, but they remain perfectly capable of deciding when and whether to adopt or adapt those norms outside of school. Students are perfectly capable of deciding for themselves how far they want to buy in. They will always have the skills. There will almost assuredly be times when they are glad to have them. And they will be able to turn them on and turn off as they wish. We all knew kids growing up who went to schools where ties were required of the boys; many of them would have their ties off within seconds after exiting the door. Some wouldn't go near a tie in the hours outside school; some found they occasionally liked to look a little bit sharper; they liked knowing how to knot a tie or match it to their outfit. Everyone understood that they wore ties in school and got to choose how to adapt that tradition on their own time.

In our experience, students usually understand and value elevated expectations in the organizations they are a part of. They like being held to high standards when it's clear those standards are driven by belief in their potential. Even the students who don't always seem to appreciate it at the time or in the moment usually come to see the value in the end. Everyone loves to tell the story of the coach or teacher who pushed them to their full potential. They often like to exaggerate how challenging it was (how many sprints they had to run, for example). But they tell the story with pride because it represents a time when someone thought they were worth investing in.

Students don't mind being held to high standards when they understand they are there out of respect for their capacity and potential (and when the standards are consistently upheld). This fact is especially relevant in a discussion of technology. Will students at first be happy about restrictions on phones in school? Of course not. Will they argue against it? Gripe about it? Absolutely! Might they sign a petition? Sure, and if so, all the better!

They are young. They don't in fact know everything about the world at age 16. Among other things, they haven't yet experienced what it will be like in school without their phones or how their learning will benefit.

So we should expect some pushback and be happy if students organize a petition drive or a protest. It means they care and have stood up for what they believe in. This is a good thing, even if we think they are wrong.

If there is a petition drive in response to a cell phone ban, we'd meet with students and say, "Tell us all your concerns about the restrictions." We'd try to ask follow-up questions to learn more and show that we think seriously about students' perspective: "So you're worried your mom won't be able to reach you during the day?" We'd present them with some data (perhaps some of the data from this book!) to think about. We'd look for at least one small compromise or adjustment that could be made in response. We might even give them the opportunity to gain or lose more flexibility based on their follow-through on the basic rules. "Okay," we might say, "We hear you. We'll find a place where you can go to check your phone twice a day. But know that students whose phones are out at other times stand to lose that privilege."

Yet in the end, despite impassioned arguments by engaged young people, we think you should decide based on what is in the long-term interest of the group. And that answer is clear. It's not the one the majority of students will want to hear at first. The job of running schools is not to do what's popular, but to do what's right. After that, the job is to go out and make sure students feel the difference in a positive way. "Buy-in," our colleague Paul Bambrick reminds us, "is an outcome, not a prerequisite." If the culture makes students feel whole, supported, and important, they will embrace it. There's no reason to think they'd know it would do that beforehand. If we focus on making school and school culture excellent, students will come to believe in it.

Doing that will require focus, follow-through, and buy-in from all staff members, and that is not always easy to accomplish. For any school, operational follow-through—its ability to ensure that chosen policies and decisions are implemented with fidelity across the organization—is the key driver of effectiveness. The challenge of reliably being able to get important things done well is especially significant now. One major reason for that is that faith in institutions has never been lower. At exactly the time we need them most, we, as a public, are more skeptical of them than we have ever been.

ARGUMENT THREE: SCHOOLS MUST REBUILD FAITH IN INSTITUTIONAL VIABILITY AND RELIABILITY

This brings us to our third argument in this chapter: that we have to be prepared to work to rekindle faith in our institutions, to let students experience schools that model how institutions can be responsive, caring, and effective, that respect their time and their worth, even when they cannot have everything they want. This is doubly important because, as education writer Robert Pondiscio has pointed out, school is often a young person's first sustained interaction with the idea of institutions. It's where they develop—or fail to develop—a belief that the things we build when we work together are worthy and beneficial, that working together to create things is what one does in life. When you don't trust an institution or believe that institutions can serve people well, it is hard to benefit from what they have to offer. If that's not challenging enough, we have to rekindle not just students' faith in our institutions, but that of parents and sometimes teachers as well.

One key step in the path forward is revealed by the Edelman Trust Barometer, a long-standing yearly international survey of trust in institutions. In describing data on the ebb and flow of trust in countries across the world—mostly ebb, honestly, as we noted in the introduction—the authors note that "the greatest trust gains to any institution come from information quality." When you share good information, people understand why you do the things you do. Even the act of sharing full information is an act of trust that shows openness and transparency.

There is a fairly wide body of research that supports a related idea: openness can help people determine how fair they believe an institution is, which matters greatly in their estimation of and trust in that institution. Furthermore, when people perceive an institution to be fair in how it makes decisions, they are more likely to accept its decisions, even if they do not agree.

Fairness can be divided into two types: process fairness and outcome fairness. Outcome fairness is whether people think a decision is right and fair on its merits. Process fairness is whether people think the decision-makers went about deciding in a way that was open, fair, and honest. Democracy offers an array of examples. The great majority of us understand and accept its decisions even when we don't agree with them because we believe the process to be fair. For this reason, aspiring office holders of integrity often respond to an outcome in which they didn't win by affirming the process: "The people have spoken." In the long run, the process is bigger than any single decision.

In fact, research suggests that people value process fairness as much as, if not more than, outcome fairness. What's more, writes David Chan, professor of psychology at Singapore Management University, "process fairness is a stronger predictor than outcome fairness in people's evaluation...of their leaders."

In other words, if schools must ask a diverse group of potentially skeptical families of wide-ranging opinions to support policies that allow the schools to maximize student academic progress and well-being, they should focus on process fairness because universal agreement on outcomes is unlikely. If people disagree but think you decided fairly, you are better off than if they all agree but aren't sure they understand or trust how you decided.

Chan suggests several key principles of process fairness to focus on. The first, he notes, is what he calls "accuracy." Are decisions made based on legitimate data and information? Are stakeholders aware of that? We might call that being fact- or research-based. If you're going to propose restrictions on cell phones in your school, it's going to be critical that you share not only the reasons why but the research behind it so that parents, students, and teachers know you've done your homework and the decision is based on more than just your own personal perspective.

Another principle of process fairness is consistency. People want to know that rules and policies are "consistently applied across people and time in similar situations." "Voice" is also critical. The decision-making process has to offer people an opportunity to speak and influence the outcome, Chan says, but having an opportunity to influence the outcome doesn't mean you do determine it. It means you get the chance to be heard with sincerity and openness before the decision is made.

Finally, Chan notes, "procedures are more likely to be seen as fair if they are congruent with the values and reflect the concerns of the people involved." Of course, it's hard to predict the values individuals bring to an organization like a school, but you can frame specific values you think your school stands for and refer to them. You can always go back to the why: *This is what we are trying to accomplish. This is why we are trying to accomplish it. These are the things we value as a community.*

In the introduction, we described a meeting Denarius held with students where he listened carefully and showed that he was making decisions based on data and with the long-term well-being of students in mind. In the process of doing that he said no to students—although, he reinforced a rule that was to their benefit, so perhaps "said no" isn't quite the right term. Several came to agree with his decision. Many more understood the decision even if they were not in favor of it. But all of them felt important and valued and heard. They became more connected and felt more belonging in the process of disagreeing with their principal. This to us is the sign of a well-run school.

Having observed many such schools, here's our recipe for rebuilding faith.

1. **Be really good at the core work of schooling.** One key aspect of developing trust is making certain to be effective at the core mission of education. People feel trust and faith in well-run organizations that appear capable of accomplishing complex coordinated tasks. Don't make it a choice between that and a responsive culture. A school that makes students feel belonging but doesn't prepare them to accomplish their dreams does not meet standard. On the other hand, keep in mind that academic excellence is necessary but itself not sufficient to the endeavor.

2. **Help people feel a strong sense of purpose.** We are, as we hope we have established, groupish. We succeed by forming a village—a group of people connected by place, sharing a clear vision of the future. Having a shared purpose this is to say. Because something is simple does not imply that it is easy to achieve. A simple goal is hard work in a complex world.

   To us the purpose has to begin with the shared pursuit of student knowledge, and the *shared* part is easily overlooked. A great school or classroom is first or foremost a culture that values learning. Student well-being is the second element of shared purpose. Schools that are positive, optimistic, grateful, and altruistic are psychologically healthy places, and the pursuit of virtues—which we'll discuss in Chapter 4 but which essentially means doing right for ourselves by doing right by the people around us—is perhaps the best way to accomplish this. As Angela Duckworth, founder of the Character Lab, puts it, virtues are "all the ways of thinking, feeling and acting that we [can] habitually do that are good for others and good for ourselves."

A school doesn't need much more than that. Achieving simple and important things in a complex and challenging world is no easy task and adding more goals can create as much distraction as benefit. Getting everyone focused on one or two key things is plenty difficult.

One important step in developing a strong sense of shared purpose is sharing a vocabulary. Language, W. H. Auden wrote, is the mother, not the handmaiden, of thought. Having words for things conjures them into being. A school should establish a shared vocabulary for the things it wants to instill and the purpose it seeks. This makes those things legible for students and parents. Ultimately, understanding and feeling connected to a purpose not only makes people happier, it also makes them feel more connected and more trusting (more on this in Chapter 4).

3. **Focus on process**. We live in a world where it is sometimes difficult to imagine a decision everyone in a community would agree with. In the final chapter, we examine what this might mean for the idea of school choice. In the meantime, we have to fall back on process. People have to feel that the decision-making process is founded in purpose and data, is transparent, and takes their voices into account.

A VILLAGE EMERGES

We close with a final observation about our evolutionary past. Likely we existed first, even before we were fully humans, in small and loosely connected family groups, probably a lot like the family groups of other primates today. As we were more and more able to coordinate, we became increasingly social, meaning more mutual reliance and probably larger groups. The greater the degree of cooperation and mutualism, the greater the chances of survival. As cooperation conferred increasing advantages on those groups that achieved it, we doubled down and evolved to become what biologists call "eusocial," a rare state of elevated mutuality where members of a species are willing to sacrifice for the good of the group, willing to help rear one another's young, willing to care for the aged. There are other eusocial species—bees are the classic example of self-sacrifice and coordination—but eusocial mammals are incredibly rare. It's basically us and the naked mole rat. And we are the only eusocial primate.

Over hundreds of thousands of years we formed something more interconnected than mere groups. Call them societies; they were mobile, often fluid groups and hunter-gatherers. You might form a group with other bands for a season and then when the prey moved on so did you, splitting into subgroups and separating until the next year. But these groups were different in their complexity and mutuality from what any other primate did.

"To form groups, drawing . . . comfort and pride from familiar fellowship, and to defend the group enthusiastically against rival groups—these are among the universals of human nature and hence of culture," biologist Edward O. Wilson writes. "People must have a tribe. It gives them a name in addition to their own and social meaning in a chaotic world." Our identities derived from our groups as much as or more than ourselves.

Adopting agriculture changed all that. It meant all your hard work was left standing in a field each night just waiting to be stolen.[11] Mutual obligation and reciprocity were even more necessary to survival, but flexibility and choice in group membership were reduced. We could no longer migrate or come and go from a group we didn't agree with. We had to form more stable communities: villages.

This translated the legacy of mutualism and community into a more fixed model. You might not like everyone in your village, but you needed each other and needed to be able to rely on each other. You might dislike your neighbor, but you were also ready to stand shoulder to shoulder when danger approached. That was what made you a village and gave you your identity. The village was the bridge between our biological past and the modern world.

We think the village is a decent metaphor for a school. We cannot come and go as we please.[12] We do not always agree. Yet we are bound together and must be willing to accept the terms of a social contract that causes us to rely on each other for mutualism and reciprocity. If dissenters march off in anger when the majority rules, everyone loses.

That initial social contract—stay and protect what is ours; work together if there is a crisis; set rules to make the place livable—ultimately became the basis of society and all of its institutions. In a successful village, young people come to accept the demands and appreciate the benefits of shared endeavor. They come to see that the former are comparatively small in comparison to the immensity of the latter. Just maybe they come to see that the demands are not a burden, but in fact a tool that allows us to bind together to maximize individual and group benefit.

A village in the end is founded on mutualism, and specifically, as Robert Putnam describes it in *Bowling Alone: The Collapse and Revival of American Community,* on *generalized reciprocity* (Putnam's term for Keohabe's idea of diffuse reciprocity). Sometimes "reciprocity is specific: I'll do this for you if you do that for me," Putnam writes. Even more valuable, however, is a norm of *generalized reciprocity.* I'll do this for you without expecting anything specific back from you in the confident expectation that someone will do something for me down the road." Generalized reciprocity—acts of generosity, selflessness, altruism—are the ultimate messages of belonging. They reinforce the strength of the group and remind everyone in the village that they belong to and are part of something worthy. In many ways the value each community creates in the lives of its denizens correlates to the degree to which it is successful at creating generalized reciprocity.

Notes

1. That death by stoning is described in the Bible—and still practiced by some cultures in the world—reflects its significance. The choice of the method of killing is not symbolic. It was probably the standard method, even if now we barely recognize it.
2. Quoted in Daniel Coyle, *The Culture Code: The Secrets of Highly Successful Groups* (New York: Bantam, 2018).

3. Evolutionary biologists refer to this as multilevel selection: we compete as a group at the same time we compete within the group. Edward O. Wilson's *The Social Conquest of Earth* is excellent on this topic.

4. Social Relationships and Mortality Risk: A Meta-analytic Review (2010), https://journals.plos.org/plosmedicine/article?id=10.1371/journal.pmed.1000316

5. Phiana Wilcox, KIPP Tech Valley Primary School, March 11, 2022.

6. Adam Grant and Francesco Gino, A Little Thanks Goes a Long Way: Explaining Why Gratitude Expressions Motivate Prosocial Behavior, https://www.umkc.edu/facultyombuds/documents/grant_gino_jpsp_2010.pdf

7. https://www.jstor.org/stable/2706740

8. It's worth noting here that humans also compete within groups, especially in terms of sexual selection.

9. It's important to note that it is also a time of massive learning loss for students, so we'll need to prioritize their well-being in ways that work in synergy with academic progress rather than instead of it.

10. We often meet well-intentioned educators who tell us that the answer is for schools to teach students to make better decisions about social media. This is folly. Do we really think a few assemblies by the adults telling kids to "be smart" is going to make a difference in the face of what is for all intents an addiction? Do we really think we're qualified to do that work? We are not counselors and social psychologists; we are teachers. Perhaps we could if we spent a tremendous amount of time on the topic, but schools have a specific job in society. Our job is not to address all social ills but to teach students academic knowledge.

11. Interestingly, hunter-gatherer societies often struggle with the idea of ownership. A newly killed carcass can be saved or taken with you. The incentive is to share it—to share everything. There is no benefit to keeping it.

12. In the last chapter of this book we will discuss the relevance of increased choice in schools.

Chapter 2

A Great Unwiring

Doug attended high school in the 1980s. In addition to this making him the "senior" member of the team, as we tactfully put it, this gives him some stories to tell from a different era. Here's one that his own kids find jaw-dropping:

He and his classmates were allowed to smoke in high school.

Actually, smoking was more than allowed. It was more or less enabled. There was a student smoking area with ashcans. It was marked on maps of the school.

Smoking was legal, after all, and one common argument was that it wasn't really the school's place to restrict it. People also argued that teenagers would smoke anyway. Why not give them one place to do it so there weren't butts everywhere on campus? Why not make it convenient so they weren't also late to class?

It sounds crazy now, but at the time the administration argued that high school students were adults entering a world in which, it was noted, there would be tobacco. They would have to learn to make decisions about tobacco. The administration's goal was to educate students to think for themselves.

They didn't really do much educating in practice though. There were posters about making smart choices and an occasional cautionary video, but we all know how well those work. Plus, if teachers were supposed to "talk to students about tobacco," they didn't really know how. Occasionally one might remind students that they shouldn't smoke, but they were there to teach math, history and art. Plus many of them were smokers themselves. A few occasionally allowed students to bum cigarettes from them. From the students' point of view, this earned them status. Students liked to be "treated like adults."

All in all, the argument was that it was clearly better not to come on too strong with the restrictions. The smoking area reflected school's acceptance of and respect for young people's autonomy.

At least that was how they explained it. It's possible they just didn't want to make rules about smoking because they didn't want the unpleasant job of doing something teenagers would have resented. Teenagers are good at making it difficult emotionally to do things they resent. It's also possible that they hadn't thought that a rule could be beneficial *even if some people broke it.*

All the while, everyone knew the truth about cigarettes. The data on the long-term health effects was readily available; it had been for years. The upshot was that a lot more people became smokers. Needless to say, they paid a very high price for that decision.

It was their decision, of course. They'd probably be the first to tell you that. But it does seem odd, looking back, that the school made it *so easy* to access a demonstrably harmful product that was *designed to addict young people.* And the 16- and 17-year-olds whom everyone was so eager to christen "adults" were of course not adults. They were teenagers. Their prefrontal cortex would not fully develop for nearly ten years (around age 25). This made them especially susceptible to addiction because they were at the point in their lives when they were most influenced by their peers and most likely to make decisions that ignored danger and long-term consequences.[1]

Of course, the teens wanted to be seen as adults. They argued this especially vociferously when it might result in additional freedoms like staying out late, but the educators really should have been able to see the difference. Really, it's shocking that they just went along with it.

As you might have guessed, this story isn't really about smoking in schools in a bygone era but is intended to make a point about cell phones and social media in schools today—specifically tolerance of something so damaging and addictive to young people. We also hope to point out that the arguments about why schools can't or shouldn't restrict cell phones are similar to the ones made about cigarettes at Doug's school. Educators argue that schools shouldn't restrict cell phones because it keeps young people from learning to manage their phones for themselves, because rules don't work, because it fails to treat teenagers like adults.

And, sadly, as there was then with smoking, there is damning data on the danger of the product and of teens' particular vulnerability to it.

The analogy to smoking is flawed of course. People interact with cell phones and social media differently than they do with cigarettes. Cell phones are more harmful in some ways and less harmful in others. They are more directly disruptive to the cognitive processes of learning, for example, and are far more ubiquitous: absolutely everyone has one and, unlike cigarettes, left to their own devices students would and do use them in the classroom. A recent survey in the UK by Teacher Tapp, a daily survey app for teachers designed to gauge the experience and opinions of the field more accurately, asked teachers whether at least one pupil had taken their phone out during class without permission during the previous day alone. Of almost 4500 respondents, one-third said yes. Some teachers reported it happened to them multiple times every day.

On the other hand cell phones also have clear benefits. We'll merely acknowledge them here without trying to describe the obvious in terms of their capacity to provide access to information and facilitate communication in a hundred ways. And it's worth noting that while we hesitate to use the word "benefits," there were also reasons why so many people smoked. The biggest one, probably, is relevant to the themes of this book: the sense of belonging and camaraderie that came from standing in your denim jacket sharing a cigarette on a chilly morning. It made you part of a community—one for which you were willing to make certain sacrifices to belong to.

To state the obvious, then, cell phones are not cigarettes, and the appropriate response should reflect the differences. But it should also reflect the fact that in our schools we tolerate a highly destructive product specifically designed to addict young people, and distract them from learning.

Should we restrict phones, then? Yes, though the age of students should also be a factor in the extent of the restriction. There certainly should be a complete ban in elementary schools. Middle schools should probably ban them "from bell to bell," we think, with students forbidden to have phones out or on from the first to the end-of-day bell, but permitted to use them after or before school to, say, tell their parents where to pick them up. In high school a range of plausible solutions are possible, all of them more restrictive than what the great majority of schools now do. Our own recommendation is a well-enforced rule that they must be powered off and in a backpack or bag (not a pocket) during the day, except possibly in a designated area where students can go *briefly* and at limited times to be in touch with their parents, for example. The rest of the school should be phone free. A slightly more activist stance would be to say: we should never see them during the day and we presume that students will text their parents as needed before and after school. (You could allow them to text from the main office in an emergency.) We'd love to see that but recognize that the challenges might be prohibitive for some schools. Either way, permitting cell phone use (and saying we are treating young people like adults when we enable their addiction) is not a viable policy in an institution committed to learning and building well-being.

We note again that the job of restricting something teenagers don't want restricted is a difficult one. Many young people won't like it at first, though we argue that in the long run many are likely to see the benefit. Some parents and teachers will push back. And once a policy is set, there will still be teachers who opt to raise their status by letting students break the rules (possibly the same ones who were available to lend you a smoke back in Doug's day).

It's not going to be easy. But our students require schools that reconnect them to their peers, support their mental health, and address the historic academic losses of the pandemic. Schools that hope to address that many serious challenges at once must accept the necessity of smartphone restrictions.

PLUSES AND MINUSES

We'll step down briefly from our soapbox briefly. While much of this chapter shares the *how* and *why* of taking a strong, restrictive position on smartphones, we also seek to make a balanced and two-sided argument about the role of technology more broadly. The equation has changed since the pandemic. There have been changes as a result of it that can be critical in helping schools succeed in the immense challenges we face. Here again we take Jean Twenge's guidance. She has been tracking patterns in the social behaviors and patterns among young people via detailed survey instruments for years and has seen her share of trends. Even though she describes a wave of depression and anxiety resulting from the smartphone epidemic, she *also* notes the necessity of seeing any issue as complex. Her research describes positive and negative outcomes of universal cell phone adoption—both the increased isolation of young people but also some resulting benefits: a dramatic reduction in teenage pregnancies and deaths by auto accident, for example. "There's a natural human tendency to classify things as all good or all bad," she writes, "but with cultural changes, it's better to see the gray areas and the trade-offs."

So we intend to make as balanced an argument as we can—one that talks about the gray areas and the trade-offs. Increased familiarity with and broader adoption of new technological tools during the pandemic can benefit schools. Besides, smartphones and social media aren't going away. A book that argues we should roll back the clock to a time gone by is a work of fantasy. In the real world the question is: How can we maximize what's good about the technology that pervades our lives, and simultaneously mitigate the downsides and minimize the costs?

A complex social trend playing out across society is complicated. There are more responses required than just restriction. So in addition to arguing that schools must summon the will and the fortitude to protect young people's well-being by restricting phones, we will start by examining ways technology can help address challenges and build community and connection.

NETWORK EFFECTS AND ZOOM

The term "network effect" describes the way a technology's value and utility increase exponentially when it becomes widely used. Something that's not very useful when only a few people use it becomes a game changer when everyone does. In the 1990s a few people had fax machines and the ones that existed were used among a small and quirky set of early adopters. Then, suddenly, they crossed a threshold. Faxing became universal. You could rely on every business to have one. People bought fax machines for their homes—they were indispensable. Fax functionality was built into copier machines and embedded on laptops. The more people used it, the more valuable it (briefly) became. Suddenly you had to have fax capability to communicate: a case study in network effects.

One silver lining of the pandemic was the network effect it brought about for a variety of technological applications, most significantly videoconferencing. Before 2020 only a minority of the populace knew how to use it. In the span of a few weeks, basically everybody learned how. Suddenly Zoom went from obscure to universal. Now you can presume Zoom usage, and that's a change that's actually quite significant.

To be clear—and with no disrespect to Zoom and Teams and Google Meets, which were godsends during the pandemic—we hope never to need to use them in lieu of teaching students in person again, but in their universal form such tools are highly effective at reducing barriers to meetings. This makes it easier for parents to be involved, makes it easier for students to be able to connect with teachers and resources outside of class, and makes missing class less onerous.

Parent meetings are critical to effective schooling, both in their plural form (a group meeting) and in the singular (a discussion with one parent or set of parents). Making it easier to meet "face to face" means making it easier to share information and easier to earn buy-in and get feedback. We can communicate culture and values and, just as importantly, invest in process. *Here is how things will work. Here's why we're doing what we're doing.* These discussions are far better on Zoom than in a newsletter, or in addition to a newsletter. It allows us to solicit feedback, for example, either intentionally or incidentally. This is especially important in a time when trust and faith in school are low.

In the last chapter we talked about process fairness being as important as outcome fairness. We will need to design intentional cultures and make rules—potentially challenging rules like those that restrict cell phone use during the school day—at exactly the time when institutional trust is at its lowest. Using Zoom (and recording meetings using it for those who can't attend) makes process fairness much easier to achieve. A process that informs people of why, and that makes people feel listened to, heard, and understood even when they disagree, is critical to building and ensuring trust and credibility. Reducing the transaction cost of meetings where those things can happen is a huge benefit to school leaders and families.

Trying to configure schedules and availability is one of the biggest challenges to getting face to face with parents and caregivers, and lots of schools are finding that, having moved meetings online for the pandemic, they are inclined to keep many of them that way after. First, attendance is usually higher because the transaction cost of getting to school is lower. Watch where people are connecting from at a typical meeting in Denarius's school and you'll see them at home with small children they'd otherwise struggle to find care for, and sometimes logging in from work. Parents will be on the call from an Uber or walking home from the subway. Most of these are cases where the parent would otherwise be unable to attend. This doesn't mean there shouldn't be parent meetings in school; one of our rules of thumb is that a remote meeting is usually valuable in direct proportion to the rate at which we have *also* met with parents face to face and they have been in the building. So a mix of settings is ideal. And if we had to choose, we'd rather have all those parents with us in the busy moments of their lives than not.

Doing meetings through Zoom also means we can record and share for those who are unable to attend. This can be especially important at the beginning of the year when establishing policies. A teacher or a school leader can set it out exactly how he or she wants. If people don't attend, the whole story is still available. This means you can make your case (here's why we do homework like we do; here's why we restrict phones and what will happen if your child breaks that rule) much more richly, with graphics and discussion and in your own voice. "It allows us to share our vision, policies, and expectations, but also to gauge input and feedback," one school leader told us. "It's our first opportunity to build trust and assure parents and families that our academic program is both rigorous and joyful, while also explaining what's required to keep that promise." You can put that in writing, but hearing it directly from the school is and always will be a little different.

ACCESS FOR PARENTS

Parents have had "their own emotions and challenges in dealing with the pandemic," noted Jody Jones, senior school director and senior director of school support at Uncommon Schools. Lots of times they'll say, "'I can't meet right now. I have to deal with this thing; I have to deal with that. That's always a challenge but it's a bigger challenge now with so much on their plates." When we're able to make a meeting a lot simpler for parents, we get to yes a lot more frequently. Conferencing software like Zoom does that for one-on-one parent meetings and it's no small thing.

The transaction cost of a meeting or conference at school is often high for a parent—with driving from work over to the school, plus arranging child care or coverage at work, it can cost two or three hours of a parent's time—not to mention lost pay from time out of work. If a school can show busy parents their child's work on screen at a cost of 30 minutes, they can meet more easily or more often, at times that are more convenient (both to parents and to teachers or administrators, who can also meet from other locations) and this builds goodwill and ensures alignment and understanding. We don't have to wait until things are really bad to justify a meeting. We can offer parents a 15-minute call to preview an upcoming unit and record it so parents can watch it any time. All of that means it easier to push out information and build transparency—critical organizational goals.

We learned of another way schools can disseminate information and emphasize transparency from Lagra Newman, principal of Nashville's immensely successful Purpose Prep. During the pandemic, Newman decided to offer a Facebook Live tour of the school during the day for parents. She—and later staff members—literally grabbed a phone and walked through the school, visiting classrooms with the camera rolling. The message was: *We want you to know what happens here. It's important and we will go out of our way to make it easy for you.* What a gift for parents to be able to see what their children were up to, what teachers were like during the school day, without leaving work to come down to the school. The transaction cost of transparency—and thus buy-in and understanding—was dramatically reduced. You can see an example of one of Newman's Facebook Live tours in the video *Lagra Newman, Facebook Live.*

The context parents get on Newman's tour is as valuable to the school itself as it is to parents. It's hard not to notice, for example, how joyful and also how orderly and productive the classrooms at Purpose Prep are, and how consistent they are as Newman walks from class to class. Suddenly a parent sees and feels why the school does things the way they do and what the results are. They have a clear sense of culture and methods. If I am a parent and you call me about my child having an issue in class (perhaps she's calling out in class), I suddenly have some context beyond my own experience in school (perhaps it was normal then for students to call out in class) to understand why calling out persistently might be a problem and how outside the norm it is. I can also see that the school is well run—that the benefits it delivers in its social contract with parents are worth working for.

Pushing out information like this makes parents feel welcome and important, builds faith in the institution. It helps parents understand and align with the school's vision and priorities. Seeing is, if not believing, at least understanding. Notice, for example, how much choral response there is in the first class, how attentive the culture is, how much eye contact among students, and how much joy and energy and learning. You can see and feel the enthusiasm! A parent who has reservations about their student being asked to track the speaker, for example, is much more compelled by an argument that it builds the fabric of connection and community when they have seen and felt the culture in the building.

This is doubly important because, as one school leader told us, in the wake of the pandemic, most of her parents have never set foot in the building. They don't have a sense for the place and its rhythms at all. This means that when they have conversations, they have far less context for how things work and what's typical. A parent who has a good mental model of the school and what it looks and feels like is a parent with whom every conversation starts ten steps farther ahead.

Some other key aspects of the video:

1. It's live! Notice that it's not pre-taped. As we've mentioned, this makes it feel especially authentic and transparent, and more personal too. At the outset Newman greets individual parents by name as she sees them log on, cementing a sense of connection for them as well. People feel valued when they feel seen. This sort of event would still be possible, but not quite as effective at connecting, if had been pre-taped.

2. Parents get to see their own child's classroom but also many others. Again, this demonstrates how consistent the school's approach is; there is a model. Newman even explains during the video why it's important that students are learning the same thing across second-grade classrooms. If I am a parent, now I see more clearly why there are schoolwide policies. But as a second-grade parent I also get to see what third and fourth grade will be like. I see the through-line of all the things students will do in the future that they are getting ready

for now. If the school is challenging students to do hard things—to write more, to read complex texts—the rationale becomes clearer when parents can see very concretely what the future will hold.

3. It offers existence proof of the culture. Several of your co-authors have used parent classroom visits as a tool to support a student who was struggling to meet behavioral expectations. *Come in and let's watch your child's class together for 30 minutes.* When parents come to observe, they see the norm of the room and they get to see their child in context. In some cases, with the parents standing in the room, the child struggles. With parents and school leaders observing we can gather data, share observations, and discuss next steps. Sometimes, though, the child is perfect when parents are there, and this demonstrates that the child is capable of meeting the expectations of school if he or she chooses. *Now we know he or she can do it* is an important moment of realization because many parents only know their own child. Of course they sometimes wonder if their child can successfully meet the school's expectations. Seeing them do so and seeing other children do so affirms that they can, and that consistency, support, and the belief that they will succeed are the key pieces of the puzzle.

One of the best parts of the video is that pretty much every student is reading and reacting appropriately to the school norms. If a student is disruptive, it allows Newman to have conversations with parents in which they understand more clearly that disruption is outside the norm.

It turned out this video was just a starting point. The Facebook Live sessions were so successful that Newman and her colleagues continued them *even after access to the building was restored to parents.* It made it easy for them to keep in touch. Every parent who attended felt like they had a clearer connection with staff. Every subsequent conversation was a follow-up with someone they knew a little better and who knew the school a little more. Connection with parents matters, and welcoming them into the school, even virtually, is a great way to build faith and trust.

As a side note, there's a bit of accountability for the school too in making a video like this. It only works if the culture really is strong and positive, and students are attentive. Of course parents would be bothered to see their children in a school where classrooms were not orderly. Committing to more transparency also helps focus a school on making sure it is living up to its promises.

ACCESS FOR STUDENTS

Advances in technology made during the pandemic also make it easier for students to access resources outside of class time. If teachers offer afternoon office hours online, they're often easier for students to get to. Study sessions before a test are one useful way to use Zoom meetings to support rather than supplant classroom instruction. Reducing transaction costs—making it easier to get to such activities—will make some students more likely to attend.

Teachers can also share asynchronous learning materials to help students improve their studying, to catch up if they struggle, or to avoid falling behind if they miss class. A network effect similar to the one Zoom experienced also made Quizlet, Kahoot, and other quiz functions familiar to most students, and this makes the critical learning tool of retrieval practice far more flexible. This is beneficial from both an academic and a well-being standpoint. A student who feels hopelessly behind with little chance of catching up is a student who is likely to become rapidly disconnected from the classroom community; there is far less opportunity to participate meaningfully and cement connections with peers. After enough time spent struggling in isolation, a student is likely to seek allies in rejecting class and community norms.

Absences are also more frequent and longer in a world of postpandemic protocols, and returning from an absence can be disorienting. Missing a week of class can cause students to fall far enough behind that, unabated, they can struggle with ever catching up. But technology can help. "Pre-Covid you'd have an absent student and you'd have to wait for them to come back and teachers would have to try to find the assignment to give it to them," Jody Jones observed. "But now when a student is absent, it's so easy to post their work [i.e. on Google Classroom] and to let them know what's happening." Often, she noted, they come back to school already caught up and engage positively in lessons that much quicker.

During the pandemic administrators at Park East High School in New York City designed the academic schedule with significant chunks of asynchronous time to address Zoom fatigue. This caused math teacher Lauren Brady to think about how she might use the time she wasn't in the classroom to help her students. She started editing the videos of her classes into condensed versions that students could review.

Now that the pandemic is over, she's continued with the videos. She videotapes her lessons on Screencastify into 10- to 12-minute videos: the extended highlights version of the big game. She then uploads them to Edpuzzle, where she intersperses a variety of questions. The result is a high-quality review tool that students who've missed class can access to make sure they don't fall behind. But students who are struggling also use them to review and catch up. Brady will allow any student to retake any test in algebra or AP statistics as long as they review a certain number of the video lessons.

And Brady has found the process valuable in unexpected ways. First, she says, "Sometimes the condensed lessons are better," for two reasons. Her video lessons include some multiple-choice questions of the solve-this-problem sort, but also open-ended thought questions. (What's your hypothesis? What do you think the correlation is likely to be and why?) In a typical lesson, even a student who does every problem might not answer all of these "thought questions." Maybe they raise their hand to answer once. Maybe they think vaguely about a few more of the questions. On the video version, the video pauses when she gets to the questions. Now, "every student answers every question," she says. "That's a big advantage." (She recommends about one per minute of video.)

She also notices how much time can easily be cut from lessons—time she spends repeating an idea a second time, or time she spends chatting with students about semi-connected topics. The process of reviewing through students' eyes helps her to think more deeply about how she teaches live.

The review videos work to supplement a lesson, not supplant it. They work because they capitalize on Brady's existing relationship and because they are perfectly aligned to her tests and lessons. They build off and amplify what she does in class but they wouldn't work as a substitute. However, they're a great way to make missing class far less costly to students. And though they are time consuming to make, they are evergreen. "They took me a lot of time to make but I'll have them for most of the lessons I teach next year as well." What students "miss" when they are absent in the future will be far less than a whole lesson. And she notes that it would be easy to team up with other teachers who teach the same topic and reduce the workload by rotating video duties.

Better academic supports through both synchronous and asynchronous technology can make students feel more connected when they are out of school. Technology can also support with another theme of this book: the importance of making sure students feel seen. Eric Diamon, assistant superintendent for middle schools at Uncommon Schools in Newark and New York City, noted that in returning post-pandemic it was doubly important to find "opportunities to see and celebrate students." Posting and celebrating student work via technology can dramatically expand the reach and thus the positive culture-building and emotional benefits of such efforts. Instead of just posting great work by ten students on a wall to make them feel like their efforts are important, their work can be posted online where hundreds can see it. Families can share it with relatives in other cities. Adding a bit of tech to posting student work can "allow for some really powerful relationship building for students—to know that teachers will celebrate them," Diamon noted.

MANAGING THE DOWNSIDE

So there are lots of ways technology—and expanding familiarity with its platforms among families—can help schools accomplish their mission. But schools also have to recognize the double-edged sword it creates and so we return again to the topic of restrictions—delving now into the details of how and why.

Barring some compelling (and rare!) reason, phones should not be present in the classroom during instruction. How much cell phones are restricted beyond that is more open to question. While it might seem like the simplest solution is to say, "No phones in class, but you may use them on your own time," the reality might be less simple. There is still an immense benefit to students in having time phone free outside the classroom when social interactions can be maximized. It's also important to be aware that phones used between classes mean students will be thinking about what they post and share (or what was posted and shared about them) in the classrooms before and after. Teacher Tapp's survey, for example, found that in schools where students were allowed to have their phones out some of the time, they were more likely to take them out in class than they were in schools where the restrictions were more comprehensive.

But the issue is broader yet. When young people are around their phones, when others are using them around them, when their phones are visible to them and thus capture some of their attention, it influences behavior.

The times when students can check their phones in school, in other words, should be more exception than rule. The more of a universal expectation "phones away in school" is, the more consistent and clearer it is, and the easier it is to build a habit around it. And that means building a habit of more connected and social interactions and more focused, attentive thinking. If it's inconsistent—if the rules change depending on where you are in the building, if it's left up to individual teachers to decide the rules—it's going to be a battle every time. Expectations will devolve to the lowest common denominator because a decision to enforce restrictions will appear "personal." In all likelihood viable restriction is not going to happen under those terms. Building a "flexible" system where teachers have to ask for or announce limitations on phones ("Okay, we're going to have a no phones lesson today," or "I know I sometimes let you use phones but I'm going to ask you to keep them off today") is a recipe for resentment among people who do the right thing and for getting very little done for the first ten minutes of that lesson while students complain and argue and slow-play putting their phones away. And of course it is likely to awaken resentment. In the face of that kind of difficulty and with the payoff perhaps half an hour of phone-free instruction, frankly most teachers are not going to do it.

Much better to simply make it a consistent schoolwide policy: "We never have phones out during lessons here." Or "We never have phones out during the day here." Yes, students may initially argue. But the massive transaction cost of pushback happens once, people get used to it, and then you have a year of high-quality instruction that builds community.

A restriction is different from a limitation, we note. A limitation might say, "You can only use your phone in the following ways or under the following circumstances." A restriction says, "During the following times, your phone may not be present and must be turned off."[2] How extensive the restrictions are is a reasonable question. If you want to allow access to phones at specific non-classroom times during the day, that's reasonable. The right answer probably depends at least in part on the age of your students. For a primary or elementary school, a full ban is a no-brainer. The rule should be: "No phones visible during the day, ever," full stop. We're inclined to think that's the case for middle schools too. It's not unreasonable to say students may have their phones out to communicate with their parents about staying after for activities or how they're getting home, during a clearly demarcated ten minutes at the end of lunch or the end of the day. Just remember that a small window often becomes a large one. Ten minutes becomes twenty. A student says he wasn't able to during his ten minutes and couldn't he do it now. Another student says it's an emergency. Suddenly the expectation is inconsistent. It seems like more flexibility will be easier but the opposite is true. A bright clear line is often best.

High school is by far the trickiest and most challenging case. It's a building full of near-adults who expect and deserve some autonomy, but they are the most likely to have strong dependency and the most likely to use social media platforms that can be anxiety-inducing to their peers. So yes, some flexibility is often warranted for high school students, but allowing young people the "freedom" to limit the quality of the education they and others receive and to contribute to a climate that erodes community and connection is not a viable choice.

Living the Cell Phone Challenge

We asked Denarius, currently principal of a high school, to reflect on the realities and challenges of setting and enforcing restrictions with young adults. Here are his thoughts.

Right now, cell phones (and all technology devices, including smart watches and earphones) cannot be seen or heard during the school day. If they are, they are confiscated until the end of the day. During arrival, there is a staff member who asks to see that students' phones are powered off and stored in their backpacks. However, implementation has been shaky. Sometimes the staff member assigned to the arrival post does not always check that phones are turned off. Sometimes students power their phones back on in the stairwell as they head upstairs. We need to be sharper. Other adults are required to confiscate cell phones if they see them. Most of them are pretty good at this, in part, I think, because they believe that everyone else is also doing it. You need staff to trust each other to get follow-though or it simply won't work.

Even so, I believe many students have their phones on during the day and use them when we don't see them. When they do, they are telling us they kind of accept the tradeoff of risk. And maybe that's rational. If they are caught, the consequence is that they don't have their phone for the remainder of the day and can pick it up during dismissal, but because they are not supposed to be on their phones anyway, the downside isn't huge. This is something I will probably discuss with them so that if the consequences increase, they'll understand why. Either way, the decisions

I make about technology are something we frequently talk about—both in groups that I deliberately convene to hear students' opinions and in individual conversation. For a policy that asks them to change their desired behavior this much, it's especially important to always be communicating about it. We have to listen most to young people when we disagree.

In reflecting on the year, I've confiscated many phones with little to no pushback from students. I don't make it personal, and I don't get mad. You know the rule, you know I care about you, and you know the consequence. If you're consistent, kids understand that.

When I've brought the question of what we should do about phones to the kids, the dialogue has led me to believe that they are actually okay with some form of restriction so long as they in turn have a protected time to check them maybe once or twice during the day. It's almost as if their willingness to hold to the policy is strengthened by us acknowledging their reality: they're deeply anchored to and maybe even dependent on technology and phones; life seems unfathomable without cell phones, although many people have lived quite the opposite experience. So we've taken this idea into consideration as we plan for next year. They want to be understood and to know that we are considering their thoughts and perspective in our decision-making. If the goal is that kids are not using their phones and instead are making meaningful connections with people in our community, we must meet the challenge with some grace— that is, time during the day to allow phone use. Partial restriction, if you will. But the tradeoff has to be what happens if the policy is not upheld. If we say students can use their phones during lunch and study hall, and they still break the rule, maybe requiring their parents to pick them up is a fairer consequence. I'll save that for the next conversation with kids, teachers, and staff. Whatever the policy, all stakeholders will have an opportunity to share, and we will listen. Then we'll make a call that we hope will land.

Before we go on, we pause to note that rules limiting cell phone access during school are generally simple, but the implementation of them is not. They are challenging policies to enforce for at least three reasons.

First, there is a significant incentive for some staff to be non-enforcers, to be the teacher who looks the other way. Teachers may succumb to the temptation to be well liked (we think they will garner only fleeting appreciation). They may be conflict averse. They may not believe in the policy and prefer to subvert it. Whatever the reason, you can be confident that *someone* will not agree and therefore that the policy will test the organization's culture. Ideally we discuss policies openly and candidly, but once a decision is made, everyone supports it. The degree of enforcement you get from teachers is in large part a test of your process. Staff should feel like they've been heard and respected, like they've contributed insights into the details of how it gets done even if the policy is different from what they themselves might choose. Difficult tasks—telling students they have to put their phones away; taking students' phones when you see them—are those most likely to reveal the cracks in organizational health. A school's leadership is going to have to be prepared for dissent.

Second, students are psychologically dependent on their phones. They will not want to give them up even if on many levels they know they should. One teacher we spoke with told us that students in his school were surveyed and overwhelmingly agreed that their phones were harmful to the purposes of schooling. They agreed that they would be better off without them during the day. But they resisted the resulting policy because, well, they wanted their phones. People who are psychologically dependent do not change their behavior simply because they know it would be good for them. And perhaps it's not just people in the grips of psychological dependence or bad habits. "Reason," as David Hume put it, "is the slave of the passions." It is characteristically human to use logic to justify rather than decide what we desire, and this is especially true of teenagers.[3] Ironically, once the restrictions have gone into place, a great many students find they are happier. As in so many cases, young people need adults to help them make a change and, in the end, they come to understand and appreciate it.

The third reason why restrictions are hard to enforce is a practical consequence of the second. Kids are smart and when motivated can be clever. This makes enforcement difficult, especially since teens are generally more technologically adept than adults. One common way to restrict access is to have students turn their phones in somewhere, either in the morning or before class. Several colleagues who used this approach warned us that students would bring extra "burner" phones to turn in and keep the real one, or say they had left their phone at home and didn't have one to turn in. Students will be highly motivated to keep their phones. Some will naturally take pride in proving that any system of limitation—especially one enforced by a school—can be circumvented. That's normal and natural. Several of your co-authors hereby admit to having taken great pleasure in proving that "it" could be done—almost no matter what it was, just so long as "it" was a rule in school. Despite our not-infrequent success, we have no doubt that we would want similar rules today to many of the ones we broke long ago for sake of the young people we serve and care about.

Collecting phones raises several challenging logistical issues. Where will they be kept? How do you identify each phone and its owner? What will you do when someone says their phone has disappeared? So while we think it's feasible to collect phones, and while schools that can't be assured of reliable and consistent follow-through from all staff may have to, we generally think it's a better bet to spend the time and energy enforcing a policy of "I must never see it, and if I do, it will be confiscated." But while a school has to ensure significant diligence in follow-through and monitoring, it is not necessary to find every phone. (Note: please don't tell this to the teenagers.) We say this because one of your teachers will point this out: "We'll never catch every kid who cheats; therefore we should not have the rule." As Denarius observed in the sidebar "Living the Cell Phone Challenge," he's aware of the times and ways that some students probably cheat. He's attentive to it but balanced. He knows it's the overall culture that matters. If one student in 50 sneaks to off to check a phone in a lonely bathroom stall, his private victory is sign of a school culture that does the work required of it. It has made classroom spaces safe for concentration and well-being. The occasional exception especially when students go to great lengths to work around detection proves the rule. It is telling you that the system is mostly working. What you want to watch out for is groups of students *not* trying to hide their use of phones. Let them have the bathroom stalls.

YES, IT CAN BE DONE

Despite the challenges, thousands of schools in the UK, all of them in France and some parts of Australia, and even some in the US have successfully and even happily restricted cell phones. One of your authors Tweeted about the topic recently (yes, we are aware of the irony of using social media for this) and the replies were instructive. In fact they make quite good reading (with occasional observations added):

1. We use Yondr pouches[4] at our school. They are brilliant. Yes, students can break them open. Yes, sometimes students don't lock their phone away, but on the whole it has transformed the school. Social time is spent talking to friends and the like.

2. My last school had trays in each form room. Phones were put in at registration and collected at the end of the day.

3. We are a no-phone school, and students have them in their bags/coats, but we don't see them. If we do, they are taken away and the student is given a sanction.

4. Our students hand their phones in. They're kept in a safe in each classroom. I cannot explain the impact it has on their learning environment and their social interactions.

5. They're not "banned" but students are not allowed to take them out of pockets when on site. As with anything, the consistency of all staff enforcing this has resulted in a great culture and students really respect this!

These posts reflect some of the key themes we've tried to stress: that consistency is key; that the change in culture is usually swift and stunning; that the fact that you may never achieve perfect compliance is not a rationale for not employing restrictions. They also demonstrate the basic options for restriction policies: students turn them in to a central place in the school; students turn their phones in to individual teachers for each class; students are allowed to hold onto their phones but a policy of "If I see it, I take it" is enforced.

6. We have no-phones on campus rule. Older high school students have a designated terrace area where they can use phones. Middle schoolers must have them switched off and away. First time seen: asked politely to put away; next time or repeat phone users, parent collects.

7. My school has a strictly enforced policy this year and it's amazing how lovely the conversations and eye contact are during breaks, lunch, and passing time. After school, they're on their phones like [a drug], but all day, they get a break. Parents love it.

8. No phones at my school. We have a "see it, hear it, lose it" policy. On the very rare occasion we see a phone, the pupils hand it over and parents have to come and collect at the end of the day. Works really well for us.

9. The key has been our staff. If we see it, we take it. Consistent enforcement from all is key. Can't be "the cool teacher."

10. All phones have to be in backpacks at all times. If I see a phone, I take it, turn it into the office, and write a referral. The consequences change based on the number of referrals. First time— warning and turn phone into the office before school.

11. Phones are banned. Must be switched off during the day. If it's seen, it's a 45-minute detention. Clarity, consistency, and communication is key!

12. [Staff] collect phones from students at the beginning of the day and return them just before they leave school. Phones are confiscated for two weeks if not handed in. The system works very well and we rarely have to confiscate anything.

These comments show the details of a variety of approaches to enforcing the rule. In some cases the phone is taken if it's out when it's not supposed to be. There's no "consequence" for the student other than the phone is given back later—sometimes significantly later—or given back only to a parent. This last move can be very effective but, as we'll discuss in a moment, it's most useful when parents are carefully informed and engaged about the policy. In other cases there's a sanction—a detention, for example, sometimes on the first instance, sometimes after multiple infractions. Comments 6 and 11 share another key detail we've heard multiple times: it's not just phones away—it's *turned off* and away. Otherwise it's just too easy to grab them or hide them in the blink of an eye. Comment 6 provides some ideas for a differentiated policy: older students have a designated and circumscribed place where they can have their phones out. We also like the detail of asking politely. Comment 7 is a good example of how parents in fact support the change when they're informed of why. Comment 8 reveals a clearly thought-through process to support the policy. We heard the theme of comment 12 repeatedly: when there is clarity and consistency, students adapt quickly and negative consequences are rare.

13. We allow phones outside but not inside. By facilitating when the phones can be used, we reduce the possibility of setting a climate of deceit from the start.

14. Had a "no phone can be seen" policy for years and it's run very successfully. Once implemented you quickly move to a position where you hardly ever see one out. Clear communication on why—everyone accountable—and process in place to confiscate and escalation if repeated.

15. It's policy in all Victorian Government schools here in Australia. Start of the day till the end. No phones. Many students said that they were relieved when it came into operation.

16. My son's school doesn't play. Phones go in lockers. You are caught with one, it gets taken and you get detention. Uncomplicated, unambiguous, effective.

17. No phones at my kid's middle school. You have to hand them in to your homeroom in the morning and you don't get them back till dismissal. All the kids comply.

18. The school I used to teach at forbade them on campus, period. Parents and students had to sign something at the beginning of the year agreeing that it would be confiscated, and parents had to come inside to sign it back out. Very effective actually.

Some themes in these comments. The importance of clarity and consistency again—then students react quickly. The benefits of engagement and communication with parents. When people understand why, they are far more likely to support an initiative. That idea should be applied to students and probably to teachers as well. They too will be more likely to support it if they understand the science (we'll be presenting some momentarily). Comment 13 is another example of providing a specific but clearly circumscribed place where students can go to check their phones. Comment 15, from Australia, reminds us that such steps can be taken at scale. If governments in other countries can do it,[5] so can ours. So can a school or district.

19. Our whole school [is] "no phones in class." Keys to success include lots of groundwork: surveying parents/students/staff and sharing results; drip feed of neuroscience re impacts of phone use; versus clear policy; consistent implementation w leadership support. Interestingly, in the student surveys beforehand, the students were quite clear that they thought their in-class phone use was affecting their learning, but they were also clear that they didn't want to give up their phones.

20. We do it successfully. We simply frame it this way: red lights are restrictions that allow the system to work. They are not a punishment. Phone restriction is the same.

21. Yep, works in my son's school. Would genuinely rather get him a new phone (eventually) than try to get one back from the front office staff.

22. Our government (AUS) has mandated that phones are off and away all day. It is so nice walking around the yard seeing students actually interacting again, and no distractions during class.

23. The difference is amazing, and everyone seems happier when the phones are away.

We loved comment 19 because it stressed not just informing parents of the policy but informing them more broadly—of the science and the rationale. Notice that even students were involved in the discussion, starting with surveys. As we discussed previously, when people feel like *process fairness* is in place—they are listened to, and their opinions valued—their perception of *outcome fairness* shifts; they are more comfortable supporting decisions they don't agree with; they understand that there are necessary sacrifices to positive broader outcomes. Students benefit from understanding the rationale as much as parents do, even if they disagree, and both they and parents are more likely to support it if they see the clear logic of it. Comment 20 shows a school that has spent time thinking carefully about the messaging and framing. Comment 21 is from a parent who's been inconvenienced by having to pick up a phone at school but still supports the rule. Majority parent support is a likely outcome of a phone restriction policy—several of us are parents and can attest that parents struggle at home to manage the pervasive and negative influence of social media. They're often happy to have the school be an ally. A few may resent the policy. There will be some angry phone calls. But most will appreciate it. They will do so silently and won't call your office, but they are out there in numbers!

There were also a few responses that were more complex, so our gallery walk ends with them:

24. One of the side effects of the phone holder—when students grab their phone on their way out—[is that] most of them walk out of the classroom checking their phone for everything they missed during that class time.

25. I envy anyone who's not had to play whack-a-mole with a classful of kids trying to spend as much time as possible on social media, messaging or video sites on their phones—sometimes with the excuse ("Can I use my phone as a calculator?"), sometimes without.

26. We have students who will actually refuse to put the phone away. They know we can't physically take it from them, and they just flatly refuse. Sadly, there are no consequences for this behavior, so some teachers just give up trying to enforce the rule of phones "away for the day."

Comment 24 reminds us that the nature of the restriction can result in perverse outcomes—as soon as they get their phones back some kids are more likely to dive in deep. Thus perhaps another argument for more pervasive restrictions. It's a safe bet that those students who grab their phones and are checking their accounts before they leave the door are, in fact, thinking about social media throughout much of class. The prospect of getting them back is a source of distraction in much the same way that—research tells us—a nearby phone is still a distraction for students even if it's turned off or turned over. An ideal policy would reduce the number of "transactions" (i.e. times to collect and give back during the day). Each such transaction requires work and follow-through and poses opportunities for lack of follow-through. Comments 25 and 26 come from teachers in schools where enforcement is not consistent and therefore difficult. They remind us of just how time consuming an inconsistent or nonexistent policy can be. And how frustrating.

KNOWLEDGE (OF THE *WHY*) IS POWER

As we discussed earlier, starting with *the why*—explaining the rationale for a policy to the stakeholders you will ask to follow and implement it—is critical to the success of any complex or controversial policy, especially one that will be as visible and challenging as a cell-phone restriction policy. The *why* should ideally be grounded in research and data so that teachers, parents, and students understand its logical basis and see clearly that its purpose is to exercise care for students' best interests. When people feel faith in the process, they are more open to outcomes they may not initially agree with. Taking the time to make a full and transparent case at the outset will save far more time and effort in the long run.

In the section below we've tried to make a model case for restriction based on three primary reasons. We hope it's useful in building one of your own. We note that it repeats some discussion points from the introduction. We've done this so you won't have to go searching and can find the relevant information in one place and perhaps even share the arguments directly with students, parents, and/or teachers.

The *Why*, Part 1: The Attention Problem

The first reason why cell phones warrant restriction in schools is because they fracture attention. They make it harder to focus fully on any task and to maintain that focus. This is not a small thing. Attention is central to every learning task and the quality of attention paid by learners shapes the outcome of a learning endeavor. Reading a challenging book, completing a lab, solving a complex math problem, writing a paper: these things require sustained concentration and focus for a significant period of time. The more rigorous the task, the more it requires proficiency at what experts call selective or directed attention. To learn, and learn well, you must be able to maintain self-discipline about what you pay attention to.

"Directed attention is the ability to inhibit distractions and sustain attention and to shift attention appropriately," Michael Manos, clinical director of the Center for Attention and Learning at Cleveland Clinic recently told the *Wall Street Journal*. The problem with cell phones—especially those armed with social media—is that young people using them switch tasks every few seconds. Better put, they *practice* switching tasks every few seconds, so they become more accustomed to states of half-attention, more and more expectant of new stimulus every few seconds in an endless wave. When a sentence or an idea requires slow, focused analysis, their minds are already glancing around for something new and more entertaining.

"If kids' brains become accustomed to constant changes, the brain finds it difficult to adapt to a nondigital activity where things don't move quite as fast," Manos continued. Reading is the first activity *where things don't move quite as fast* that should come mind for all educators. And though all of us are at risk of this—and though you probably recognize some of these changes in yourself—young people are especially susceptible. The prefrontal cortex isn't fully developed until age 25.[6] This is the region of the brain that exerts "top-down control" over the brain via "descending feedback signals"[7]—that is, impulse control and self-discipline—any conscious decision to decide what we give our attention to. Thinking and learning are in many cases a battle between temptations in the environment and the efforts of the prefrontal cortex to focus us.

Tech companies are what education writer Daisy Christodoulou calls "attention merchants." Their goal is "capturing attention and reselling it at a profit." Social media and almost anything you experience on your browser are businesses—very big ones. The business model involves putting you in a state of poor concentration and impulsivity for a large portion of your day, so you are a suggestible consumer. To do this they must subvert the prefrontal cortex's ability to divert your attention to anything else. They succeed only if they can "make using their website or app a frequent and automatic habit," for millions of people, Christodoulou writes, "and they've mined the insights of behavioral psychology to . . . make their product [and the states of attention to cause us to jump to it at the slightest flicker of thought] habit forming." Because they are free to the user, it's easy to overlook the fact that their goal is to make money from your behavior. There is a familiar adage in the tech sector that expresses this idea: "If you're not paying for the product, you are the product." Attracting a manipulatable form of people's attention is known in the sector as earning "eyeballs," which rather creepily expresses the idea that the portion of the body central to guiding attention can be functionally detached from the part of us that processes it. Manipulating attention to sell you things is the purpose of the endeavor of social media, but of course being sold things isn't the only outcome, or even the worst one.

Anytime young people are on a screen they are in an environment where they are habituated to states of low attention and constant task-switching. This is the case even if they are not actively on social media, though of course most young people will at a minimum be fighting the impulse to check social media as soon as they turn on their phones *even if that was not their original intent in checking them.*

As we noted in the introduction, in 2017 before the rise of the newest generation of maximally disruptive products like TikTok, a study found that undergraduates (more cerebrally mature than K–12 students and so with stronger impulse control, it's worth noting) "switched to a new task on average every 19 seconds when they were online."

And of course the brain rewires itself constantly based on how it functions. This idea is known as neuroplasticity. The more time young people spend in constant task switching and searching for novel information, the harder it becomes for them to develop or maintain the capacity for sustained periods of intense concentration. Our brain is constantly rewiring itself to respond to the ways that we use it. If we send our brains the signal that we need them mostly for tasks involving a frenzy of distraction and half attention, they will rewire to expect and be responsive to those settings. This is to say that after a time, the risk is that our phones are within us. A brain habituated to constant states of half attention and impulsivity rewires to become more prone to those states. Without mitigation, our phones—and certainly social media and gaming apps—socialize us to fracture our own attention.

This affects us most when they are near but even when they are not in our hands.

"If you want kids to pay attention, they need to practice paying attention," is how John Hutton, pediatrician and director of the Reading and Literacy Discovery Center at Cincinnati Children's Hospital, put it, and the first step to that is to enforce a break from devices that destroy it. An institution with the purpose of learning cannot ignore an intruder that actively erodes its prime currency.

The *Why*, Part 2: An Anxiety Machine

Cell phones armed with social media are addictive thanks especially to the advent of the Like button starting in 2009. Getting likes delivers a small surge of dopamine—a neurochemical that makes us feel a tiny bit of euphoria. This biochemical response to affirmation is surely connected to the evolutionary importance of group formation. Seeking group approval is too important to leave to the decision-making parts of our brains; we are wired to reward social approval and connection chemically—which ensures that we reliably heed the call.

But our phones take it up a level. Like buttons deliver what is called "intermittent variable reward." The dopamine surge is unpredictable. You can't rely on it. Research has shown that such uncertainty "keeps us checking and checking more than a definite reward," writes Christodoulou. You begin to obsess over getting likes and other forms of electronic approval because they are connected to "the inner gauge that tells us, moment by moment, how we're doing in the eyes of others," explains Jonathan Haidt.[8] You can score yourself through the eyes of others—or at least subscribe to the illusion of that—and get constant updates. If there's anything we hope you've gotten from this book, it's that we should take the phrase "in the eyes of others" seriously. The combination of unpredictable reinforcement and a device that scores our popularity and degree of inclusion for others to see is an addiction machine.

Again the cost of this is shown in Twenge's research. "Teens who spend six to nine hours a week on social media are still 47 percent more likely to say they are unhappy than those who use social media less," she writes. "The more time teens spend looking at screens, the more likely they are to report symptoms of depression. Eighth-graders who are heavy users of social media increase their risk of depression by 27 percent," Twenge writes. "Teenage loneliness was relatively stable between 2000 and 2012, with fewer than 18 percent reporting high levels of loneliness" she and Haidt wrote. But in the six years after 2012—when cell phones became universalized and social media began to include approvals and like buttons, rates increased dramatically. "In 36 out of 37 countries, loneliness at school has increased since 2012," they report. "They roughly doubled in Europe, Latin America and the English-speaking countries." But much of that data was from pre-pandemic years.

A CDC report published in late March and based on surveys of 7700 teens in 2021 rang the alarm even more clearly. It warned of an "accelerating mental health crisis" among teens, with 44% saying they feel "persistently sad or hopeless." As recently as 2009 that number had been at 26% and even in 2019 it was significantly lower (37%). Roughly 20% of teens said they had contemplated suicide. This number too represented a dramatic increase, but the numbers hid a gender disparity. Social media is an anxiety and isolation machine *for girls in particular*. "Boys tend to bully one another physically," Twenge writes, "while girls are more likely to do so by undermining a victim's social status or relationships. Social media give middle- and high-school girls a platform on which to carry out the style of aggression they favor, ostracizing and excluding other girls around the clock." For what it's worth, among the hours that a typical teen spends online every day, boys are likely to spend proportionally more of it gaming while girls are likely to spend proportionally more of it engaged in social media, which might be one more reason for the disparity. Regardless, rates of anxiety and depression are often almost twice as high for girls as for boys.

It's worth noting that a lot of the engineering done by tech firms is specifically designed to reduce the influence of other social networks, especially the family. Posts that disappear as soon as they are read make the social media interactions of teens invisible to adults and parent proof—especially the toxic and brutal ones. Parents never see them, so a supportive adult is far less likely to know or be able to help process the pain and anxiety. A staple of social media design is the offer of anonymity. Not being accountable for what you say brings out the very worst in human behavior.

We hear some educators arguing, "It's up to teenagers to learn to manage their phones," or even more implausibly, "Schools should teach young people the skill of managing technology." This is patently unrealistic. Schools are not designed to address psychological dependence, and it's hubris to think that the average teacher can—in addition to everything else he or she is responsible for—now suddenly master the art of battling a creation of tech engineers that has addicted a generation via a few pithy lessons, presumably done in all the spare time left over from everything else they're teaching, as if it were more or less like teaching kids to use a microwave. Changing the behavior of people who are psychologically dependent on their phones is difficult, exhausting, and time consuming. Some teachers *might* be able to do it with quality training and strong curriculum if it was the only thing they set out to do. But it's not. It's magical thinking to propose that an epidemic that has doubled rates of mental health issues and changed every aspect of social interaction among millions of people is going to go away by having teachers stand in front of the room declaring, "Kids, always use good judgment with your phones." Restricting phones is a far better strategy.

In a 2021 editorial Twenge and Haidt argued essentially the same thing: that schools *must* restrict phones if they care about young people's well-being.

The *Why*, Part 3: A Single Phone Affects Everyone

Cell phones affect behavior when they are present even if people are not using them. "Smartphones and social media don't just affect individuals," Twenge and Haidt point out. "They affect groups. The smartphone brought about a planetary rewiring of human interaction. As smartphones became common, they transformed peer relationships, family relationships and the texture of daily life for everyone—even those who don't own a phone or don't have an Instagram account. It's harder to strike up a casual conversation in the cafeteria or after class when everyone is staring down at a phone. It's harder to have a deep conversation when each party is interrupted randomly by buzzing, vibrating 'notifications.'" They quote the psychologist Sherry Turkle, who notes that we are, now, "forever elsewhere."

"Forever elsewhere" is what we hear echoes in the words a college student shared about his life on campus recently. "Often I'll arrive early to a lecture to find a room of 30+ students sitting together in complete silence, absorbed in their smartphones, afraid to speak and be heard by their peers. This leads to further isolation and a weakening of self-identity and confidence, something I know because I've experienced it."

But a phone user's actions in a group setting shape the thoughts and experience of nonusers in other ways. Among other things, it distracts them; research suggests that simply having a phone nearby causes the user and others to think about what might be happening on their phone. Most psychologically addictive behaviors are this way. And of course, "causes everyone to start thinking about what's on their phone" is not neutral. It is just as likely laced with anxiety since so much of social media interaction is as well. What exactly are the other people in the room texting? Young people are keenly aware that the person across the room who appears lost in their device while you're talking could just as easily be mocking them, their comments, their attire to others in the room—for consumption then or for mean-spirited commentary later in the day.

The social behaviors of phone users reshape the broader social norms of every room they enter. "Even when they do see their friends," Twenge writes, smartphones allow and encourage them to "avoid certain social interactions." They are less likely to send a welcoming glance to greet a friend, less likely to overhear and laugh at a funny remark. Glancing down at their screens in public places, they make those places less connected and more isolating. There's nothing more isolating than feeling alone and ignored in a crowd. "At school people are quieter," a high school senior told Twenge in *iGen*. "They are all on their technology ignoring each other . . . they seem like they don't want to talk to me because they are on their phones." And of course the natural response, now, is to take your phone out and look busy as well.

Group-based interactive activities that create community and connection provide an antidote to the world of social media; yet another result of increased phone use is the decline of participation in almost every other activity. Teens are far less likely to hold an after-school job than they were a few years ago, for example. They are less likely to engage in after-school activities like drama club or jazz band. And nonparticipation influences peers almost as much as the individuals who, immersed in an online life, no longer choose, say, to try out for the school play. Demand shapes supply. When fewer people participate in communal life, there are soon fewer ways to participate in communal life. There are fewer school plays to try out for, fewer science clubs, fewer debate teams. We speak from personal experience here. One of us has a child who loves after-school gatherings like the science and Spanish clubs. They provide social connection as much as a setting in which to engage her curiosity. Over the course of the past school year, however, about half of those clubs simply ceased functioning due to dwindling attendance. When only three or four kids show up to a meeting, it's not much fun, you can't do much, and there's not really a group to feel like you belong to. After that it's only a matter of time before just one or two show up. At that point, just before it goes defunct, the last act of the club is often to reinforce the loneliness and isolation of those last few students who are there in the room seeking connection and belonging and finding none.

BUILDING IN THE ANTIDOTE

More than merely providing a respite from screens and social media, schools can provide an antidote to the drawbacks of the online world. When Sam Eaton and her colleagues at Cardiff High School in Cardiff, Wales, welcomed students back from the pandemic, the school's rules included restrictions on phones. But the school didn't just tell students what they *couldn't* do. It made it easier for students to do positive, enjoyable things that rebuilt their social connections and relationships with their peers. The school's staff devised a variety of settings where students could interact during recess—for example, tables to sit at with cards and board games provided, ping-pong tables, spaces for other outdoor games. It gave students something explicitly social to say yes to.

Frequent informal interactions while playing games are a great way to rebuild social skills and rekindle feelings of connection. Playing cards requires eye contact and reading facial expressions. There are funny under-the-breath remarks and momentary disappointments over losing a hand. There are lots of low-stakes opportunities to get feedback on whether what you said was well-suited to the moment— gracious or funny or made you sound like a sore loser. That sort of thing rebuilds the interactive skills that wane when the phone dominates young people's lives. Students can use those skills to build positive relationships. It also provides a stronger feeling of connection than just standing around wishing you had your phone.

This picture of students playing chess in the courtyard at Cardiff High School is a good example. Small tables have been set up for serious players; there's a giant set for those who want something a bit more lighthearted.

This giant Jenga set facilitates short lighthearted interactions with a more impromptu group of peers.

Add to that ping-pong and card tables (cards provided!), as seen in these pictures.

Suddenly students have a whole range of informal but constructive ways to connect and interact. There are constant small signals about greeting and belonging and turn-taking via eye contact, facial expression, and body language. If you are a student, you look around and you see those things and the resulting connectedness everywhere, in a dozen different ways. You are reminded of how human interaction works. And it's easy to feel belonging because there's likely to be something for everyone.

Family-style meals are another example. They have been a godsend since the pandemic, Jen Brimming of Marine Academy in Plymouth, England, told us. Lunch at Marine Academy means kids and one or two adults around a small table in easy social and socializing chatter. It doesn't have to be formal or topical; the adult doesn't lead a discussion of current events. It's lightly structured togetherness, eye contact and talking as a group for a sustained period. People have a place to belong to. Some schools actually serve meals family style or include family-like responsibilities; when one of us ate at Michaela School in London, students brought over a tray with the meals and others bought a pitcher of juice or wiped the table afterwards. Other schools let students get their lunch cafeteria style but provide a warm and welcoming seating face-to-face that makes the sorts of interactions that let all students feel connected far more likely. Everyone has someone to talk to.

You can see that in the pictures Jen sent us.

Note the eye contact, the group interaction, even the slow pace implied by a conversation involving an adult and a real knife and fork.

Sam and Jen's schools have both made small adaptations of familiar activities to create what we think of as antidotes—activities during the school day that work to facilitate positive interactions that counteract isolation. They recall for us the data from Jean Twenge's research we shared in Chapter 1 showing that certain activities correlate negatively to anxiety, loneliness, and depression such as playing a sport wherein young people engage in purposeful shared endeavor, cooperation, eye contact, and turn-taking, not to mention managing disappointment and success. Things like that do more than just disrupt screen time; they replace it with something actively curative.

The school day is full of moments that could be optimized—recess or lunch as at Sam's and Jen's schools, but also arrival, dismissal, passing time, or morning meeting. Our caveat would be that quality has a greater effect than quantity. Better to have one or two really meaningful interactions per day than several that don't quite come off and only sort of build culture. Poorly run activities tell students that the institutions of their lives are fragile, weak, and unable to connect the people within them, just as a poorly run class with low academic expectations suggests to them that their time isn't especially valuable.

And of course, schools can provide more antidote time via more or better extracurricular activities as well—vibrant well-run clubs, teams, and interest groups.

In Chapter 5 we'll describe more extensively how Charlie Friedman, executive director at Nashville Classical Charter School in Nashville, Tennessee, and a group of teachers redesigned extracurricular activities after returning from the pandemic. One of the key things was to focus on audience-building. "We really focused on giving those students a chance to perform," he noted, but the performance feels more meaningful if a lot of people come. Yes, you want your parents there but you want your peers there as well. You'd like a few friends and maybe a few classmates you'd like to know a bit better there. "We thought a lot about how to incentivize and encourage people to come and watch performances and games," Friedman said. Of course not every kid was able to participate, but the interesting thing was that by building the audience experience they not only made it more fun to perform, they made it more fun and meaningful to attend. You felt belonging when you were engaged and connected in the stands. Singing and chanting and celebrating together can be as meaningful as performing together.

That said, it's important to also offer extracurriculars where participation does not require a specific cultivated talent. Many of the most common extracurriculars like sports and music are based on activities that reflect a lifelong commitment. As athletes and musicians ourselves we love these activities and fully endorse them. But the downside is that if you are 15 and looking for something meaningful to add to your life and haven't played soccer or sung all your life, those things are out for you. So clubbish activities that you can join based on enthusiasm and interest and still feel belonging are also really important.

Speech and debate have been critical additions at Strive Prep in Denver, Elisha Roberts told us. Anyone can join; it just takes willingness. And it features all the social benefits you'd want: eye contact, teamwork, turn-taking. But Roberts also described one of the small routines that facilitators used to build community. "You count however many kids are in the class. It starts completely silent and then one person has to say 'one,' and then you have to listen and feel for who is going to say 'two,' 'three,' and so on. Seeing middle schoolers do that and be in tune with each other and be trying to get to 25 and to say, 'Oh, we couldn't do it in 30 seconds.' There was a connectivity that was playful and simple but powerful in terms of socioemotional connectedness." It reminds us that small moments can be built in anywhere, that in fact a school might assemble for teachers a list of simple collaborative games they could play in two minutes or less at down times—before class, at communal lunch, in the hallway, or as a reward for a great class discussion.

The CDC's survey bore this out. Teens who said they felt connected to people at school were "far less likely to report poor mental health than those who did not feel connected at school." We don't have to find everyone a best friend; we just have to make them feel seen, cared about, relevant, fully present in the life of the institution and the perception of their peers. A well-run school "can be a protective factor" in students' lives, the CDC's head of adolescent and school health, Kathleen Ethier, told the *Washington Post*.

We note especially the term "well-run." No one feels a connection to and belonging within a poorly run place that wastes their time and can't get things done or that can't cause people to behave positively. The chess tables and ping-pong at Cardiff High School only work if pupils reliably respect and protect the equipment and if the school can make sure there's a fresh supply of unbroken ping-pong balls and full decks of playing cards. Orderliness is surprisingly central to belonging. Doing things well, especially including the core of the daily work of school—having classes that are well-taught and productive and feel meaningful to students; having the institution efficient in running core activities and reliably able to do what it sets out to do—those things also affect the belonging students feel.

"I think folks want to be claimed," David Adams, CEO of the Urban Assembly's network of 23 district schools in New York City told us. "There's this idea that teenagers don't want to belong to things. Yet they go out into our communities and . . . are claimed by antisocial groups. It's okay to claim them and say, "You're ours," but we have to understand that there is a contract that is part of that. People want to be a part of something and we can help them do that If we can deliver on our part of the contract."

Too many students go unclaimed by schools. This has always been true, but it is doubly challenging now when young people live with a clever device in their pocket forever whispering to them that it will find a place for them in the world. That device can deliver a million bright and alluring "interactions" no matter where they are.

Consider how this has rewired two small aspects of young people's lives compared to those of a generation ago.

One is the decline of waiting, and therefore mind-wandering. Think of how much time you spent waiting when growing up—for a ride from your mom or for a bus; in line at the pharmacy or the department of motor vehicles—all of them spent with "nothing to do" except observe the people around you, the traffic going by, wander through the thousand almost-nothings in your head (some of which became ideas and beliefs after a time). Young people today never do that. There's less waiting anyway (you wait in a virtual queue) but if they do they simply scroll through their phones instead. There is no mind-wandering downtime.

Another difference is the end of one of previous generations' most anxious moments: having to eat alone in the school cafeteria or a restaurant. Movies from the sixties, the eighties, even the aughts, are full of cafeteria scenes where the protagonist stands with his or her tray at the entrance to the cafeteria and . . . Well, we didn't need more than that to know what the scene was about. Now young people simply take out their phones and engage in another world. They eat alone all the time.

The convenient accessibility of a simple form of connection, we are saying, has rewritten the equations of social interaction in ways that are complex (not always good; not always bad). We cannot outcompete the phone based on convenience—on the speed and variety of interactions. Having lunch alone and scanning Instagram is less painful than eating alone and having nothing to do but look around and chew, so of course young people (and adults!) chose it. But compared to having lunch with friends—to laughter and smiles and familiar patterns—it is paper thin.

We compete with that device to claim young people, to cause them to decide they belong at least in part with us. As institutions (the most important institutions in society, we'd argue), we can only hope to compete based on quality—on rich interactions that bring humanity and camaraderie into the foreground and make those the characteristics of the places where we learn. There are fewer and fewer places to have a laughter-filled lunch with friends. That is just maybe the window through which we climb and claim kids to school (and implicitly to community and shared endeavor).

After all, there is a reason why technology (despite the Ted Talkers announcing the arrival of a seamless future of frictionless, learner-led, at-your-own-pace learning) showed during the pandemic that it could not come near the classroom—even the flawed version of it we offer most young people—for learning outcomes and resulted in massive learning declines. It matters to be in the room with other people, to read the body language of others as they present or listen, to feel the room when the insight drops. The classroom is still the room where it happens because of the power of individual connected to group and all of the signals that creates. If we can build enough flesh-and-blood connection into the day (we will take up that topic in subsequent chapters), we may find even the students initially opposed to giving up their phones to be glad they did.

Notes

1. Today, young people can't rent a car until they are 25 because insurance companies recognize that they are less adept at considering the long-term consequences of their decisions.
2. If you want, you can add an *unless clause,* so in unusual cases teachers can turn off the default—as in, phones are restricted unless the teacher has made (or requested) a special exception—but honestly we recommend against it.

3. For an excellent discussion of the research behind ex post facto reasoning—making a gut decision and then using the rational brain to justify it—see Jonathan Haidt, *The Righteous Mind*.
4. Yondr is one of several companies that make secure pouches for cell phones so they can be turned in before class.
5. France has also banned cell phones.
6. The development and maturation of the prefrontal cortex occurs primarily during adolescence and is fully accomplished at the age of 25. The development of the prefrontal cortex is very important for complex behavioral performance, because this region of the brain helps accomplish executive brain functions. https://www.ncbi.nlm.nih.gov/pmc/articles/PMC3621648/#:~:text=The%20development%20and%20maturation%20of%20the%20prefrontal%20cortex%20occurs%20primarily,helps%20accomplish%20executive%20brain%20functions
7. https://www.ncbi.nlm.nih.gov/pmc/articles/PMC2752881/#:~:text=Taken%20together%2C%20these%20observations%20suggest,information%20that%20is%20behaviorally%20relevant
8. Haidt is quoting the social psychologist Mark Leary here.

Chapter 3

Rewiring the Classroom: Teaching That Amplifies the Signals of Belonging

This image, taken during a discussion among students in Denarius Frazier's classroom (described in Chapter 1), tells a story about how classrooms can encourage students to send signals of belonging to one another, and the power those apparently tiny signals have to shape classroom culture in significant ways. Those smiles of support, those affirming gazes of Vanessa's classmates—they are no small thing, we contend.

In a moment we're going to delve more deeply into the video of that lesson and several others to unpack key details of how classrooms can be wired to signal connection and belonging, how they can be made to feel so dynamic and engaging that students feel swept up in something, and how classrooms can make students feel important, like part of something bigger. But we want to pause first to make an important point.

You will see connection, community, joy, and belonging in all of the classrooms we show you. We hope you will study them carefully alongside us to unlock the magic the teachers have wired into the culture. But please do not fail to observe that these classrooms are all also academically demanding, rigorous, and knowledge-rich. They ensure emotional and psychological fulfillment *while also fostering the highest rates of learning and achievement.*

These are classrooms that prioritize learning—more than the average classroom, arguably—and yet students still feel connection and belonging throughout. In many cases those feelings come about *because* of the learning they are doing. So we want to be clear: the question we should be asking is not *How do we wire classrooms so students feel belonging and connection?* It's *How do we wire classrooms so students feel belonging and connection while making sure they learn as much as possible?* It cannot be a choice between the two.

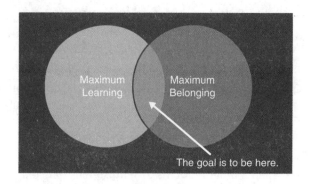

Fortunately, there's more synergy than conflict between these two goals. Remember that the psychologist Martin Seligman's formulation of happiness includes three pathways that create it: pleasure, engagement, and meaning. When those three things combine, the feeling of well-being is strongest. Of the three pathways, people are most likely to perceive the connection between pleasure and happiness, but most likely to actually be made happy by experiencing engagement and meaning. A 2009 study by Seligman and Stephen Schueller found that while all three contributed to an individual's overall sense of well-being, pursuing engagement and meaning was more strongly related to well-being than pursuing pleasure.[1] When we lose ourselves in a task and we feel like what we are working toward is important, we are happy.

HIS STUDENTS ARE SO MOTIVATED

It's hard to watch the video of Denarius's class and not be impressed by his students. Each time Denarius asks a question they throw themselves into the task with energy and spirit. "We're a little divided," he says to students a little less than 30 seconds into the clip. "Turn and Talk: Why?"

The moment that phrase leaves his mouth, the room crackles to life. Every student enthusiastically discusses the problem with a peer without a moment's hesitation. A more rational response (at least in many classrooms) might be to turn to your partner and observe what they do first before expressing any willingness (or enthusiasm) to discuss the question on your own part. Are they really going to talk to you about sine and cosine? You wouldn't want to be too eager if your classmate was going to roll her eyes or scoff at the conversation. If that was what students were doing in Denarius's classroom, things would literally *sound* different. The response would be far more muted: the sounds of voices would be tentative at first and build only very slowly, or not at all.

But that's not what happens here. Students seem utterly sure that their peers will want to talk math. There isn't a second of doubt or hesitation. And of course, having seen their peers' response to this Turn and Talk, they will be even more confident next time. They will have internalized one more data point that the norm in Mr. Frazier's room is enthusiastic scholarly engagement.

Later, when they discuss the problem as a group, students talk *to* each other, not *past* each other. They listen carefully. They build off one another's ideas. Each student's comments seem important, which means that *they* feel important.

It's an impressive group of young people. In fact sometimes a colleague will watch the video and say something along the lines of, "Well if my students were like *that,* I could work miracles too," but to see the video that way is to mistake the outcome for the cause. We understand why you might make that mistake, mind you. Denarius appears to do very little except simply step back, ask a question, and smile in anticipation of the room exploding into engaged intellectual debate.

But of course, as anyone who's ever tried it knows, the reality is far more complex. If you "did what he does" here without laying the foundation he has carefully lain, you'd get a very different result. Yes, we think almost any group of students will engage this positively if the environment is just right, but it also takes a great deal of intentional design and engineering to create just the right classroom environment. The moves Denarius makes in the video are carefully if subtly executed and the moves that we don't see because they happened before this lesson took place are twice as important—and doubly intentional.

What we are seeing is an exercise in positive social engineering, which is to say Denarius has thought very deeply about the culture he wants his room to express and how he can bring it into being. In fact, what we hope to convey in this chapter is that classrooms are first and foremost cultures, and the interactions among students, especially in the classroom, must be deliberately orchestrated to build a sense of connection, belonging, and shared scholarly endeavor.

To go a step further, engineering classrooms this way is quite possibly the single most important thing schools and teachers can do to help address students' need for connection and community. After all, in a typical seven-hour school day, students might spend six of those hours in classrooms. A school can invest in its socioemotional programs and extracurricular activities (in later chapters we'll discuss how to do that, so know that we are in favor of those things) but unless the classrooms come to life like Denarius's does, unless the six hours per day of sitting in lessons makes students feel important, accomplished, connected, and successful, the other pieces are only going to help so much. The classroom remains the fundamental site of interaction in school. There is no way to have an inclusive school culture worthy of every child without weaving reliably great culture into the overwhelming majority of classrooms.

On the whole young people are historically behind academically and are historically isolated socially. Leading schools and classrooms that create opportunity and foster well-being sufficiently to address this dual crisis necessarily demands a level of intentionality about the culture that we hope to show is evident in Denarius's classroom. Your classroom (or classrooms if you lead a school) will of course feel slightly different, will bring to light a culture with different emphases and tone. But in this chapter we argue that it should have the same level of intentionality; we like the word "engineered" to describe the level of design that's necessary to creating the optimal learning environment. Every classroom should ensure that students work hard toward important goals with focus and engagement, uninterrupted by distractions, within a group of peers who signal caring and support, especially when members of the group are in the midst of scholarly endeavor.

We think that's possible and we're going to show you a series of classrooms that prove it. We'll study why they are that way and focus on a handful of things that matter most from a point of view of connection and belonging in Denarius's classroom and others like it. (Our discussion draws heavily on terms that readers of Doug's book *Teach Like a Champion 3.0* will be familiar with. For those who aren't, we'll try to explain them briefly as we go, but if this chapter speaks to you, you will need that book as well.)

"SNAPS IF YOU AGREE"

Let's start with a tiny and seemingly inconsequential moment. About 1:15 into the video of Denarius's classroom, a student named Folusho (in the back row, wearing a sweatshirt) responds to her classmate, Vanessa. "Okay," she says, "I agree with Vanessa. I think [example] A is finding the reciprocal, and reciprocal and inverse are not the same thing." As she says this, something that might seem odd happens. Three or four classmates start to snap. A few seconds later you can see Fagan, the girl in the center of the screen, nodding along as she snaps. She's looking around, trying to establish eye contact with other students to encourage them to join in and snap too.

Folusho (left) answering; Fagan (right) snapping and nodding at peers to encourage then to join her.

The snapping is a system of positive reinforcement Denarius has established. Students snap to show support for a classmate when she is speaking. The "support" can signal a variety of subtly different things. On an intellectual level it can express, "I agree with you" or "I got that answer too." On a more emotional level it can mean, "I support you; keep going; you're doing fine."

Perhaps this seems at first like a bit of a gimmick. It isn't.

Speaking to a group of people is anxiety inducing, but also necessary for optimal learning. Almost everyone feels at least mild tension when they speak in front of a group, doubly so teenagers, who are keenly sensitive to status and peer acceptance. For the great majority of us, the moments when we start to speak are moments when a small voice asks,

"Do I sound stupid right now?" or perhaps less anxiously, "Is what I am saying making sense?" If we feel right away that we are succeeding and winning approval, that can be a huge motivator to persist in talking and to talk again in the future. On the other hand, if we're plagued by doubts, if we think it's going badly and that we've just embarrassed ourselves in front of others, it will make us want to speak less.

This is a constant challenge in classrooms. Talking in public about ideas is central to learning about them; it's also central to building cultures of belief. If I never see people in my peer group talking about sine and cosine, I will likely think those things are not for me either. If my peers are always talking about sine and cosine—and the electoral college and juxtaposition and resistance and adagio—then I will come to believe that those things are mine too.

So it's important that as Folusho starts to talk, she instantly gets subtle but consistent positive feedback from her peers. *You're doing great*, they're saying, even as she's talking. Her classmates are able to simply and *without interrupting her* express the idea that they support her. It's a tiny signal that reinforces her feelings of success and builds between them a sense of membership in something meaningful and real. Using a shared code demonstrates that they are part of a group. Using it to praise a comment about finding the inverse of sine says that the group values the scholarly.

You can hear these snaps of support and affirmation throughout the video: when Brittany weighs in about 1:45 into the video and again at about two minutes. There's snapping for Vanessa when she changes her answer just after 2:15. You could argue that this is as important a signal as the smiles and glances of affirmation that we described in Chapter 1.

Note also that Denarius specifically asks for snaps at 2:30: "I agree that A is the answer. Snaps if that's correct." He's reinforcing the signal, making it more of a habit for all students to use it, and making everyone feel like they are participants in getting the right answer. Their sign-off (Yes, we all agree. That's correct.) affirms the groupishness of the moment. Just maybe it's not fully correct until they've all affirmed it in this small way. A room full of teenagers is a room full of people looking around to determine what are the unspoken norms of thought and belief to which they should adhere. In that setting every single person in the room has just affirmed: *I understand how to find the inverse of sine. I care about finding the inverse of sine.*

Snaps for that, we say.

There's even a hilarious moment (well, we think it's hilarious) at about 2:45, where Omowunmi is speaking and one student in the back snaps "wrong"—at least in Fagan's eyes. Maybe his timing is off. Maybe it's too loud. But Fagan glances back as if to let him know, "Hey, that's not how we do it."

Side note: We're pretty sure we could make a movie just about Fagan and her incredible efforts build connections and shape norms behind the scenes in this video. Like so many kids in your classrooms, she is a connector, a team builder, a captain. She and a thousand kids like her are all-in on culture building if we can give them a truly worthy culture to help build!

In fact what Fagan's reaction to the "wrong" snapping—and the moment when she is rounding up snappers to support Folusho—tells us is that she perceives this system to be hers. *She wants it done right!* Denarius has carefully installed and explained the system. He has set initial rules for how to use it (and how not to!) but now there's shared ownership. Students are constantly initiating it of their own accord without Denarius's input. They value the way it shapes the classroom, now—the positivity, the mutual support, the connection it creates. It lets them be actively involved when someone else is talking.

Anytime students remind each other of their community's deeply held beliefs, values, principles—"how we do things here"—it makes that community and individual's commitment to it stronger. Students take intellectual risks and persist in Denarius's class in part because they get this small signal of affirmation from their peers. They engage more fully as listeners because they get to send signals of appreciation to their classmates and because looking to praise things you find insightful causes you to see them more often. Denarius has given students a way to build a team, to signal membership and support to one another, and they have embraced it. They *like* feeling like a team.

The snapping seems like a small thing, but it's not.

One reason it's not a small thing is that in many cases, how a student's classmates respond to her efforts to participate is as important as, if not more so than how her teacher does. In *Motivated Teaching*, Peps McCrea reminds us that our perception of social norms is the single biggest influence on our actions and motivations. The older the student, we'd argue, the more important their perception of the group norm is in shaping their behavior. Teens will seek to do what they think other teens do.

Further, McCrea notes, the more we feel we belong to a group, the more we become invested in its goals and conform to its norms. Students signal (to others) and reinforce (to themselves) their membership when they snap along with peers. This makes them more vested in the culture.

Imagine: You are sitting in a class room where your peers' actions are telling you: *We enjoy and value discussing trigonometry*. It's a norm, an unwritten assumption or rule within the group. The more you feel you're part of that group, the more tiny things you do to express your membership in it, the more your peers appear to make an effort to signal that you belong, the more you feel pleasure, engagement, and meaning as you do things. All of these things cause you to internalize the norms of the group more deeply, and in this case the more you feel like you are an *enjoys-and-values-discussing-trigonometry* kind of person. It recalls an observation of Daniel Coyle's: "Belonging feels like it happens from the inside out, but in fact it happens from the outside in." You feel like you belong because you act like you belong. Tiny signals are as important as big ones.

Meanwhile, Denarius says nothing during most of these interactions. We don't see him build the system; we don't see all the moments at the beginning of the year when he explained to students when to snap and how to do it right (quickly two or three times only, etc.). It looks like he's passive, but he's far from it.

To design the procedures in a classroom, to make them routine, to invest students with a feeling of shared ownership in them when possible, to ensure that they engage in and feel engaged by them: these are among the most important skills of any teacher but especially the teacher who seeks to shape his or her students' perception of school and their relationship to it. To shape norms and build students' buy-in to those norms is to build culture. That's what makes Denarius's classroom exceptional. To put a fine point on it, we will not succeed in addressing the academic and social needs of young people in the wake of the pandemic unless we actively build optimal learning cultures. We've chosen to begin studying how this works with such a seemingly mundane norm—peer-to-peer snapping—to show that even a very small behavior can be immensely influential in achieving that goal.

WE CALL THIS "PROPS"

We call the classroom systems that encode snapping and other forms of affirmation "Props." To give props is to give recognition, approval, acknowledgment, or praise to another person. There are a variety of potential versions beyond snapping that a teacher can use to allow students to express mutual affirmation. Two other common versions are "sending shine" and "sending magic." When students "send shine" to one another they make a small gesture on their hands with fingers wriggling like sunlight entering a room and direct it at someone they wish to show support for.

This image shows students in a video we'll discuss shortly "sending shine" to a classmate as she answers a question. Sending shine is similar to snapping because it expresses appreciation, but some teachers prefer it because it is silent and because the name makes the purpose explicit: a signal we send to support someone and help them succeed.

It's not either/or of course. Sending "shine" can coexist with snapping (the classroom we took this picture from uses both). But it's also important to be careful of having too many Props. Better to have one that works really well than several that don't build pitch-perfect culture. We like snapping a bit more with older students. The percussiveness of the snaps is especially affirming to the speaker (they can hear and almost feel it, even if they aren't looking) and the signal is gratifying to send so people like sending it more. It's also more "grown up." You may doubt that, but if we start snapping in our workshops with adults, we often find it spreading throughout the room even though we don't ask people to use it. People just like the way it feels.

With any signal, teachers have to remain attentive to how students use it. Someone will always want to overdo it; it can become silly, a form of subtle disruption, if not used with discretion. So you'll need to be ready with phrases such as "Hold your snapping please," or "I love the snapping, but it has to be shorter and quieter. I promise your peers will still feel it" to gently correct.

With younger students, we're inclined to favor sending shine. It's cheery by name so asking for it feels upbeat: "Send David some shine." Plus snapping is more likely to go awry with very young students—they're not quite as experienced socially and don't know quite as intuitively when it makes sense to use it. So shine at younger grades and snapping at older grades is a decent rule of thumb, but you can see the full array of possibilities in the videos we've shared. Ideally this will allow you to imagine different approaches to defining and amplifying these tiny signals so they are clearer and more evident.

In the video *Christine Torres: Props*, Christine is teaching vocabulary and we see her use "shine" twice. First as a student, Etani, hesitates in answering a challenging question, Christine asks her classmates,

"Send Etani some shine." They do so enthusiastically, and you can sense the support Etani feels before she nails the question. In a second example from Christine's lesson, there's another challenging question and here Christine models sending "shine" herself. Several other students choose to join in. It's feels organic in the way students choose to express their support.

Sarah Wright is also teaching vocabulary in the video *Sarah Wright: Props* and her students are fired up to try to use their new words. She calls on Akeem, and several students (his neighbor to the right in particular) show their support for his enthusiasm by sending enthusiastic magic. It's worth noting that almost out of habit Sarah makes the magic gesture herself in calling on Akeem.

In the video *Rousseau Mieze: Props*, Rousseau has chosen two students' written work to share with the class. He playfully asks the class to "snap it up" for them to honor their effort. The result is compelling.

And finally in *Erin Magliozzi: Props*, Erin's students spontaneously "shine on" Jas to support her as she answers. After she gets it right, they snap their approval. She's got both systems firing! To be Jas or any other student in a classroom like Erin's is to be supported, encouraged, connected, and reminded constantly that you belong.

"HABITS OF ATTENTION": THE HIDDEN POWER OF STUDENTS TRACKING EACH OTHER

When we discussed the photo taken from the video of Denarius's class in Chapter 1, we focused on the power of what Vanessa's classmates were doing as she acknowledged her error—looking at her, smiling, sending nonverbal signals that they approved of her—and how they show their approval of her when she shows her scholarly side. The signals come via eye contact, facial expression, body posture, and, as you've now seen, even snapping. Their actions influence her willingness to take academic (and social) risks. Her response to her mistake is exemplary, mature, and humble; it reflects a young woman of character. But it also reflects a room in which psychological safety is combined with a palpable feeling that learning is a team sport. The room brings the best out of her; her response is hers but not hers alone.

In fact, eye tracking and nonverbal signals of affirmation and inclusion are present throughout the video; you can see it happening over and over. Recall the moment we described earlier, where Folusho is speaking.

Her classmates are turned to face her—Fagan, who is characteristically snapping along and trying to encourage others to snap, is an exception. One other student is looking at the problem on the board. But the norm is clear. We engage one another with our eyes when we talk.

To frame the vocabulary a little tighter, the concept of looking at the speaker is called *tracking*. The broader set of behaviors—showing one is interested, focusing and directing one's own attention in the most productive direction—is called *Habits of Attention* (that's the term Doug uses in Teach Like a Champion 3.0 if you want to read more about it). Like Props, it too involves giving recognition, approval, acknowledgment, and appreciation to another person. When we see it happening, we think of the social contract. A tiny demand (let's look at each other; let's do what we can to show we're interested even if we're sometimes not) and a massive payoff (we build a place where lessons light the room on fire, where we belong, and we maximize our chance to achieve our dreams) if we can get everyone to embrace it enough to build a visible norm.

The norm is evident in Denarius's room. You can see students using Habits of Attention while Folusho speaks, while Brittany speaks, while Fagan speaks, and while Jevaughn speaks.

And of course they also track Denarius. Some teachers see the benefit of peer-to-peer tracking but hesitate to ask for it themselves. They worry that it is authoritarian to ask students to track them.[2] Why, we ask, would we have a system that shows everyone in the room respect and affirmation, that reminds them that their voice matters, and exclude the teacher? Why would we want to signal that the teacher's words weren't also important? There are myriad reasons why tracking the teacher is beneficial to students (it helps them pay attention, for example; this and other reasons are summarized in *Teach Like a Champion 3.0*) but we would like to observe that signals of belonging and the consequent emotions also affect teachers. The same rules of biology apply. Feeling appreciated, supported, and affirmed in your classroom makes you happier and more confident, more connected to students emotionally, and almost assuredly a more successful teacher. It makes you a teacher who, like students, is not afraid to take the risks inherent in a learning! Should students track the teacher as well as peers? Should they reaffirm the social contract implicit in a positive learning environment with their teacher too? Of course!

It's worth noting that a teacher's gaze is also an important signal. (That it's obvious does not mean it's not worth reflection.) Of course giving students eye contact when they speak shows them we are listening. It's an important habit, and a great way to model for students which signals to send and how, as you'll soon see Fran Goodship do in a video from her classroom in London, England. But it's also a habit you seek "in the aggregate"—you can't be looking at the speaker every moment when you are responsible for a class of 30. In fact, occasionally gazing around briefly while students are talking can be a reminder to others that you are looking to see if they are engaging (and it's important to make sure everyone is on task). We'll see an example of that in Fran's classroom as well.

But symmetricality of gaze is also worth some reflection. Wharton Business School Professor Ethan Mollick recently wrote about a study by So-Hyeon Shim and colleagues,[3] which found that, in Mollick's words, "when leaders gaze positively at group members who might otherwise be left out, other people in the group listen to that person more." Similarly, when we work with teachers, we often remind them of how important individual eye contact is and asks them to include it when practicing such common tasks as giving directions or asking questions. Establishing eye contact with a wide range of individuals, even fleetingly, is far more effective than looking generally "at the group."

You can see Denarius do this quite clearly in the first moments of his video. "Go ahead and take 30 seconds to silently, independently evaluate the two solutions that I saw," he says. As students study the problem, Denarius is not looking past students at the back wall for example. He is not looking down at his notes or at the board. He is not sweeping smoothly across the room in a scan. He is looking around the room with his eyes fixing very briefly on individual students. He is "looking at their eyes" and in so doing both affirming them—I see you and acknowledge you—and helping them to feel lovingly accountable.

Getting Started with Habits of Attention

Habits of Attention is a powerful tool, in particular because it multiplies and magnifies belonging signals in the classroom, but implementing it so that it becomes a consistent and vibrant routine is easier said than done. Success requires careful design and execution. Here are some implementation notes based on the experience of teachers like Denarius.

First, like any system, Habits of Attention requires buy-in—from teachers, from students, and sometimes from parents. There's a decent chance you'll have some skeptics among your stakeholders so the first step is making sure everyone understands the *why*. As we discussed earlier, process fairness leads to outcome buy-in, even when people aren't at first sure they agree, and the first principle of process fairness is making it clear to stakeholders that decisions are based on research, sound principles, and shared purpose. Take the time to explain the benefits, of course. (Pro tip: Show a video or two: *This is what we're shooting for. . . .*) But also ask teachers and possibly parents about their reservations. Be ready to respond, listen carefully, and, if necessary, look for opportunities to explain or even add points of flexibility in the details of implementation you ask for or the degree of variation you allow. That said, we are also for starting small on flexibility or even promising flexibility if needed after an initial trial period. We say that because we aslo think buy-in is an outcome, not a prerequisite. If implementation is strong, people will change their minds. Implementing the system well so classrooms feel vibrant and inclusive is the thing that's most likely to cause people to believe that the system is worthwhile. If that doesn't happen, fewer people will be convinced.

That said, here are two areas where you can potentially offer flexibility if teachers express concerns:

- There's a variety of language that teachers can use to ask for tracking and the differences can be meaningful. For example saying, "Class, give me your eyes" or "Class, give Vanessa your eyes" feels different from saying, "Track me, please" or "Track Vanessa, please." Some teachers may prefer the directness and clarity of the latter; some may prefer the hint of gentleness in the former. Giving them the latitude to express the idea differently may make some reluctant teachers more comfortable or help others feel like they can be more authentically themselves when they make the request.

How we ask students to attend is also an opportunity to share their rationale more clearly, and this may also be useful to teachers or students. Here's some useful language:

- "It's important that we're tracking now."
- "Make sure to show Vanessa your appreciation by tracking."
- "Check to make sure that your eyes are on Vanessa, please."

The first example allows a teacher to remind students by emphasizing the importance of the moment. The second reminds students of the purpose (never a bad thing). The third as a reminder assumes the best—that is, it presumes that students who aren't tracking have merely forgotten and reminded will choose to embrace the norm.

It can also be helpful to remind teachers that tracking, and the other pieces of Habits of Attention, are default systems. That is, we should install them so we can use them simply and easily whenever we need them. But we can also turn them off temporarily. Letting teachers think of phrases they'd use to turn off the default—and having an open discussion about when it would be okay to do so—can also build buy-in. Here are two examples of phrases to turn off the default that we especially like:

- "No need to track if you're taking notes or looking at sources."
- "Eyes or note-taking. Your choice during this discussion."

Process fairness applies to students too (obviously), though it's a bit different because of course students don't get to decide whether something will be a policy in most cases—including this one, where we think the benefits are important enough that it's actually not up for, say, a vote. What if 15 want to try it and 15 don't? Systems only work when they are universal. (Of course, it's reasonable to offer flexibility to students who are neurodivergent or have other specific learning needs—that's a different situation.)

So rather than asking for input beforehand about something they won't have enough experience to judge with, why not ask for input *during*?

Here's our recipe. It focuses on older students because we think younger students are much less likely to push back.

1. Roll it out carefully. Explain the *why* behind it as you do so. Consider showing students a video so they can see what classrooms are like with Habits of Attention in place. Focus explaining on the social contract: the long-term mutual benefit and the small daily demands.

    "I think you will be surprised by how much this changes the feel of the classroom, how supported and encouraged you feel. And I am confident that it will help build an environment where you learn more and help each other to get closer to your goals. And soon enough it will become a habit."

    We recently discussed with one school leader the benefits of adding a group-based explanation ("We build these habits because we are responsible to one another; here is how you make your neighbor stronger") to an individual-based explanation ("Here is how this benefits you, personally"). This helps students to see the social contract at work and understand that it is the broader culture that is the goal.

Regardless, the key at the outset is not necessarily whether students agree fully—they don't really know enough about it to judge yet, having not tried it—but whether they *understand*. If they believe you are doing it for their long-term benefit and if they believe the case you make for it, you're ready to move forward. Most teenagers get that teachers are there to help them do what is in their long-term interest, even if they don't get up every morning wanting to do those things. None of the four of us liked writing papers as teenagers. We rolled our eyes and complained. But then we got down to it because we understood why writing essays would help us and we believed it to be true. Teenagers know that school requires the application of self-regulation over their very human desire to do what's more pleasant. If they understand the *why*, and if you are clear and consistent in asking them to follow through, they will very likely give it a chance.

2. Try it for a few weeks. Make sure to work for solid follow-through so students are experiencing a high-quality version of Habits of Attention. Make sure they are using it to discuss topics of real merit and importance. Buy-in is an outcome, not a precondition. Let students talk about something important or work on a challenging problem together in a way that feels meaningful and they will be more likely to perceive the difference.

3. *Then* ask for their feedback, focusing not so much on whether but on how:

> "We've been doing this for a few weeks now. Answer as your most mature selves, the ones who want to achieve and think about your future success: How's it going? Does it feel different? Do we need to adapt anything to make to work better? Turn and talk to your partner to discuss."

This would be another case where you might show a video. "Great, let's watch Denarius's students. What can we learn from watching them that we can use?" (Note if you discuss with your students: All of the students in Denarius's class went on to college. Fagan, the hero of the movie, has just graduated from a top school!)

4. Make tiny changes as needed but *stick with it*.

In the video *Christine Torres: Building Tracking*, we assembled a series of examples of Christine asking her students to track. Notice how she periodically acknowledges them when they meet the norm. Notice also how incredibly engaged her students are. When she asks a question, almost every hand shoots up. These data points are almost surely connected. You can also sneak ahead and watch *BreOnna Tindall: Habits* to see how she builds an outstanding culture of belonging using Habits of Attention, Props, and the next technique we'll discuss: Habits of Discussion.

HABITS OF DISCUSSION: TALKING TO, NOT PAST, EACH OTHER

Let's go back to the moment in Denarius's class where Folusho responds to what Vanessa has said at the start of the discussion. As we noted earlier, Folusho says, "Okay, I agree with Vanessa. I think [answer] A is finding the reciprocal, and reciprocal and inverse are not the same thing." Her words reflect another apparently mundane but crucial belonging signal that is constantly communicated by and among students in Denarius's classroom.

Folusho begins by making clear reference to Vanessa's previous comment. She references what Vanessa said briefly ("I think A is finding the reciprocal" is a restatement of Vanessa's point), credits her by name, and then describes how her thoughts connect (*I agree and intend to extend her idea*). In doing so she has communicated the importance of Vanessa's words. She was listening to her classmate carefully and thinks her words matter. That may sound trivial, but too often in classrooms the opposite occurs. A student like Vanessa speaks and the next student to talk doesn't give the slightest indication that the previous comment mattered or ever occurred. Perhaps her point is totally unrelated. The message is: no one thought that was worth responding to. Sometimes a student will actually begin with a phrase like, "What I was gonna say was . . ." The subtext is: "What Vanessa just said, to the degree I was even listening, irrelevant. My comment is exactly the same as it would have been if she had never spoken." The response by their peers for thousands of Vanessas, suggests their comments are largely irrelevant to their peers. Just as often this message is delivered by silence. If after your comments no one responds at all, if they provoke no indication that they appear relevant or valuable to your peers, you soon learn to stop speaking.

Just as we are all frequently in Folusho's shoes, wondering as we speak if our words make sense and buoyed by the indication in the snapping that we are doing fine, so too we are all frequently in Vanessa's shoes—asking ourselves after we speak: Should I have said that? Did people value, hear, or care about what I said?

The anxiety that your words will be ignored is a much more prevalent part of our lives than it was 20 years ago—times a thousand for young people. The Like button is the driver of compulsive social media use. Young people post their thoughts and then check their likes and then check and check again because they yearn for confirmation that their peers valued what they said. This should remind us of how powerful affirmation is and how much we crave it after we speak. We speak because we want what we say to be relevant to others—at least that should be one of the major purposes of speaking—and afterwards we are waiting for the room to tell us whether it was.

In the classroom, the answer to the question *did people value what I said* comes primarily from peers rather than the teacher—especially for students above the primary grades. Like the signals we discussed in Habits of Attention, it is communicated in a language of signals that are often overlooked. The average student looks out across the room, having just answered a question, and just as likely sees precious few signs of response or interest. If signals of affirmation occur, it is an accident. Mostly this serves to remind her that she is disconnected from many of her peers—or at least she is when she is engaged in the work of the classroom. She leaves the room and is primed to affirm or earn belonging with peers in other ways.

Wondering whether your words were ignored, irrelevant, or scorned is a strong disincentive against participation. Or it can be a strong incentive to turn a discussion into an argument in which the purpose is to win, to prove that your words mattered. That divides people, rather than connecting them.

Interestingly, if Folusho had disagreed with Vanessa but in doing so had said something like, "I saw it differently from Vanessa," she would still be affirming what Vanessa said—responding with respect, validating the importance and relevance of the comment. That might seem paradoxical but it's still important: *She doesn't have to agree to make Vanessa feel affirmed and important.* If she responds to Vanessa but respectfully disagrees with her, she sends far more positive reinforcement, far stronger signals of belonging, than if she shared an opinion that was in agreement with Vanessa but made no reference to her contribution. Doubly so if she rephrased a bit of what Vanessa's said. ("I saw it differently from Vanessa. I don't really think this is a reciprocal.") She would be demonstrating that she was listening carefully to what Vanessa had said and thinking about her argument. Listening carefully and responding to someone's ideas is a belonging signal, even if you don't agree with them. (In fact it can make it easier to disagree cordially.) Because such signals are subtle, we often overlook it when they fail to occur, but they are crucial to building an optimal classroom culture.

Is it necessary to point out that listening is not just a critical skill but possibly a dying one? Careful listening is one of the first things that goes in a world of fractured attention. It is rarely modeled in the click-bait world of social media, where the goal of much communication is not to engage in substantive discussion but to score points, garner likes, and "call out" those who disagree. Is it necessary to point out that when we aren't listening to the people we're talking to (or at), conversation drives us apart instead of connecting us? Glancing at our political process should give us pause to think about the way we run discussions in the classroom: points given for loud and emphatic opinions forcefully stated, but few if any for listening well, seeking to understand, or resisting the temptation to assume one has found the "obviously" right after just a few seconds of reflection. We live in a world where people fold their arms and turn away after they stop speaking; the message is that they are so committed to their point of view that potential responses don't really matter, could not possibly influence them. The social and political costs of this are immense and we should be careful not to reinforce it in our teaching.[4] The fact that social media socializes people to talk past each other, to dismiss one another's words, makes it doubly important to build an affirming environment in the classroom.

This technique that Denarius uses to do this is called Habits of Discussion. It involves students making a practice of referring to or rephrasing a previous comment, referencing by name the person whose point it was, and situating their own argument in connection to it:

- "I agree because . . ."
- "I disagree because . . ."
- "Another example of what Vanessa is talking about is . . ."
- "I'd like to build on what Vanessa said earlier . . ."
- "I saw it differently from Vanessa . . ."
- "I think you could interpret that slightly differently . . ."

If you listen carefully to the video of Denarius's class and others we feature here, you can hear such phrases again and again.

Jevaughn, speaking after Omowunmi's explanation of the solution about three minutes into Denarius's lesson, says, "Now that I think about it, I agree with Omowunmi. . . ." Could anything make Omowunmi feel more affirmed for her effort to explain what she thinks the class has learned?

Fagan uses a subtler example about a minute and a half into the clip. Typically, she's pretty into the debate but even so she begins, "Also, you could just work it backwards." The word "also" is a tiny reminder to the room that she is picking up where Folusho left off.

Even Denarius uses the technique! "Yeah, so I agree with Omowunmi and Jevaughn," he says, putting a bow on the discussion.

Belonging is a flame, Daniel Coyle tells us, one that needs to be constantly fed by tiny signals. The habit of affirming, restating, and reacting intentionally to previous speakers sends a constant stream of those signals, even when the speaker disagrees.

THE TOOLS IN SYNERGY

Between the systems for snapping, eye-contact with speakers, nonverbal positive reinforcement, and verbal affirmation, Denarius's classroom is literally full of signals that build belonging. And those signals are frequent because he has created systems to communicate and magnify them. They are most evident when students engage in scholarly work that reflects their ambition and purpose.

You can also see a lovely model of how these three techniques come together in the video *BreOnna Tindall: Habits*. After some initial writing and a Turn and Talk at the beginning of the video, BreOnna calls on Adriel to share first. It's a Cold Call so it's doubly important for Adriel to feel the love. "We're going to go ahead and Track Adriel," BreOnna says, "So snap it up for Adriel." She's smiling warmly here, both at Adriel and his classmates.

Here's what it looks like as Adriel (on the far left) prepares to respond.

The signals of belonging and support are both visual (tracking and smiling; everyone looks sincerely interested) and auditory (a rolling wave of snaps). The snaps even buy Adriel a moment to compose himself.

A side note here: some people argue that Cold Call (calling on students who have not raised their hand to volunteer) is harsh and invasive. We argue the opposite. Asking Adriel his opinion and singling him out for a chance to speak tells him that his voice matters. "Of all the people in the room," BreOnna is saying, "we'd love to hear what you think, Adriel." There's almost nothing that could be more inclusive, and by facilitating his success through Props, Habits of Attention, and Habits of Discussion, BreOnna is helping to build his confidence. When he does well, as he does here, he's also rewarded by spontaneous snapping from his peers, and he is suddenly far more likely to think that speaking in class is something he can do well. He's far more likely to volunteer.[5]

Renee gets called on next and again we can see and feel the warm glow of her classmates' focus shifting toward her. The image here shows what their signals of belonging look like.

Notice how carefully BreOnna models the body language of interest and attentiveness throughout. They're good at it in part because she models it so carefully. There's spontaneous snapping while Renee speaks and class-wide snapping (reinforced by BreOnna's nonverbal reminder) afterwards. The video closes with Nylah answering and again she is affirmed by earnest eye contact, the appearance of genuine interest, and a rolling wave of snaps.

Habits of Discussion are also hard at work. BreOnna asks Tano to "build" off of Renee—that is, she reminds him to use Habits of Discussion to refer to Renee's idea. And we can see the work she's done to teach connecting phrases like the ones we provided above because Nylah begins, "I'd like to respectfully disagree with you. . . ." She's taken the idea that if we disagree well, it can still connect us in a community and reinforced it by including "respectfully" in the phrase. This not only makes Tano feel affirmed, but it may make Nylah more likely to share her true opinion because it does not seem to imply a conflict with a peer.

YES, BUT HOW DO I DO THAT?

The challenge of the videos we've been watching is that the systems Denarius and BreOnna rely on are already deeply embedded in their classrooms by the time these lessons occur, so it's hard to see the steps they took to set them up. It would in some ways be more helpful to see them on day one, rolling out and explaining: *This is how we'll snap for each other. This is how we'll strive to look at each other. This is how we should connect our ideas in discussion. Here is why we will do those things.*

While we don't have first-day video of Denarius and BreOnna— while in fact there is no single first day but rather a series of days when the ideas were explained and tirelessly reinforced—we do have first-day video of Habits of Discussion from Ben Hall's classroom. (See *Ben Hall: Habits of Discussion Rollout.*) Ben teaches at Ipswich Academy in Ipswich, England, and the video shows him not just using Habits of Discussion for the very first time but showing his students how it will work and letting them experience a successful discussion.

Buy-in, as our colleague Paul Bambrick observed, is an outcome, not a prerequisite. So Ben's goal in the video is not just to explain Habits of Discussion to his class but to have them *feel what it's like* to have a collaborative conversation about a challenging topic. So he's chosen to begin installing Habits of Discussion with a lesson with real content to discuss: the death penalty in Britain. Importantly, this is a topic they have spent several lessons studying. When participants are well-informed, discussions are fact-based and connected. When participants lack knowledge, they fall back on emotion and sometimes invective. This pushes them apart more than drawing them together. Obviously, that's not what Ben wants.

Not surprisingly, then, his first move is to ask students to review their notes and familiarize themselves with arguments they'd made for and against the death penalty. Interestingly, they've had to do both. That is, he has asked them to make a case in writing for *both sides of the issue* before he asks them to argue their opinion. We love this move. So often, we note, young people are encouraged to share their opinion right away—and this quite obviously forces them to formulate an opinion about an issue instantly. But smart people, we note, often delay forming an opinion on an issue until they have gathered all of the evidence and reflected on it for some time. There is no rush—or shouldn't be.

As a side note, a belief in the value of delaying making up one's mind could be reflected in the language a teacher uses during discussion. BreOnna asks Tano to "build"—she doesn't encourage him to take sides, just expand. Denarius asks students to "agree, disagree, *or build*." These phrases stand in contrast to the phrase "agree or disagree" that we more commonly hear teachers use. By itself, "agree or disagree" suggests that those are the only two options: one side or the other; argue for or argue against. Adding the option to "build" specifies a way to participate and reflect without deciding, subtly suggesting that it may still be too early for formulating opinions.

Ben gives his students a bit of time to look over their previous thoughts but interestingly they are so familiar with Turn and Talk that they assume that's what he's asked them to do and the room instantly bursts into peer discussions. Ben quickly steps in. "Sorry, guys. I meant to be clear. Don't discuss it. We're looking and thinking now." Notice his exemplary use of the technique Assume the Best[6]— Ben presumes his own lack of clarity was the most plausible explanation for students not following directions and shows that was the first thought to cross his mind. And even though there's been a miscommunication about the task, we can already tell from the response that this is a classroom where students read the norm to be active and engaged participation. This, as we will discuss, is in large part a product of clear and well-installed routines for commonly occurring tasks like Turn and Talk.

After a bit of discussion, Ben next uses the Turn and Talk his students were expecting. He's allowing them to rehearse points they might make in the whole group first, in a lower-stakes environment. Rehearsal, in this case, means not only that you get to say it once and sort out your words so you are clearer and more confident if you say it later, but also that you get to see how a peer responds. You can look for signals of affirmation—nodding or following up on your point enthusiastically—to tell you a bit more about your initial thought and perhaps help you to refine it.

After the silent review and the brief rehearsal via Turn and Talk, Ben introduces Habits of Discussion. Notice that he explicitly calls it a model, implying that it's something they'll use over and over. He presents a slide that contains three especially important pieces of information.

First it outlines how the discussion will work. Ben will ask someone to open. Others will weigh in. Someone will be chosen to summarize. He's going to be Cold Calling, so students are doubly incentivized to listen carefully. It's especially nice that he's provided a last step to discussion that focuses on connection rather than division. The discussion ends with a summary of what we—all of us—said and talked about rather than one person stating a final opinion of a single perspective.

Second, Ben gives students potential "roles" they can play: Instigator, Builder, Challenger, Summarizer. There's subtle brilliance to this.

Naming the roles helps students to understand the purposes of what they might do in a discussion. He names some things that might not be obvious: builders, who expand ideas, are an important part of a discussion. And in Ben's classroom, disagreeing isn't arguing, it's challenging. That's a much more collegial and group-oriented framing. And the idea of calling them "roles" allows students to participate in the discussion with a bit of psychological safety. He has asked them to take a position, to express an opinion, but it's a "role". A student who says something that does not perfectly express what they think can step back from it a bit afterwards (I was just playing a role). Perhaps they were even the instigator just to choose that role. It allows students to distance themselves from every opinion they express. They can disagree or make a mistake or change their minds without making it seem personal. If friendships are strained by disagreement that might emerge, there's an easy way back: I was (or you were) playing the role of challenger.

In fact, after Andy opens the discussion, Ben calls on Sam using language that reminds everyone that he will be playing a role. "Sam, what would you like to be?"

Sam responds, "I'll be a challenger and I disagree with you, Andy." He very clearly refers to himself as playing one of the roles Ben has outlined. He appears to find the lowering of stakes reassuring and accepts it. Perhaps he's going to see Andy on the playground at recess in an hour and wants to keep the discussion of sensitive topics at arm's length. In playing a role, he can disagree or experiment with ideas at minimal risk.

Notice next the useful starter phrases Ben provides for students to use on his slide. These echo the sorts of phrases we heard students using in Denarius's class. They show students how to connect their ideas but also subtly prompt them to think about ways to engage a discussion beyond merely arguing for or against. Yes, there are "I agree/disagree because" starter phrases, but there are also phrases like "Building on that idea," "Linking to that idea," and "It could be argued that . . ." The last phrase in particular is a beautiful example of a tactful and subtle way to raise a dissenting opinion while respecting the other person's opinion. (I'm not saying I know for sure or that I hold this opinion; I'm just saying that someone could argue it.)

Notice crucially that Ben projects the slide and keeps it up on the screen for students to see throughout the ensuing discussion. It's no coincidence that students use these phrases throughout. (Many of them are highlighted in yellow in the video's subtitles.)

Should we bring the death penalty back into UK law?

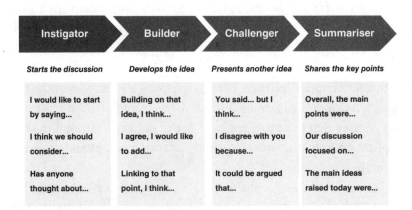

Instigator	Builder	Challenger	Summariser
Starts the discussion	*Develops the idea*	*Presents another idea*	*Shares the key points*
I would like to start by saying...	Building on that idea, I think...	You said... but I think...	Overall, the main points were...
I think we should consider...	I agree, I would like to add...	I disagree with you because...	Our discussion focused on...
Has anyone thought about...	Linking to that point, I think...	It could be argued that...	The main ideas raised today were...

Ben Hall's Habits of Discussion slide, reproduced here so you can borrow and adapt it.

Notice that Lily, invited via Cold Call[7] to share her perspective, summarizes what Rhys has said rather impressively, even though she disagrees. She demonstrates both that she understands his argument and that she sees it differently; she shows respect and appreciation even while she challenges her classmate. You could argue that community is built in that moment, even though there is open disagreement. That is truly a rare thing these days.

Next, Joe is invited into the conversation, and he references both Andy's and Rhys's comments. Rhys, Sam, and Lily have all spoken since Andy offered his opinion and, it's worth noting, Joe still remembers it! Certainly this sends a clear message to Andy about the influence of his words. It also suggests that the importance the process places on responding is having an effect on students' listening.

It's also worth noting that both Lily and Joe are not using the phrases exactly as Ben has proposed them, though other students do. As we noted at the outset, he's given them a model and they are already adapting it. This is important because when we discuss classroom systems, sometimes people say that it entails scripting people's behavior and subverting their autonomy. *It's telling them what to say.* But this underestimates students. People copy briefly and then, because they are smart and independent-minded, begin to adapt and internalize almost immediately, making any system their own. We see that with the snapping in Denarius's classroom. You might argue it's scripted or perhaps even proscriptive, but in fact the students use it in their own style and adapt it. That's what's happening with the "scripted" phrases here. A script is a great way to learn a model, but it doesn't remain a script for very long. It's the same with the phrases Ben has provided here. We're not even through the first application and students are already adapting the phrases to make them their own.

Back in Ben's class Sienna is speaking now. She begins by "building off of Lily's idea," again a reference to a previous comment demonstrating listening and affirming her classmate's contribution. We can't see Lily, but she must feel important in this moment. Very quickly—in a span of five minutes—students have figured out how to use Ben's model to talk to one another, to weave comments into a discussion.

The clip ends with Ben calling on Katie to summarize. Frankly, she crushes it, ably describing the range of viewpoints expressed by her classmates in a way the people who held those opinions would probably accept as accurate. Notice the way that she even self-corrects slightly. She beings, "We discussed that most people think . . ." but then she reconsiders. Actually the room was pretty evenly split. What she had assumed was the majority was in fact not quite so clearly so. "A lot of people think we should . . ." she says, suggesting how carefully she's listened to the arguments and how well she's been able to read the overall position of the room. She also appears quite comfortable with the disagreement. This is not a room where opinions are motive tests. It's safe to have a conversation. We shouldn't discount this. Many or possibly most students do not think it is safe to share all of their opinions in classrooms. A recent survey of almost 20,000 college students by the Foundation for Individual Rights in Education, a nonpartisan nonprofit group, found that more than 60% self-censor their opinions in classroom discussions.[8] Those numbers obviously aren't for K–12 classrooms, but they suggest a larger social problem that is almost surely present in our schools as well and that has deep psychological effects. It's hard to feel like you belong in a classroom where you can't express your opinion openly.

HABITS OF (LITTLER) DISCUSSIONS

Habits of Discussion is important enough that it deserves another video, and the one we'd like to share is especially valuable because it shows how the technique can be used (and taught) with much younger students. Crucially it also shows how a teacher can pay special attention to interpersonal and conversation skills that are especially important to young people right now (and sorely lacking for many).

In the video, Fran Goodship of Solebay Primary Academy in London is hard at work teaching her year-one students how to have a discussion. A useful point for context: our video of Fran was shot in the first weeks of the 2021–22 school year, which means that many of Fran's charges have never spent a normal school year—or indeed a normal social year—as children. That is, one without isolation and limited social contact.

Fran has asked students to talk about why a character in a story named Matthew might want to be invisible. Notice that, like Ben, she tells students that they are going to have a discussion so they can be aware of the context in which the skills she is teaching will apply.

She starts by calling on Tiber. Notice the instant response from his peers. They turn and face him and he is affirmed by signals of belonging. But notice Fran as well, and how demonstrably she is modeling the sort of body and facial language that shows interest and connection. Here she is tilting her head in a show of interest as Tiber talks:

There are several reasons she might do this. First, while it true for older students that the social cues from peers are usually far more influential in shaping motivation and behavior than the responses of teachers, that is less clearly the case for younger students who, obviously, are much more interested in pleasing their teacher and who are much more likely to attend to her in particular. So it's important that Fran send signal affirmation to him as well, especially as his comments stretch to thirty seconds or so. "You're doing fine," her attentive body language is saying. But of course she is also modeling to his classmates how to look interested and affirming. And in fact throughout the lesson she makes a point of modeling in a slightly exaggerated way *how* to send nonverbal signals of belonging. Younger students don't yet know what is implicit to Denarius's students. What do I do with my face and body to show I appreciate what you are saying? Fran models that throughout.

Tiber's a bit nervous perhaps and he says quite a bit but hasn't really answered the question. This is common among younger students (and sometimes older ones) and highlights an important discussion skill—attending to the question we are asking. It's much easier to work together toward figuring something out if what we're talking about is clear, so Fran brings Tiber's attention back to the question. She also signals to a classmate to put her hand down so Tiber can continue without anxiety or distraction. We've spoken about positive signals of belonging. It's also worth noting that a hand raised while you are talking can be a signal to a speaker that people in the room are "done" with what you've said, and have decided it's their turn to respond. In that case it's a good bet they are no longer listening. It's a significant disincentive to talk.

After persisting bravely, Tiber starts to get the group closer to answering the question. Notice the snapping that Fran uses here. She hasn't installed the system of props fully yet but is beginning to model to familiarize students with it—*it's something that happens when you are doing well.* She also very briefly wiggles her fingers at him. She's in the early stages of familiarizing them, in much the same way, with the idea of sending "shine."

She's now called on Isha, and the significance of the language she uses to do so—"Building . . . Isha . . ."—should now be clear. It's a cue for Isha to connect her idea to Tiber's and to weave together a conversation. Again as Isha begins answering you can see clear and slightly exaggerated body language modeled by Fran. She's making a point of showing what "interested" looks like. She's even touching her ear to suggest to students: *This is what I look like when I am listening carefully.*

Fran is incredibly attentive to her eye contact, to making sure Tiber and Isha know she's listening carefully but notice that at least twice as Isha is talking Fran very briefly glances at other students as if to remind them that they should be tracking Isha too.

Isha has suggested that, in the story, Matthew is embarrassed by the fleece he is wearing. Fran, in response, makes another brilliant move to amplify belonging signals. "Put your hand up if you think Matthew was embarrassed in paragraph one," she says and every hand goes up. She wants Isha to know she's done well and is on the right track, but she wants the signal to come from her peers. Peer approval is powerful, we've noted, even if in the primary grades at least it may be slightly less so than the teacher's approval. But here Isha gets both. Her move here also accomplishes a bit of what Denarius achieves when he asks his students to snap if they agree with the final answer. They get to affirm their agreement with Isha's insight and feel more connected to the norms Fran is building.

After a quick summary of the discussion so far, Fran calls on Jamillah, asking her if she agrees with Isha and Tiber. Notice that she points to Jamila to orient her classmates to where she is and remind them to track her—this directs their attention so they listen better and also results in Jamillah feeling listened to. She wiggles her fingers a bit, "sending magic" style to make being called on feel a bit more celebratory. That's a lovely detail to add given that it's a Cold Call. The Cold Call is clearly an invitation—what's more inclusive than asking someone their opinion?—but the lighthearted gesture adds to the positivity.

Zara is next and again Fran asks her to build on what Jamillah has said. There's so much consistency here from Fran. Again she's modeling what positive nonverbal listening looks like. Again she's asking students not just to participate but to connect their ideas.

Unprompted, Zara comes through with a beautiful connecting phrase: "I would like to add to what Jamillah said," showing that she has already internalized the details of how one converses in a way that connects ideas and honors other participants.

IT MIGHT GET LOUD: ADDING TURN AND TALK AND CALL AND RESPONSE

In the first weeks back from the pandemic, things were going well at Marine Academy Plymouth, in Plymouth, England. "We'd come a long way in terms of routines in the classroom," Assistant Vice Principal Jen Brimming told us. Familiar procedures like Everybody Writes[9] and Cold Call got all of the students involved in class regularly. There was a lot of thinking going on and the thinking was usually of good quality. But it felt a little less energetic than the teaching staff wanted it to be. It felt a little quiet. "It was a bit like a cathedral," Brimming said, "really productive but also fairly silent." This observation is important from a belonging point of view. We want to make students working hard and enjoying learning to be visible to one another. If they don't see clearly how engaged their peers are, it won't influence them as much. There won't be something clear to belong to.

One of the keys to happiness, Martin Seligman reminds us, is engagement—losing oneself in an activity that draws you in with energy and momentum. People (including Seligman) often use the word "flow" to refer to this. The term was coined by the psychologist Mihaly Csikszentmihalyi, who studied it for much of his career. Flow states, Csikszentmihalyi points out, are profoundly pleasing to humans. Losing track of time, engaging fully, especially as part of a group, is a powerful draw, perhaps, as suggested in Chapter 1, for evolutionary reasons related to the importance of tasks like persistence hunting in our survival. Either way, Csikszentmihalyi observes, "the experience is so enjoyable that people will continue to do it even at great cost, for the sheer sake of doing it."[10]

If we want students to feel connected to the classroom, it's important for them to feel the kind of momentum and forward progress we see in Denarius's classroom where students bound quickly from task to task while also thinking deeply and learning extensively. Most often that comes about via familiar routines guided by clear, crisp directions: "We're a little divided. Turn and Talk with your partner. Go."

So Jen and her colleagues set out to build momentum. They wanted the sound of classrooms to communicate vibrancy and belonging and they chose two routines to add to their arsenal: Turn and Talk, and Call and Response.

Another side note: there is an implicit presumption that there should be an overall ethos to how teaching works and classrooms feel across the school in the staff's discussion of the school's overall feel and this too is no small thing. It's hard to build culture by yourself. Things like Habits of Discussion or the moves Jen and her colleagues decided to try are much more powerful and much more likely to take hold if they are happening schoolwide. If students walk into any classroom and expect to build off of speakers and show their appreciation for their classmates' ideas nonverbally, they will pick up the habit quickly. If it happens in some classrooms but not others, it will be far less likely to become second nature to them. Denarius's classroom and BreOnna's classrooms also give credit to their colleagues who were working on the same set of culture-building tools and whose shared commitment helped them succeed.

Done well, Turn and Talk makes a habit of having short discussions with a partner. That, in and of itself, is a good way to build connections. But Turn and Talk also lets students rehearse ideas before a whole group discussion so they are more likely to engage and feel connected during those activities. And even beyond that, Turn and Talk sounds like community. Think of the sound of the room when Denarius released his students to the Turn and Talk at the beginning of his lesson. The room crackles to life. That sound is also a signal to students—about energetic engagement, by the whole class, on cue. It says energy and positivity and belonging.

And don't sleep on Call and Response. In every culture on earth, people sing and chant to cement their membership in the group. Group singing and chanting are explicit parts of worship in every religion. When we sing or chant together we are visibly and audibly in unison. We affirm our connectedness and the idea that we are a meaningful group. The historian William McNeil coined the phrase "muscular bonding" to describe "the sense of euphoric connection that is sparked by performing rhythmic movements in unison to music or chanting."[11] Everyone feels its pull, he posited, and marching, dancing, or chanting together were part of the key institutions that framed society and identity. Think religion, the military, politics, sports.

Done even briefly, communal chanting or singing can have a profound effect, but it's also something our rational, individualist selves are likely to overlook. Still in its ability to send belonging signals to the group, Call and Response recalls again Daniel Coyle's observation: "Belonging feels like it happens from the inside out, but in fact it happens from the outside in." Students feel like they belong because they act like they belong.

You can see these two techniques bring Jen's classroom to life in the video *Jen Brimming: Reprehensible.*

Jen starts by introducing the word of the day, *reprehensible.* She signals nonverbally for students to repeat it Call and Response style.

They all see that everyone else has responded with enthusiasm. We are five seconds into class and an active, engaged culture has already been reinforced. Immediately after, she asks students to jot the definition in the books and they snap to it with energy and spirit. They've taken two discrete actions within 12 seconds and a student in the room has seen everyone around him participate twice in that span of time. The sense of flow is palpable and a norm of active, engaged, connected participation has emerged. There's also a pleasurable sense of team. Some people presume that students won't like this sort of thing, that Call and Response is somehow a bit controlling, but the students, for their part, appear quite happy with it.

After two students are called to read the definition and an example, Jen asks students to jot down their "first thoughts" about why stealing from a charity is reprehensible. Notice the formative language. No one hesitates to write "first thoughts" out of fear they will be wrong because the phrase suggests they will refine their answers anyway. The word "jot" also lowers the stakes. It's hard to miss the effect of the fast start here. It's engaging and energetic and draws students in with its momentum: it's a case study in building flow. In Jen's class you're always thinking or chatting or writing. It's the class where you look up and suddenly 45 minutes have passed.

This is useful as a reflection in a time of socioemotional challenge. Teachers may be tempted to start class by "checking in": asking how students are in an unscripted manner. Going around the room attempting to engage as many members of the class as possible: "What about you, Casey? Good weekend?" One downside of this is that the lesson starts slowly. Students may tune out. Students may feel like their time is not being put to good use.

We're not saying there isn't benefit to checking in with students. We are wondering if there's a better time, in many cases, than the beginning of class. Get started right away, we say. Engage students. This will make them happy. If they are busy, they will feel that you value their time and this tells them they are important. You can see that, perhaps, in their response to the Turn and Talk Jen sends them off to about one minute into the video. We've seen a lot of rooms bursting to life in response to a crisp Turn and Talk delivered with clear, sharp, speedy directions but this one may take the cake.

Terry-Anne is called on to answer and the belonging signals that surround her should now look familiar. The class—reminded to track by Jen as she calls on Terry-Anne—turn and smile encouragingly. After Jen asks, "Do you agree?" the snapping expresses affirmation of Terry-Anne's answer. At about a 1:45 there's another speedy and engaging Turn and Talk, again with punchy language to release students to the task. In this case (and the previous one) Jen has let students raise their hands before the Turn and Talk—they've signaled that they'd like to answer and now she presents Turn and Talk as an opportunity for everyone to do so. The room is practically bursting with energy and a group ish vibe—all of us together in an almost orchestrated way knowing exactly how to do the tasks of learning is actually fun. Phoebe offers to answer. She's rewarded with tracks and snaps—this time spontaneously from her classmates. It feels like a round of applause but faster. Who wouldn't want to participate?

By the time she asks students to make a connection to a new word, Jen's got every hand in the air. When Katie answers "hypocrite" the class repeats it in unison. (Repeating vocabulary words is extremely helpful as pronouncing them is critical to reading them and using them in future encounters.) Next there's another round of Turn and Talk, with the student called to answer afterwards greeted with tracks and rewarded with snaps, belonging signals over and over, energy and momentum, not to mention a palpable and almost predictable rhythm to class. It's fast-paced and engaging. Students know what's likely to come next. It feels like basketball or soccer or tennis practice—both in the pace and the team-like coordination and connection.

As we see in Jen's class, Turn and Talk and Call and Response can facilitate belonging, causing socializing students to participate frequently and with spirit. This can cause them to see their role in the classroom differently. Belonging often happens from the outside in, Daniel Coyle reminds us. I see myself participating enthusiastically and start to perceive that I am enthusiastic about school.

MEANS OF PARTICIPATION MAKES "HOW TO PARTICIPATE" TRANSPARENT

Means of Participation is a phrase we use to describe the format in which you want students to answer your question. "Do you think Jonathan is the villain in the story?" is a very different question depending on whether you'll ask students to answer it by writing out their "first thoughts" quickly on paper (i.e. Everybody Writes), Turning and Talking with a peer, answering in unison via Call and Response, or being called on to speak aloud (either as volunteers or via Cold Call). Planning how you will want students to answer a question is often as important as the question itself!

Choosing the right Means of Participation for a given question is most powerful when 1) we signal which Means of Participation we want students to use clearly and transparently, and 2) the procedures for each Means of Participation are deeply encoded in routine. Then they can engage unselfconsciously and energetically like Jen's students do.

So as you watch Jen's video, notice that it is always clear to students the format in which they should answer, how each form of engagement is familiar to them, and how Jen cues them consistently and transparently. It's the same four or five Means of Participation over and over in different combinations. She starts with a Call and Response, two Cold Calls, and an Everybody Writes. She signals the Call and Response with a gesture (hand by her ear). Students know what this means. Because it's so clear and they know how to do it, everyone calls out energetically and unselfconsciously. Cold Calling or taking volunteers is Jen's default (i.e. students assume that that's how they'll answer unless told otherwise) so she doesn't need to signal it. But her phrase "Jot down your first thoughts" delivered rapid fire releases students quickly into Everybody Writes, a routine they know well. The cue, in a sense, is part of the routine and she delivers it crisply and quickly so the room snaps to life (watch the back row react if you doubt us).

"Turn and talk with your partner, go!" works much the same way: it releases students to a familiar activity with a clear signal. They know exactly what to do and are more engaged in answering the question because the process is a habit. The material they are learning remains foremost in their conscious thinking. With this kind of clarity and familiarity the room bursts to life almost no matter which Means of Participation she chooses because students like knowing how to do things. They like not worrying whether they'll be the only one to join in.

One thing you might be noticing from Jen's class and several others (like BreOnna's, Denarius's) is how common Means of Participation work in synergy. There are frequently recurring pairings and sequences. A brief written reflection into a Turn and Talk is a regular sequence in classes like Jen's. Having written an answer gives you lots to talk about. So is Turn and Talk into whole group questioning, especially when it starts with Cold Call. If everyone has talked their ideas out, they'll be more confident and have more to say when called on. And again, when you send them to the Turn and Talk, they probably know there's a decent chance a Cold Call is coming. So they're ready.

A participant at one of our workshops came to this conclusion in notes that looked like this.

Ask the question (repeat x2)
↓
Silent Solo (thinking time)
↓
'You have 30s. to Turn + Talk'
↓
'Hunt' for good answers
↓
Count down to end the talking time
↓
'Track' ← needs implementing first
↓
Cold Call from the answers you've heard during 'Hunt' or address misunderstandings you've heard.

Silent Solo is the phrase that cues the activity of a quick independent minute of writing. That's part of what's so smart about what this teacher wrote. She's already thinking about the familiar phrases to cue the activities.

Planning for Belonging Cues

Darryl works extensively with schools to help them define and achieve their own vision of strong culture. The visions schools develop in working with him are aligned but not exactly the same. The details of how they implement culture vary. He offered these notes on planning to establish a culture of connection and belonging in your classrooms.

There are several important questions leaders and their school communities might consider to begin shaping their culture of connection and belonging. The first series of questions are about defining the cues for connection and belonging you want students to receive within the school community.

- What are the deeply held beliefs, principles, and mindsets your school community, and the larger community, holds about connection and belonging?

- What are the connection and belonging cues we want students to receive in our classrooms?

- What role do stakeholders play in embodying, upholding, and protecting our culture of connection and belonging?

- What happens when stakeholders' behavior falls outside our expectations for fostering a culture of connection and belonging?

These questions are important to answer, because they provide a foundation for which schools can begin to define and communicate the culture they hope to establish. As we shared in Chapter 1, when you share good information, people understand why you do the things you do. In that case the community—or much of it—will rally around your culture, especially when they understand that it is grounded in connection and belonging, if they understand its principles, the behaviors and signals to observe for when it's thriving, and the actions that might compromise it.

One of the pitfalls to avoid when pursuing a culture of connection and belonging is skipping the step of defining your cues. We can only build investment and trust if we're open and transparent with our stakeholders when these cues have been defined. If we are to restore faith in our schools within the communities we serve, we need to be providing more rationale, more definitions, and when necessary, more research for why we're working so hard to build a culture of connection and belonging for our students.

The second set of questions here are about how we orchestrate and send signals that reinforce the cues we've established to foster connection and belonging. Denarius explains that when he's circulating and giving his students feedback, it's a signal to amplify the cue that he has high expectations, cares about the quality of student work, wants to share their progress with them, *and* he's always going to be meticulously prepared to respond to their work so they can all experience progress/success. He's not simply checking to see that they're working, though that's part of it; he wants students to feel like his classroom is a place where they can experience success and thrive as a learning community.

Questions to Define Your Signals

- What are the signals we'll use to send these cues throughout our lessons and throughout the day?

- How will you teach/roll out expectations of belonging and connection to your students?

- How and when do you send these signals within your lessons, during transitions, or during events?

- How will we roll out, reinforce, and maintain these signals?

- What happens when students and/or teachers send signals that conflict with the cues we've named as a school community?

ACTIVE OBSERVATION: HIDDEN DRIVER OF RELATIONSHIPS

In the clip *Nicole Warren: Busy* you'll see a lot of things that by now look familiar. Nicole gets things off to a fast start. She asks for eyes up (i.e. Habits of Attention) and then immediately sends her students into a math song. That they love the song is pretty evident in their body language. Needless to say, they are also affirming their belonging to the group.

A few seconds later they're off to a Turn and Talk about the one thing they want to remember about rounding. The task explodes with energy. She's cuing a familiar routine with a familiar phrase. There's another little chant—a bit of Call and Response—before they pass out their independent practice packets. But notice also the second half of the video when Nicole circulates as students are working quietly at their desks. She's both responsive and present—responsive meaning she sees their work provides useful and timely feedback that helps them succeed (and feel successful), and present in that she is not distracted and is able to bring a full range of emotions. She is able to perceive things about students' moods and progress quickly.

This is in part because of her clipboard. She is taking notes on students' work so she can remember where they are. She has a clear answer to all the problems on the clipboard so she can check it easily and compare their answers to it. Her working memory is free to watch and connect with them.

This technique is called "Active Observation." It means taking notes in writing as students work and preparing an ideal version of the right answer that you can look at while they work. It frees you to think about your students as you circulate and you can see this in Nicole's class. She connects over and over through the content with students. They feel her caring and a connection to the teacher because of how she gives them feedback and that is in some ways a product of her preparation and her careful note-taking.

PUTTING IT ALL TOGETHER

You can see a final version of many of the ideas we've discussed in this chapter come together beautifully in the video *Erin Magliozzi: Keystone*, from Erin's classroom at Memphis Rise Academy in Memphis, Tennessee.

Observing carefully—notice she is holding a clipboard—as students work independently, Erin notices that Jas has found the correct answer and makes a note to Cold Call her. This is an example of what we call "hunting, not fishing." Erin has chosen Jas for a Cold Call based on her careful observation of student work. She knows Jas will get to shine. She will be successful, feel successful, and push the class in a productive direction with a good answer. As a result she Cold Calls without hesitation. As she does so, students turn and track Jas. They're sending magic. You can feel the love.

Jas answers well and there's snapping in affirmation. (Erin's got both snaps and shine working in her classroom.) Erin has also added a third signal to her classroom. Her students give her a thumbs-up to confirm that they've finished taking notes on Jas's answer. Not only does this let them indicate and thus reaffirm their engagement, but Erin uses the signal to give them the ideal amount of time to complete their task—not so short that it's rushed, not so long that pacing and flow suffer. Flow and thus belonging are accentuated by this signal. It also affirms their engagement: yes, we're ready; yes, we've all taken notes.

A side note here on note-taking. When Erin asks everyone to get Jas's answer down in their packets, she's done something useful in a variety of ways. Writing the answer encodes it in memory and it engages everyone in a productive task in a way that's unambiguously visible to everyone else. Everyone sees everyone else scribbling away. A norm has been set. But it is also a strong signal of affirmation. Think for a moment of what it feels like to be Jas. You are called on. Not only do you get affirmation from your peers, not only does your teacher tell you you've done well, but then everyone writes down what you said. Writing something down says it is important. This is a clear signal that your words carried weight. In fact, the only thing that could be more powerful than her classmates being told to write down what she's said would be making a comment and observing as your classmates spontaneously write down what you said. Message: what you said is so important I had to write it down. In classrooms where teachers consistently ask students to write things down because they are important, it becomes a habit and students are all the more likely to spontaneously initiate it of their own accord.

Like most things in the classroom, a behavior like that is made possible by a teacher's planning and the conditions are set for that here. Students in Erin's classroom all have a packet in which to write. She has made a habit of writing frequently and built the norm that everyone will write when asked. As with other norms, as students get used to it they start to own it. Pencils in hand, taking notes frequently, with space provided, they are far more likely to respond to Jas's words by writing them down of their own accord. That will be good for their learning and great for Jas's feelings of belonging in the classroom.

After they write down Jas's answer, students start to spontaneously signal to Erin that they're ready to move on. As you no doubt by now recognize, as they do this they are signaling their desire to keep going and making the norm of engaged participation visible.

From here students are off to three minutes of independent work with a partner. Erin walks around, clipboard in hand, making notes and giving feedback. She's not explicitly trying to build relationships and make kids feel seen and important; she's trying to teach them the content, but it clearly has that effect. Notice the affirmations, the snaps she gives to students, the "code" she establishes with one student so he can communicate his status privately.

Notice also that she takes careful notes of students who have good answers whom she can call on: Corey and Jaquie. There's another Turn and Talk, a bit of silent work, and then perhaps five minutes after she saw their answers, there's a lovely appreciative Cold Call for Corey and Jaquie, punctuated by snapping and shine. They're incredibly productive in Erin's classroom but there's so much support and belonging, both from peers and also from Erin, who's playful and warm and caring as she circulates, in large part because she's taking careful notes. She's not walking around for five minutes trying to remember whom she wants to call on and why.

SUMMARY: TECHNIQUES THAT AMPLIFY BELONGING

In this chapter we've tried to describe and show examples of a handful of teaching techniques that we think are especially crucial in building classrooms that embrace students and make them feel connected to peers and to the work of school. They're techniques that, taken together, increase and amplify a wide array of seemingly mundane signals that tell students they belong, that school is for them, that they are cared about and connected in school. At the same time these same tools help ensure that young people get the outstanding education they deserve. As we noted before, we refuse to countenance a trade-off between these two goals.

Briefly, the techniques we've described here are:

Props: A system that allows students to affirm each other nonverbally as they learn. We've described how snaps and "sending shine" can do that. You can perhaps imagine more. We think it's an especially important place to start the discussion because it appears so small. We hope to have shown that classroom culture is often built of small things that are easily overlooked.

Habits of Attention: The intentional application of our most foundational evolutionary behaviors—how we look at each other and how we encourage or discourage the things people do around us with our eyes, our expressions, and our attention. "The aspects of things that are most important for us are hidden because of their simplicity and familiarity," the philosopher Ludwig von Wittgenstein wrote. "One is unable to notice something—because it is always before one's eyes." We spend so much time reading our status in the group in the fleeting gazes and glances of our companions that we hardly notice how profoundly it influences nearly everything we do. Attending to it is one of the fastest ways to make people feel a part of the work of schooling.

Habits of Discussion: The deliberate shaping of the norms of how we talk to each other. "To" is a key word there. So much of communication now subtly dehumanizes and disconnects people—young people especially. We talk past one another. We talk at one another. Amplifying signals that we are really with the people we are talking to, that we are connected when we talk is a necessity we feel ever more strongly as we look out at a world full of missed opportunities for connection.

We discussed **Turn and Talk** and **Call and Response** together, though they are separate tools. One is a system to leverage short energetic peer-to-peer chats to bring energy and vigor to classrooms and build confidence in talking about academic ideas. Call and Response is the creation of opportunities to answer in unison—a fun and engaging act of togetherness we are apt to overlook.

When we combine Turn and Talk and Call and Response with a few other systematic ways to ask students to participate in the classroom—especially **Cold Call**, Volunteers, and **Everybody Writes**—we have a system of systems. **Means of Participation** is the name for the technique that combines these participation systems intentionally and signals them clearly to students so they can participate joyfully, energetically, and unselfconsciously and so lose themselves in the classroom and just possibly experience the state of flow—one of the most joyful mental states that humankind experiences.

Finally we discussed **Active Observation**—how the act of carefully attending to what students are doing in class lets us give them meaningful feedback simply and easily. This builds relationships and a sense of belonging through the work of learning. Doing well also frees our working memory as teachers so that we can be as attentive to the experience of individual students as possible.

You can study these techniques and others more deeply in *Teach Like a Champion 3.0,* but of the 63 techniques in that book, these are the ones we would emphasize most in response to the current state of society and the greater than ever needs of young people to connect and learn more successfully.

CODA: ORDERLY CLASSROOMS ARE CARING CLASSROOMS

One topic we have not discussed explicitly but which is implicit in every technique we've described, every video we have shown, and every moment of belonging created by the teachers in them is the necessity of orderliness in the classroom—humane and carefully designed orderliness, of course, thoughtfully reinforced by a caring and reflective teacher, but orderliness just the same. Every joyful moment you see in Erin's or Denarius's or BreOnna's or Jen's class begins with the fact that students are routinely on-task and reliably follow directions. They understand and respect the standards of behavior set by the community for the benefit of the group.

When Erin tells her students to work independently at noise level zero (i.e. silence) on the last question in her lesson, for example, there is the hum of silence in the room. In that moment her students are learning as they deserve to learn—with focus and without distraction. Erin circulates and interacts with students as they work. She could not be half so attentive to her charges if she was distracted by a student who refused to follow along and was instead making "hilarious" burping noises, or two who insisted on talking during the silent work time, or yet another who marched out of the classroom and thus caused Erin to follow.

The sense of togetherness and belonging that thrives among students—the belief that the teacher sees them and cares about each student's progress; the sense that classmates support one another's efforts to succeed—exist not despite but because of orderliness that Erin (and her school) have established.

Her students work in a room that honors their time and effort and tells them, in its orderliness and productivity, that they are important. By contrast, nothing could express more clearly that students simply weren't important to the institution (and society) than allowing their time and their opportunity to be wasted in a classroom where disruptions or distractions large and small were tolerated and even expected.

Or consider two additional clips, *Denarius Frazier: Help* and *Madalyn McLelland: Write It Down*, that demonstrate what is often the unspoken truth of classrooms. Teachers can only be fully responsive to students to whom they can give their full attention. As a result disorderly classrooms hurt the most vulnerable learners, the ones who need their teacher's support the most.

In the videos both teachers spot, and then spend significant time helping, students who are struggling academically. Notice how carefully they are able to attend to those students.

Denarius spends more than two and a half minutes helping a single student grasp the concept he's struggling with, and during that whole time, no one turns around to gawk, no disruption breaks Denarius's concentration. He doesn't have to redirect anyone. Every student remains productively on task. It's quiet so he can whisper and ensure privacy for his student.

The student, Denarius recalls, was a hard-working and curious young man whom he enjoyed teaching but who had knowledge gaps in his basic procedures dating back to middle school. He would make a mistake in his calculations, get a strange result, and become lost.

That's the case in the video. Walking by, Denarius notices his student doesn't have anything written on his paper. This strikes him as strange because they had been working the problem for some time. Perception—noticing that something was off with one student in a room of 30, is the key, and research tells us that perception relies on working memory.[12] If your mind is engaged in thinking about or forestalling or scanning for a dozen things that might go wrong, if the room is noisy and distracts your attention, your working memory will be engaged elsewhere. You will be unlikely to perceive the cues that can cause you to recognize that a student is struggling or confused or frustrated.

But Denarius notices right away and stops to investigate and explain. After a bit of discussion he believes the student has understood, but having started to walk away, glances back and again notices a dearth of "signals" he would expect to see if the student grasped the problem: pencil moving, the student flipping through the book or his notes, say, maybe just a change in posture. It's hard to describe with certitude exactly what signs we read in situations like these that communicate a student's emotional status, but only a calm, poised teacher whose mind is free to attend to such details and who is not battling distractions is likely to perceive them.

Or notice how pitch-perfect Madalyn's tone is, how her short, lilting phrases "Pause. It's okay. Write that down!" get a frustrated student back on track. You can't bring that kind of nuance to your tone if you're also raising your voice slightly, struggling to be heard. You can only be the geography whisperer if you can actually whisper and you can only do that in a quiet classroom.

Both of these beautiful, supportive, and patient interventions begin with perception—Denarius and Madalyn *notice* that a student is struggling. Because their rooms are orderly, it's easier for them to see when something is "off." When things are calm, when you're not distracted, when there's a clear task and a clear expectation for how to complete it, suddenly you notice the look of confusion on a young man's face or that one of your students is stalling and not completing her work.

The sense of orderliness and predictability, combined with their meticulous preparation, make it possible for Denarius and Madalyn to respond to individual students' needs and avoid the assumption that students who appear disengaged or off-task don't care about completing the tasks before them.

As you surely know, building orderly climates is not simple. It is 10 times more challenging now, as so many students have returned to schools not just distracted and anxious but also out of practice at structure and expectation, having had far fewer interactions with institutions that socialize exchange and reciprocity. They are behind academically and have ground to cover. And just maybe they have been led to believe that being asked to meet expectations or accept the terms of a social contract is unreasonable, that to accept authority is to tolerate authoritarianism.

But authority is not authoritarianism; its careful exercise is an absolute necessity to the running of just, fair, humane, and effective classrooms. The argument that authority is akin to authoritarianism is an example of what the psychologist and writer Rob Henderson calls a "luxury belief"—an idea that confers social status on people who hold it but injures others in its practical consequences. The students who are harmed most by the idea that schools should not set and enforce clear rules for young people are the young people themselves, especially those who as a result do not learn how to control their impulses, delay gratification, and exert self-discipline, those who are left at the mercy of peer social norms that are powerful, negative, and costly.

We write further in Chapter 4 about some of the ways schools can think about how to address the root causes behind some students' nonproductive behavior. We agree, strongly, that schools must do better in how they respond when students behave counterproductively. But we also think it is a grave disservice to tell students it is okay to make a habit of behaving in ways that are counterproductive to the groups in their lives. Learning how to thrive within an institution and balance one's own goals and needs with those of the group is immensely valuable to people who expect to accomplish things as parts of groups in the future—that is to say, to almost anyone who wants to accomplish anything of value to society.

It is a gift of schooling for young people to learn how to join productively in the endeavors of their lives. The people who are harmed most by the belief that schools should not set and enforce rules with consistency and caring, in other words, are the students who behave poorly as a result.

Some nonproductive behavior is a result of the difficulties students face in their lives outside of school. Some of it, let's be clear, is not; people behave the way they do for a wide variety of reasons. You simply cannot say, "Student behavior is the result of X," unless X is "a thousand different things." In fact, one of the challenges with environments that are disorderly is that they make it more difficult for schools to allocate the appropriate resources and time to students who truly require extensive support because they are spending them on young people who are fully capable of choosing to behave differently. What's beautiful about all of the clips that we've watched is that the orderliness the teachers have instilled allows them to be especially attentive and responsive to the psychological needs of their students.

Notes

1. https://www.tandfonline.com/doi/abs/10.1080/174397610037941
   30?journalCode=rpos20#:~:text=Engagement%20and%20meaning%20correlated%20more,with%20educational%20and%20occupational%20attainment

2. Elsewhere in this book we discuss the devastating costs to young people when adults confuse the exercise of authority with authoritarianism.

3. https://journals.aom.org/doi/10.5465/amj.2017.1507#:~:text=Thus%2C%20a%20leader's%20subtle%20positive,positive%20attention%20from%20a%20leader

4. See Doug's article "Teaching the Art of Listening in the Age of Me, Me, Me," https://www.tes.com/magazine/archive/teaching-art-listening-age-me-me-me

5. Doug discusses this more along with the data to support it in *Teach Like a Champion 3.0*, p. 282.

6. See *Teach Like a Champion 3.0*, p. 497.
7. See *Teach Like a Champion 3.0*, p. 282.
8. https://chronicle.brightspotcdn.com/10/2d/a28062aa41b4bc2ac d088fa79da1/2020-college-free-speech-rankings.pdf
9. See *Teach Like a Champion 3.0*, p. 324.
10. https://www.sbp-journal.com/index.php/sbp/announcement/ view/142
11. https://fs.blog/muscular-bonding/; https://bigthink.com/the-present/muscular-bonding/
12. See Daniel Willingham, *Why Don't Students Like School?* (Jossey-Bass, 2009).

Chapter 4

Wiring the School for Socioemotional Learning

One common theme of the post-pandemic world is the increased interest in socioemotional learning (SEL) among schools and educators. Not that SEL wasn't plenty familiar to most educators already, but two years marked by increased stress, isolation, and loneliness for thousands of kids "turbocharged" interest in it, as education policy expert Rick Hess recently put it.

Not only have many young people been through challenging and difficult experiences, but in many cases long periods of isolation have resulted in diminished social skills that have left them less able to manage everyday conflicts and challenges now that they're back in schools. Doug recently met with school leaders in Texas and asked them about the emotional and psychological status of their students. Had they come back to school behaving differently? Of the more than 180 people in the room perhaps 3 or 4 did not agree that students had changed. One leader described how students were impatient with each other and how misunderstandings or small slights escalated quickly. "Even with their friends, the slightest things cause a flareup."

"They struggle to show each other the basic empathy they all need,"[1] another said. There were academic effects too. "They give up much more quickly in the face of difficulty than kids did before the pandemic," an administrator opined and the room nodded as one. And in particular, they reported that classroom behavior was dramatically worse—the rate of disruptions was higher, the basic willingness to do as asked was lower, and highly emotional responses to the setting of limits were more frequent.

So it's an especially critical time for schools to ensure that students thrive not just academically, but also psychologically and emotionally. That idea is a "variation on a historical theme," Hess and Tim Shriver, board chair of the Collaborative for Academic Social and Emotional Learning, recently wrote. "Since the dawn of the republic, teachers and schools have been tasked with teaching content and modeling character."

A few weeks after Doug's meeting in Texas, we convened a group of school leaders to ask their opinion their students' emotional well-being. "On a socioemotional level, we have seen less development and maturity from students than we have in previous years at a particular grade level," Rhiannon Lewis, a school leader at Memphis Rise in Memphis, Tennessee, told us. "The ability to self-regulate is a bit less developed, and we can only guess that this is due to the lack of socioemotional support during the pandemic that has left this long-term impact." David Adams, CEO of the Urban Assembly's 23 district schools in New York City, noted:

> "I've seen students become more sensitive in interactions. The notion of how to interact, that there are social norms that are guiding you—my students are really having difficulty navigating conflict. Escalation comes a lot faster than it used to. Persistence is another challenge—persisting in work, persisting in relationships. Some of the things that were more taken for granted need to be really more explicitly taught."

Adams's comments reveal one of many carry-on effects for students when they struggle to connect with each other and resolve minor difficulties. It means disrupted relationships between and among young people. Losing a friend over some initially small incident seems especially sad in a time when young people so badly need every valuable connection.

So an increased emphasis on SEL is a worthwhile response to the present context, and in this chapter we'll try to sketch out specific approaches and general rules of thumb for rebuilding social and emotional capacity in students. But we also offer some caveats, because helping students navigate challenging situations is challenging in and of itself. SEL interventions can be faddish. They can be rushed into service with little evidence to support them. And there's the risk that we'll be lured into believing that a single action or program can solve the issue we face. Most likely to help, we think, is the careful selection of manageable strategic efforts that focus on rewiring daily social interactions and cognitive habits to build socioemotional capacity in students. In Chapter 3 on rewiring the classroom, we talked about the need to maximize frequent, often small signals of belonging. In writing about building socioemotional health, we argue for wiring the building to send constant, often small signals to reinforce mindsets and behaviors that foster well-being.

One benefit of that approach is that it can help us avoid what UK education writer Joe Kirby calls hornets: "high-effort, low-impact ideas" of the sort that schools may do out of best intentions. Good schools, Kirby notes, have to avoid doing every good thing so they can focus on the most important things and "put first things first." A hornet isn't a counterproductive or ineffective idea. It's a moderately helpful thing that keeps us from focusing on activities that help students more. Resources are finite, even when our hope and caring for young people is unlimited. Using up time and effort on moderately useful activities tires out staff and degrades their ability to teach well and be emotionally present for students.

More SEL is not necessarily better, in other words. Consistency, quality of offerings, and return on effort should be the goals. We have a lot to accomplish in schools right now—it's a once-in-a-generation learning crisis as well—and most importantly, only well-run activities build students' sense of belonging and well-being. A class to build SEL skills two or three mornings a week with every teacher in the school leading a section might be a difference maker, but only if all of those teachers were well prepared with excellent lesson plans that are interesting and helpful to students. If the teachers aren't prepared and don't teach well, if the room in which we're talking SEL doesn't walk the SEL walk and make students feel signals of belonging and inclusion like we saw in Chapter 3, it won't help much. Indifferently run activities don't move the needle much. And well-run activities—as Chapter 3 also showed—require planning, preparation, and training.

Rather than pressing every lever, we should choose the most effective ones. This applies to everything we do in schools, but it's especially relevant in a discussion of SEL because another challenge is that it can be vaguely defined and because positive outcomes can be presumed to result from good intentions alone.

Consider a recent report by the highly regarded Collaborative for Academic, Social, and Emotional Learning (CASEL) called "10 Years of Social and Emotional Learning in US School Districts."[2] It defined SEL as "the process through which all young people and adults acquire and apply the knowledge, skills and attitude to develop healthy identities, manage emotions and achieve personal and collective goals, feel and show empathy for others, establish and maintain supportive relationships and make responsible and caring decisions." That's a sprawling definition to put it mildly, and a goal with a definition that excludes nothing is problematic operationally. What activity can a staff member propose under the aegis of improving SEL and have school leaders realize that it's of secondary importance or not germane at all?

The report's approach to data doesn't help much either. Its retrospective analysis of ten years of investment in SEL across multiple large districts offers little insight on which methods or ideas worked best and delivered maximum return for effort. They highlight a small number (three) of less-than-overwhelming data points, including a district that "reported an overall improvement in school climate, as measured by student responses on the annual climate and connectedness survey . . . [of] four percentage points (from 68% to 72%) and student perceptions of caring others increased by two percentage points (from 63% to 65%)." There's no analysis of the correlation to specific actions, never mind causation.

A tiny improvement in a subjective survey instrument in a district where dozens of factors (including randomness) could have driven a marginal perception of change does not exactly build an unimpeachable case for the report's conclusion: sustained districtwide focus and expanded funding are required. Such a strategy doesn't make it more likely SEL programs will work. It merely opens the idea to concept drift—if everything is SEL, nothing is. And it makes it more likely that wide-ranging nonstrategic efforts will be ineffective or consume scarce resources.

A final caveat: it's important to remember that teachers are not trained mental health professionals. We should be cautious about presuming their capacity to delve into areas where social workers and counselors are better suited and more qualified.

START WITH VIRTUES

Fortunately, we think there is a path forward—one that starts with but need not consist exclusively of character education, an element of SEL that involves the intentional naming and reinforcing of virtues that make the community and its members more likely to thrive and succeed. What are virtues? you might ask. University of Pennsylvania psychologist Angela Duckworth describes them as "ways of thinking, feeling and acting that we [can] habitually do that are good for others and good for ourselves." Implicit in that definition of virtue is both an individual and a group dynamic—one reason why we think character education is so important. Virtues are "positive personal strengths"[3] that help individuals succeed, that help them feel happier and more fulfilled, and that also build community. A school full of character and virtue is likely to be a place where people feel valued, important, and connected.

To clarify, there are a variety of approaches schools can take to socioemotional learning; we will describe several in this chapter and our assumption is that different schools will have different needs. But we argue that one foundational piece of the solution for many schools is an emphasis on building virtues though character education. For some schools, rebuilding atrophied social skills or investing in mindfulness will also (or alternatively) be important. In other cases, providing interventions for a narrower group of students who struggle most will be critical. Of course, there are other beneficial programs schools can consider. Many of them are excellent and we don't propose what we describe here to be comprehensive. Rather, we offer an approach we think can deliver immense benefits in well-being and belonging to a large number of students at a manageable cost of time and effort and can be implemented by most educators without significant additional training. It's a sensible approach that can add broad value at a time when schools are pulled in a dozen directions.

KNOWLEDGE, PERCEPTION, AND REASONING

Character education focuses on instilling virtues that allow individuals and communities to thrive. To do that, the Jubilee Centre on Character Education's "Character Education Framework" advises, schools should emphasize virtue *knowledge* (helping students to understand what virtues are and why they are beneficial), virtue *perception* (helping students to notice virtues more readily as they occur in the world around them and how they shape the community), and virtue *reasoning* (supporting students in making decisions about when and how they apply those virtues in their own lives).[4]

That's a compelling recipe for long-term learning, but character education has its skeptics too. To some people the idea smacks of paternalism—how can one person say what characteristics are virtuous? To others it smacks of politicization—character virtues will be a vehicle for proselytizing values in an agenda that is not their own.

We argue that we are always teaching values, whether we realize it or not. By seeking to focus transparently on a set that is as close to universal and as optimally beneficial as we can get, we can mitigate these concerns. We should seek out traits that the greatest number of parents (and hopefully students) place value on and that we have reason to believe will really help students, doubly so if we maintain a focus on virtues that build both connection among community members and also foster learning—the ultimate purpose of school.

One of the themes of this book is being attentive to process in order to gain more buy-in from stakeholders. Character education is a perfect example of a time to be intentional about process. By being transparent about what virtues it has chosen and why, and by asking parents for input on the virtues it chooses, a school can reassure parents who may be skeptical and ensure their trust in how the school seeks to support their children. To state the obvious, this is important because our work as educators is to *help* parents to raise *their* children. We, your authors, frequently use the expression "our kiddos" or "our students" but that is merely an expression, a signal of our commitment to and caring for the children and families we serve. Effective character education (and SEL more broadly) requires input from and connection with all stakeholders–students, faculty, and families—but especially parents. It should reflect their values. Our private values may not jibe perfectly with every member of the school community but we can and should seek consensus values, the best possible representation of the things we all agree on most, and that is a process that will require input and listening.

So the process should start by explicitly naming virtues the school aspires to uphold and reinforce. As Angela Duckworth also points out, character education and socioemotional work more broadly are not guesswork. There is science—a great deal of it—to help guide us toward the most important virtues and traits that most build well-being and connectedness.

As a starting point in thinking about character virtues, we love this chart[5] developed by the Jubilee Centre for Character and Virtues in the UK. They differentiate four types of virtues: intellectual virtues (such as critical thinking and curiosity), moral virtues (such as compassion and respect), civic virtues (such as service and civility), and performance virtues (such as teamwork and perseverance). Even before we get down to a discussion of which virtues matter most, the idea of seeing them in categories, each with a broader purpose, is helpful. It helps to answer the question of *why*. Our goal is for young people to be equipped to "pursue knowledge, truth, and understanding," to be prepared to "act well in situations that require an ethical response," to be able and willing to contribute to "the common good" in a variety of situations, and to have a set of "enabling" skills like determination and resilience that can help them accomplish the first three—and most other goals in their lives. To us as parents, family members, and educators, the power of the chart is as much in those categories as the individual virtues. Reading it helped us to see the broader purpose in character work and how different parts fit together. We suspect that a parent—even a skeptical one—glimpsing such a framework would feel reassured and informed.

THE BUILDING BLOCKS OF CHARACTER

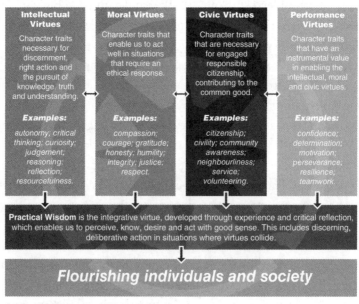

Source: [6] / University of Birmingham

So start by choosing and naming virtues, but remember that understanding "why"—the purposes of the virtues in a well-lived and healthy life—is critical. We don't personally recommend choosing *all* or even most of the virtues proposed in the Jubilee Centre's framework. There are far too many to focus on and reinforce well. A few key ideas deeply understood and valued are better than a list of terms. And frankly, some are inevitably more important than others. Choose a handful—we'd suggest five to seven—that align with your mission and are most compelling to the parents in your school's community, and then build them into the fabric of the school. For what it's worth, we think the authors of the framework would agree. In describing "examples" of virtues that would fall into each of the four categories, they show that their assumption is that people will chose, select, and prioritize these or others. We like that too because the words matter. Do we, your authors, perceive a difference between diligence and perseverance, for example? Yes, we do.[6] Which word you pick—and how you define it—matters.

BUILD THEM INTO THE FABRIC OF YOUR SCHOOL

Once you've chosen virtues, the next step is to *build them into the fabric of the school*. The key to instilling beneficial habits of mind for young people is to reinforce them throughout the school day. Strong character and healthy mindsets are far less likely to thrive if they only come up during a specific block of time! Character can and should be reinforced while community members are doing other things; perhaps it's best reinforced that way. After all, if you truly value compassion, you should value it and look for it everywhere. It's better to show appreciation for it throughout the school day than to design an hour, twice a week, when we attend to things like compassion. It can start there perhaps, but the important part is the message that we should always be thinking about the people we want to be.

Another way of putting this is that to be successfully instilled in the life of a school, virtues should be taught, caught, and sought;[7] that is, students should understand what they are and how they are beneficial, then the school should set out to increase their visibility so that they are clearly valued and are more readily apparent as community norms. Over time, the culture should attempt to socialize students to internalize the virtues—to seek them because they perceive them to be part of who they are or want to be. They should also be modeled intentionally and consistently by the adults.[8]

Making sure virtues are taught means providing not just definitions but also examples and applications. This might start at a schoolwide community meeting or perhaps a grade-level meeting where the reasons why the virtues matter are shared, perhaps with a few personal stories from the adults. We're big believers in active practice when learning vocabulary in academic classes. Active practice means giving students the definition of a term (rather than asking them to try to guess at it) and then allowing them to apply it in challenging situations. Jen Brimming did that with the word "reprehensible" in the video from Chapter 3. Students are engaged because they are asked to apply a term they know in complex and challenging cases: Why is it bad to steal but reprehensible to steal from a charity? Why is being a hypocrite reprehensible? Which characters from various books we've read are reprehensible and why?

Building knowledge of virtues could look similar. At a grade-level or schoolwide meeting, you could explain briefly that gratitude means showing appreciation and thanks for the things people do for you, and then ask students (perhaps via a series of Turn and Talks) to reflect on a series of questions about it:

- What's a situation in which a student might show gratitude to a teacher?

- What's a situation where a teacher might show gratitude to a student?

- Saying "thank you" is a common way to show gratitude but there are other ways. What's a way you might show gratitude that does not involve saying anything?

- How might you show gratitude to someone who found your dog after it ran away? How might you show your gratitude to them if it turned out they didn't speak any of the same languages as you?

- What's something people forget to show gratitude for?

- What's something a pet might show gratitude for, and how might he or she show it?

- Do we always have to express gratitude to a single person? Try to think of an example of how and why you'd express gratitude to something other than one individual.

Questions like these require thinking and reasoning on one hand and discretion and adaptation on the other. They grow students' understanding of a concept but also ask them to think about how they would apply it in their own lives. How each student answers the last question is a personal reflection. Later you might ask students to think even more deeply about it:

- What's a time when you didn't show gratitude when you wish you had?

- Describe a time when someone showed gratitude to you that you still remember.

We say "later" in describing when you might ask this second group of questions because there are very few concepts we can master in one interaction. Learning requires constant discussion, reflection, and expansion over time. We need to keep talking about virtues to make them meaningful. Better to spend ten minutes discussing gratitude five times over the course of a month than to spend one hour discussing it once and then letting it drop.

We were struck recently by a video we observed of Equel Easterling teaching virtues in his classroom at North Star Clinton Hill Middle School in Newark, New Jersey. His session was focused on introducing the concept of gratitude. (As we'll discuss later, research somewhat suggests that gratitude is perhaps the single most powerful virtue for student well-being.)

Equel starts by asking students what gratitude is. They provide examples and descriptions. Then he defines the term formally and asks them to reason about it based on a video: How were the people in the video showing gratitude and why was it valuable? Notice the degree of peer-to-peer discussion and the degree to which the environment is full of belonging cues—how students listen carefully to one another, reference and build off of one another's ideas, and generally make each classmate feel like their words matter. As we noted before, an intervention designed to enhance socioemotional health only works if the environment emphasizes student well-being as much as the content does. As the video closes, Equel's students put gratitude into action immediately, writing letters to a teacher so they feel the benefits of expressing appreciation right away.

But, again, even a thoughtful reflection isn't enough on its own. Behaviors and mindsets are made habits via frequent application. A virtue becomes part of the fabric of a school community via repeated application and the magnification of constant signals that affirm its importance. The research on this is clear: the perception that something is a norm among group members is the biggest influence on motivation and behavior. Job one is ensuring that the institution and the people within it are always looking for examples of virtues and have systems to make them appear as visible and valuable as possible.

We'll discuss that idea more in a moment when we discuss the "mechanisms" of culture building, but we pause here to note that encouraging students to demonstrate virtues allows them to feel the positive emotions that accompany positive (i.e. virtuous) behaviors. The fact that being "virtuous" generally feels good is often overlooked, but for the most part humans have evolved to feel good when they demonstrate virtuous behavior. Generosity feels good to most of us because it benefits the groups we have evolved to rely on and cements our connections to them. We have evolved to find it gratifying so that we are more inclined to do it. So helping students to engage in positive prosocial behavior is likely to make most students feel good about themselves, to recognize the parts of themselves that are already virtuous, and to enjoy the feeling of contributing to and being appreciated by the community. Students themselves are often not aware at first of how positive and affirming this feels. In fact this is a topic good virtue instruction can subtly draw students' attention to. You could add a question to a reflection on gratitude such as the one we were describing earlier that asked something like: "Think of a time you expressed gratitude to someone whom you are close to. How did you feel afterwards?" Or similarly, with a virtue such as generosity or compassion or honesty: "How did it feel to you afterwards?"

Of course, not every single student will feel good about engaging in virtuous behavior. There will always be people who show less desire to demonstrate positive behaviors and invest in shared well-being, but the number who do engage positively once they experience how it feels to do so in a community that values it may surprise you—and them! Most young people want to feel belonging. They want to feel like they are contributing members of a worthy group. They can be convinced otherwise; they can seek belonging in counterproductive groups and take on antisocial behaviors, but for the most part we think that if we—and other students—model, explain, and show appreciation for prosocial behaviors, most young people will choose to seek them.

We sometimes think of character as fixed—that a student who behaves a certain way just is that way he is. But like anything else, people (young people, especially) change as the cultures around them exert influence. They "progress . . . through a trajectory," as the Jubilee Centre puts it, which begins with their understanding virtue and then experiencing it and responding to incentives—both intrinsic and extrinsic—to make a habit of it. Ideally this process feels good, and over time virtues become for them "autonomously sought and reflectively chosen virtue."

THE CASE FOR GRATITUDE AND RESILIENCE

We love the way Equel Easterling made a virtue meaningful in the lives of his students. We love the way his classroom communicated belonging to students in the way they interacted with one another as they discussed virtues. But we also love his specific choice of virtue gratitude. Arguably he chose the single most important virtue of them all.

We've noted the necessity of making choices among the virtues to build into a school's culture. Five to seven is our target number. And that means hard choices. The list of potential virtues is long. So we want to make the case for a few virtues that we think are especially beneficial to student well-being and belonging. In fact they're so important that we think schools should find a way to make them a part of their culture in durable and meaningful ways, even if they choose *not* to pursue a virtue-based character education approach. As we noted previously, there is quite a bit of science on the drivers of well-being and happiness. There's also quite a bit of science on what causes people to overcome adversity. In that research these two concepts rise above the rest.

Gratitude, as we discussed briefly in Chapter 1, is underrated. A recent publication by Harvard Medical School noted that it is "strongly and consistently associated with greater happiness. Gratitude helps people feel more positive emotions, relish good experiences, improve their health, deal with adversity, and build strong relationships."[9] The direction of the benefit is in some ways unexpected. We presume that showing gratitude is primarily beneficial to the recipient, because showing someone appreciation makes them feel special, more important, more valued. The surprise is that it is even more beneficial to the person expressing the gratitude.

Expressing gratitude regularly has the effect of calling students' attention to its root causes: there are good things in their world worth appreciating and giving thanks for. And then one of the most durable findings of social science kicks in: "Scientists estimate that we remember only one of every one hundred pieces of information we receive and the rest gets dumped into the brain's spam file. We see [and remember] what we look for and we miss the rest," Shawn Achor writes, "and what we look for is a product of habit." Students who look for good things in their world see more of them and find the world looks like a more supportive place with a clear place for them in it. After a while this becomes a habit, Achor notes. He calls it the Tetris Effect. Like a chronic player of the video game Tetris, who starts to see its component shapes everywhere, students who practice looking for things they can appreciate and who articulate *why* those things are worth appreciating start to see reasons to feel good about their world everywhere. By thinking about why those things are worthy of gratitude, they come to understand better why some things are valuable in life. This becomes more or less automatic (a "cognitive afterimage," Achor calls it) and a kind of optimism is instilled.

This is often accompanied by physiological benefits such as a reduction in blood pressure, Emiliana Simon-Thomas, science director at the Greater Good Science Center at Cal Berkeley notes. It can "slow the heart rate, and contribute to overall relaxation." Gratitude she says is a "de-stressor" that sooths the nervous system.[10] And of course it builds social connections to bond and appreciate one another. Social connections are one of the healthiest things people can have; people with stronger, more positive social connections are routinely healthier physically and live longer. Achor writes:

> "Few things are as integral to our well-being. Consistently grateful people are more energetic, emotionally intelligent, forgiving and less likely to be depressed, anxious, or lonely. And it's not that people are only grateful because they are happier. Gratitude has been proven to be a significant cause of positive outcomes."

So when we observe Equel asking his students to write letters of appreciation, they—not the receiving teachers—are actually the ones whom the exercise benefits. It helps them to notice the people in the world who seek to help them. It causes them to feel like the world—or *their* world—is on their side. From where they're sitting, it seems like a better place.

Back in 2016, on a visit to Michaela Community School in London, Doug observed an example of an exercise in building gratitude. In retrospect, its benefits to students' socioemotional health are even clearer than they were at the time. At the end of lunch, a teacher stood and offered pupils at the school the chance to stand and express gratitude for anything they felt was important in front of the gathered group of students (about half the school). It's important to note that it was entirely voluntary. No one was required to say anything. They were not told who or what they might want to show gratitude for. It was an example of "virtue reasoning." Students decided for themselves whether they wished to express gratitude to someone, and if so, for what. And most of them did. Their hands shot into the air. Almost everyone in the room wanted to be chosen to say thanks.

Was this perhaps because, having made a habit of doing so daily, the students felt the psychological benefits? Were they responding to the fact that it made them feel happy and, well, virtuous? Contributing members of the community? Did it feel adult and mature to have the wherewithal to throw off the narrow lens of childhood (it's all about me) and embrace the people in the world on whom you relied? To affirm the presence of a village around you?

Whatever the reasons, students stood and thanked their classmates for helping them study. They thanked their teachers for expecting a lot of them and helping them. One student thanked the lunchroom staff for cooking for them—the school ate family-style meals with real cutlery and plates and (as we discuss in Chapter 2) this resulted in real face-to-face conversations. For a person used to US school meals eaten in the blink of an eye off plastic trays, it was eye-opening, a ritual that clearly built belonging and reinforced social skills.

Given how strongly many people hate speaking in front of large groups, it's worth noting that each of these eagerly proffered expressions of thanks was made impromptu and while standing in front of more than a hundred people. And yet the gratitude seemed to come pouring out of them until the teacher in charge said it was time to go back to class. The ritual seemed to give the students who spoke a sort of stature. It expressed the idea that the appreciation of a student like Havzi or Camilla, when earned, was important enough for a room full of people to hear about and take note of. Part of the message was that their appreciation, their opinion, was a valuable and important thing. No wonder there were more hands than the staff could ever call on.

Doug wrote elsewhere about how unexpected it was:

"I found myself wondering about it for a while afterwards. Here were kids . . . who might have faced difficulty at home and on their way to school. Many had left (or even lived still in) places racked by violence and difficulty. But . . . their days were punctuated not by someone reminding them that they had suffered or been neglected by society, but by the assumption that they would want to show their gratitude to the world around them.

"What did this mean? Well, first of all, it gave rise to a culture of thoughtfulness. Everywhere I looked students did things for one another. In one class a student noticed another without a pencil and gave her one without being asked. In the hallway a student dropped some books and suddenly three or four students were squatting to pick them up. When students left a classroom they said, 'Thank you' to their teacher."

It wasn't just that everyone seemed to be thanking everyone else and seeking to do something worthy of gratitude. They seemed to take pleasure in it. Many students chose to say "Thank you, Miss" or "Thank you, Sir" to their teachers as they filed out of the room after class, but the tone was always cheery. Students bounced out of class.

In writing about the power of gratitude, Shawn Achor notes that the important thing is not just to name things you are grateful for but to say—and therefore think about—why. This causes you to think about the things you value most in the world. Thus a tiny detail from lunch at the Michaela School also sticks in Doug's memory. The teacher running the gratitude session occasionally gave students feedback. "That was excellent, Camila. You were very clear about why you appreciate how hard your mother works." "Thank you, Havzi. Could you briefly say why Luke sharing his snack with you was meaningful?"

As we leave the scene in the school's cafeteria, it's worth noting a key framing of the psychologist Martin Seligman's work. Seligman found, we have noted, that happiness does not consist merely of pleasure. It consists of meaning and engagement as well. People who experience happiness consisting of all three aspects lead the happiest lives. What is true then of our grateful students is true of examples throughout the book. When people feel connected to other people and to something larger than themselves, and when they lose themselves in an activity or endeavor and when the things they work toward feel important—achievement or service or community or family—then they are happy, far happier, in fact, than if they ardently pursue pleasure and pleasure alone. Surely that has broader implications for SEL lens work.

It's worth sharing a bit more about Seligman himself here. He is the founder of positive psychology, a branch of psychology that looks to study why things go right in some people's lives. Prior to Seligman and a few colleagues making the case, psychology focused almost exclusively on what goes wrong in people's lives, why it happens, and how to fix it when it does. Obviously that's important work, but it's only part of the story of humanity. What goes right is equally important. Rather than looking at what goes wrong when people struggle, positive psychologists want to know what makes them thrive, even in the face of difficulty. Of course there are students in our schools for whom we have to ask, "What's going wrong here?" But for the great majority of our students the question is: What can go right? What can enable them to thrive and flourish? What behaviors and habits and mindsets can we instill in them to make it more likely that they do so? There are a series of things we can do in schools to take on that latter challenge, and instilling gratitude appears to be one of them.

BUILDING RESILIENCE

Another key body of research in the annals of socioemotional well-being also has to do with studies of what goes right in people's lives, but in this case why some people respond with resilience when confronted with adversity or even trauma. Given how much students have been through in the past few years, it's doubly relevant now.

Columbia University Teachers College clinical psychologist George Bonanno has written extensively on the topic, particularly in his book

The End of Trauma: How the New Science of Resilience Is Changing How We Think About PTSD. Bonanno finds that people are strong and surprisingly inclined to resilience. This does not mean that they do not suffer and struggle emotionally in the face of adverse experiences. Being upset after a difficult experience is normal and recovery often takes time, but Bonanno stresses that most people do recover, even from highly adverse events. Of course some do not; of course we need to be ready to identify those cases and provide them with access to the care they need, but the message of resilience is also clear: our children are strong. The great majority will overcome even extreme difficulty and it's important to remind them of this, and not suggest that we think they are fragile or damaged by their experiences. In fact, Bonanno's research suggests, most people follow what he terms the "resilience trajectory," a common path back from adversity or duress.

Bonanno is realistic about the research on resilience and overcoming trauma and the limits of what it can tell us. We only know a little about why some people bounce back and why some struggle for more prolonged periods or perhaps never quite get over a terrible experience. There's more we don't know than we do know, but at the core of the 'resilience trajectory,' the path back from adversity Bonanno finds—an idea called the "flexibility mindset." People who have this mindset are the most likely to thrive after hardship. People with a "flexibility mindset" tend to share "three interrelated beliefs...optimism about the future, confidence in [their] ability to cope and a willingness to think about threat as a challenge." It is "essentially a conviction that we will be able to adapt ourselves to the challenge at hand, that we will do whatever is needed to move forward," he writes. "These beliefs interact and complement each other in a way that multiplies their individual impact. And collectively they produce a robust conviction...'I will find a way to deal with this challenge.'"

If we can instill a flexibility mindset in people who have faced difficulty, Bonanno argues, we give them the best possible chance to return to a state of well-being and flourishing. As with gratitude, we think weaving the component parts of the flexibility mindset (and thus the resilience pathway) throughout school cultures and magnifying the signals that reinforce it are critical actions for educators to take.

One key additional piece of research on the topic of resilience comes from Bonnie Benard, a social worker whose books include *Resiliency: What We Have Learned* and *Resilience Education*. Benard notes that the environment, not just the individual, plays a role in responses to adversity. There are in fact "protective factors" in certain environments that increase the chances that people who are part of those communities will thrive and show resilience in the face of adversity. "The characteristics of environments that appear to alter—or even reverse—potential negative outcomes and enable individuals . . . develop resilience," Benard writes, are, first, the presence of "caring relationships." These relationships "convey compassion, understanding, respect, and interest, are grounded in listening, and establish safety and basic trust." The second thing environments that promote resilience do is send "high expectation messages." That is, they "communicate not only firm guidance, structure, and challenge but, and most importantly, convey a belief in the youth's innate resilience." Lastly, organizations that foster resilience give young people "opportunities for meaningful participation and contribution" that includes bearing "real responsibility, making decisions, expressing opinions and being heard."[11]

Reading Benard's description, we are struck by its applicability to the classrooms we portrayed in Chapter 3. They are learning places and they are "protective" places. Teacher relationships "convey compassion, understanding, respect, and interest" and so, interestingly, do peer-to-peer relationships. They certainly manage to send "high-expectations messages" consistently. They are full of firm guidance, structure, challenge, and belief. And again they clearly give young people opportunities for meaningful participation and contribution. Students have voices but perhaps most strongly of all feel heard.

The characteristics of protective places Benard describes give us a pretty good recipe for how a good school or a good classroom should run, and so again one of our takeaways is that in addition to the many things we also do, running a great school and a great classroom is also critical to positive mental health for young people. Doing our core work exceptionally well is a key part of what it's going to take to help students thrive.

HOW A MOMENT BECOMES A MECHANISM FOR DEVELOPMENT

During the pandemic, Hilary's family adopted a few regular traditions and rituals, one of which was playing a game where family members drew a card with a written question on it. Everyone around the table answered aloud. Some of the prompts were simple (*What's your favorite season?*) Others presented more of a challenge (*Who is the funniest person in your family?*). Hilary quickly realized that much of the "challenge" was socioemotional in nature, managing the human side of answering. Beyond the question *Who really is the funniest?* are considerations like: "If I answer truthfully, what if I hurt someone's feelings by saying they aren't the funniest? Do I fib? Do I not answer the question? I could say, 'Oh, everyone is funny,' but that's really the same as saying nobody is. What if I say I think I'm the funniest? Then what will people think of me?"

As time rolled on, and more and more of these conversation cards were pulled, it was not lost on Hilary how the discussions they evoked were lessons in how we understand, model, and develop character. In those dinner conversations her family wrestled with issues like honesty, fairness, and courage. A simple game provided practice and experience exploring family members' values, how they would or could exhibit virtue and model character in their daily lives.

But even more than that, the questions provided the opportunity to learn how to navigate the dynamics of relationship building and connection through frequent, low-stakes opportunities at trial and error. There were small but not always simple interactions amidst a group where safety and caring were established. *Actually no one got upset when I said someone else was funniest. They took it as an opportunity to celebrate that person too. Hmm, people didn't think it was that funny when I said it was me.*

Low-stakes trial and error in a supportive environment is a very powerful thing for learning to make your way in the world.

While these moments happened at home, they are typical of how recurring events can become an opportunity to develop the building blocks of interpersonal skill or character. The daily game became what we call a "mechanism"—a recurring setting in which questions were raised and reflections about self were normalized. Schools with strong, vibrant "protective" cultures tend to use such mechanisms especially effectively, particularly when they can infuse them with a sense of community, belonging, and psychological safety.

A "community meeting" is one of the most common—and for our money, effective—mechanisms a school can leverage. "Meeting" is a time when a large portion of the school—ideally the entire "village"—comes together; such times are perfect for stressing togetherness and reinforcing shared values, especially those values that help young people thrive and connect. If we share a culture, if we are a village, there should be times we all get together to talk about what matters most.

Scheduling short, well-planned schoolwide, gradewide or even single-classroom "meetings" is powerful in part because we can all see one another. A village conceives of itself as a village in many ways because there are times when everyone turns out for an event, when everyone can see each other. It's even more powerful when there are rituals and traditions—we greet each other in a consistent way. Or we dance, sing, or tell stories. Taken together this says, "We are an 'us.'"

Here, for example, is a picture of one of our favorite principals, Nikki Bowen, at morning meeting with her students at Excellence Girls Charter School in Brooklyn, New York.[12] Students are gathered in the school gymnasium. Teachers, sitting beside students, are engaged in a chant or song, a ritual that occurs frequently at meeting. Nikki is walking toward the center, getting ready to orchestrate the proceedings.

Notice the way students are seated. They are in groups by homeroom and in tidy rows. This manner of seating suggests the intentionality and importance of the meeting. It's carefully arranged because it matters. And students can all see one another—it helps to see "us" to conceive of "us"—and be seen. Yes it's also true that it's easier to create an orderly happy productive environment when you can tell at a glance that everyone is seated where they should be, but mostly the arrangement is about feeling seen and heard *by everyone*. You can raise your hand to speak and everyone can see you. Each class has its own place to sit. (Having a place means you belong!) There's space in the middle for people to be invited forward to share ideas or be honored or perform in some way. It's a shape built for "togetherness." Nikki circulates, talking values, cueing songs, and asking questions of students. She regularly uses "meeting" as an opportunity to call out class groups and individual members of the community for special praise.

It's not just Nikki talking, though. Other teachers often lead at meeting. Sometimes students do. And no matter who is leading, the rest of the community participates actively, often via Turn and Talk and Call and Response. It looks and feels like Jen Brimming's class from Chapter 3 but at 10 times the scale. And there's a *lot* of singing: the Hope Chant, the Respect Chant, the Optimism Song. "We woke up the neighbors each morning with our school pride and togetherness," Nikki recalls.

Here are the words to one of their school songs. See if you can spot the themes that recall the ideas in Chapter 1:

This is the school that has the girls who work hard all day long!

We're great thinkers, dynamic speakers

And we will change the world!

How will you change the world?

By being my best self!

Your best what?

My best self!

But it only takes you?

No it takes me, it takes you, it takes all of us, it takes our sisterhood.

Cuz girls are . . . smart, girls are strong,

Girls are helpful, girls are special, girls are POWERFUL!

Morning meeting is short, by the way: 10–15 minutes, sometimes less. But you can get a lot done in a short time when you have clear goals and familiar, well-established rituals.

You could use the meeting to ask students the sequence of gratitude questions we shared on page 138, for example. Or you could also use it as an opportunity to reinforce a virtue like, say, consideration. Doing that at meeting might sound something like this:

Before we head to class, I want to share two small examples of consideration I saw among students this week. One was a tiny moment many people might not have noticed. On Wednesday, I noticed a student in seventh grade drop his binder in the hallway. His papers and things scattered but it wasn't a big deal because right away and without being asked, three or four classmates helped him gather and organize his stuff. By that I mean they didn't just hand his stuff back to him, but they helped put pages back in order and held one set of notes while he put another back into his binder. I noticed Anthony Watkins, Desi James, and Lucia Rodriguez, and I know there were others. Thank you to those I recognized and those who were just as helpful but I wasn't able to see in such a thoughtful group. Two snaps, please, for those community members whose consideration made this a more supportive place to go to school, a place where you always know you can rely on your classmates.

But consideration can also be intellectual. So I just want to describe briefly the discussion I heard in Ms. Breese's grade eight history class. The topic was the Bill of Rights, and more specifically what was guaranteed to citizens under the Second Amendment. People did not agree, as is common in a democracy, but Ms. Breese's students did an exemplary job of both listening carefully and disagreeing respectfully. I heard lots of students say things like, "I see your point but . . ." David Lopez even summarized a classmate's argument that he didn't agree before he added, "But I'd like to give another interpretation." It was an exceptional example of how we can disagree and also remain a respectful and connected community. So two stomps on two for Ms. Breese's fourth-period grade eight history. One-two!

We've written out these hypothetical scripts in detail because we think the specific words and framing matter, and because we think that's how a great school leader would do it. The purpose in this case is both to "catch" students exemplifying school virtues and to make meaning of those events. Catching virtuous moments is nice. Catching them and having a great and positive setting in which to share them is better. That's the power of meeting or some other mechanism. With a good place to celebrate them, now you have an incentive to go hunting virtues.

As our examples above imply, we especially love it when school leaders call out tiny moments that might otherwise have gone unnoticed. It's important to help students see how those actions make the school better and more welcoming for everyone. We want to make it more likely that positive actions get noticed and that students understand the value in them. And while our example is from a schoolwide meeting, it could just as easily come from a grade-level meeting, or one held in a single classroom.

Another detail about the examples above: we ended them both with the larger "village" giving affirmation, in this case in the form of snaps, stomps, or claps. We think it's important to add something symbolic to show that the whole community places value on the actions, not just the person speaking. That's one reason we love "two snaps" or "two claps" or "two stomps." They're fast and physical ways we can have the school community express affirmation of people and give its blessing to an idea. Since those affirmations get used a lot, just snaps alone are not enough (as they were in Chapter 3). In meeting you need to be able to mix it up: "Two snaps and two stops for Abed!;" "Two claps and an 'Oh yeah' for Desiree."

Though as we've mentioned, "meeting" can be done at a grade level or even in a single classroom, it's ideal when it connects students across levels of the school and makes what feels like separate groups feel like one. When Denarius interviewed a group of students about what they liked and valued about his school (described in Chapter 1), he was surprised to find that 1) students loved meeting, and 2) what they loved most was the chance to see and interact with students from other grade levels.

There are a variety of ways to do "meeting" in other words, and a school doesn't have to choose just one. "We have community circles to build connectivity across a single grade-level and use a schoolwide Friday celebration to honor student leaders in front of the whole school every Friday," one school leader told us. They use a series of meetings with differing groups joining for different purposes. One theme we'd point to is that quality is more important than length. You want meetings to pop with energy and positivity. You want people to leave wishing it was a little longer. Don't belabor things. If there's more to say on a topic, bring it back again at the next meeting. If a meeting expresses our values, those values should include honoring people's time and planning things carefully.

Another way to acknowledge students who show character and virtue would be to create a simple and symbolic icon: a laminated heart made in the school colors or a picture of the mascot, for example. A school leader could say, "I'm going to put the green and gold heart on the wall outside Ms. Breese's class this week in appreciation for what I saw." Or "I'm going to put the Hawk's Crest in the spot in the hallway where those students were so helpful." Now the school has a very simple system for describing virtuous behavior (morning meeting), a system for the group to express approval and appreciation (stomps, claps, etc.), and a third tiny, simple system for helping people remember them and placing additional appreciation on them. It has built a series of butterflies, to use Joe Kirby's phrase.

VISUAL CULTURE

The idea of putting an icon—the Hawk's Crest—outside a teacher's room or in a hallway to honor the values expressed there is a great example of another crucial mechanism for reinforcing character and belonging: visual culture. The walls can talk too—and schools can design them in a way that speaks the language of virtues and values. Including quotes from current and previous students, images of students doing virtuous things, or quotes from key members of the community are typical ideas. Happily they are butterflies—extremely low-lift actions, great for a leader to delegate to a group of teachers who love this kind of thing— but have huge influence on creating a warm and supportive community.

Consider the impact of what one school we know did. They placed a large printed photo of each student with their first name at the bottom in the front hallway: name plus face. So simple. Suddenly it was ten times easier for both adults and peers to use students' names. One of the simplest ways to show people they belong is to call them by their names. If the school secretary knows your name, if the custodian knows your name, if the fifth-grade teacher knows your name even though you're in fourth grade, you feel known. And of course it's also a great memory refresher for adults. See a student and realize you're unsure of his or her name? Dash on over to the picture wall and doublecheck. Next time, you're sure to remember!

Or consider something we saw on a recent visit to Memphis Rise Academy in Memphis, Tennessee, where we noticed a system called Locker Shoutouts. Members of the community can grab a tiny appreciation form that looks like the one shown in the photo. On it, they write a short appreciation that they attach to a student's locker. On our visit we noted a student named Jaylen had received a note from one of his teachers expressing appreciation for his enthusiasm in class.

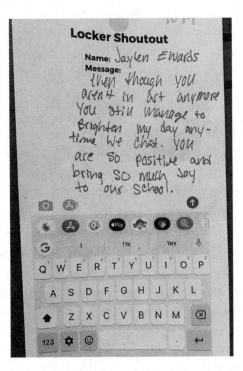

It's a simple system that makes it easy for the good things to be appreciated and made more visible. In addition to Jaylen finding the note on his locker seen here, another student, Sarah, had written an appreciation to a classmate, Magda, for helping her figure out a math problem at lunch. Yes, Magda must have felt great returning to her locker to find the small token of gratitude. Yes, Jaylen must have felt a keen sense of belonging at the school. But so too Sarah must have felt good to be able to show her appreciation. And think also about how the students in the school see the world differently, wandering down the hallway and noticing lockers dotted with appreciation for the goodness members of the community are constantly demonstrating. It makes the school feel like a more positive, welcoming, and supportive place. And since our perception of group norms is the most important driver of our behavior and motivation, it encourages students to seek to match those positive and healthy norms.

Notice, by the way, that Locker Shoutout is printed with an image of a keyboard at the bottom. That might seem strange but it's a subtle hint. Elsewhere we discuss the importance of teaching students positive social media habits. The keyboard suggests to students: *This would look just as good on your phone. This is the kind of thing that you could post to build a positive and supportive online community.*

And in fact, social media skeptics though we are, we think a school could experiment with an electronic version of the locker shoutout that could make the goodness of community members even more broadly visible and could model for students how to use social media to show appreciation rather than to denigrate.

As a principal, Denarius spent a lot of time planning out visual culture. Here are a few examples of how he used it to build culture at Uncommon Collegiate Charter High School.

At the top of this image, you can see the virtues Denarius's school has chosen. They're visible throughout the school but here are paired with images of people who've exemplified those virtues and whose stories students are familiar with (they talk about them at meeting!). In addition, taking the time to post honor roll students shows the importance of academic achievement. Notice that the materials are carefully posted, perfectly spaced and aligned, and the walls are clean and tidy. This expresses the idea that we value what is posted.

Lots of schools post quotes from famous people. We like that too. But we *love* the idea of this quotation from one of the school's alumni.

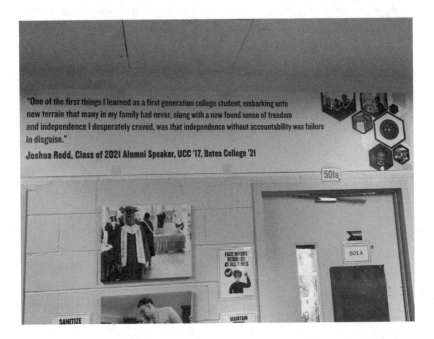

"One of the first things I learned as a first generation college student, embarking onto new terrain that many in my family had never, along with a new found sense of freedom and independence I desperately craved, was that independence without accountability was failure in disguise."
Joshua Redd, Class of 2021 Alumni Speaker, UCC '17, Bates College '21

Or check out this wall: another beautifully framed quotation from a graduate and a colorful board where people can say "thank you" to staff members. It's a triple whammy: it's beautiful, it gives students the gift of sharing gratitude, and it makes teachers happy and motivated and appreciated. It's easy and appealing to do something good for the community and good for yourself!

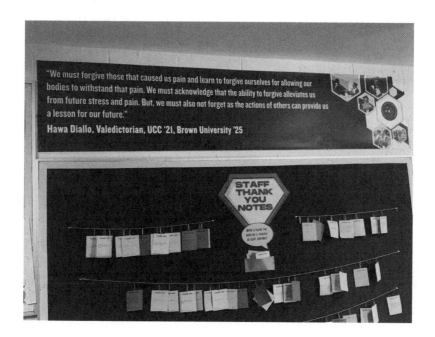

"We must forgive those that caused us pain and learn to forgive ourselves for allowing our bodies to withstand that pain. We must acknowledge that the ability to forgive alleviates us from future stress and pain. But, we must also not forget as the actions of others can provide us a lesson for our future."

Hawa Diallo, Valedictorian, UCC '21, Brown University '25

THE MECHANISMS OF WIRING

We've talked about *what* to talk about with young people to help develop their well-being (virtues! gratitude! resilience!) and shared a few examples of when and how schools might engage those conversations (meeting!). But as we've mentioned, conversations about beneficial mindsets and habits are best when they're woven into the fabric of the school—when, like belonging cues in the classroom, they are constant small signals.

So here are a few more times and places that can be harnessed as culture building mechanisms in service of SEL development.

Arrival

Check out the video *Shannon Benson: Good Morning* in which Shannon, then the dean of students at North Star Academy Clinton Hill in New Jersey, and his colleague, Anneliese Tint, greet students and parents at the door in the morning. What could better remind you that you belong than being welcomed with a warm greeting and a handshake? In most cases Shannon greets students by name (in a few more weeks he'll have them all). There are also short greetings and interactions with parents. It's a great way to build relationships and make sure parents feel welcome too.

Here are some types of interactions we see:

Small playful moments: Shannon jokes with Johnny about his water bottle.

"Everything okay?": Shannon checks in with one boy to make sure everything went okay after school the day before.

Practical details: Shannon takes the opportunity to walk over to a student's car to check in with Mom about a missing permission form. So much better than a phone call!

Tiny reminders about culture: Shannon subtly reminds Johnny how to greet an adult by saying, "Good morning, Johnny," in a deliberate tone. He's calling Johnny's attention to the fact that he is modeling the greeting he expects back.

Teachable moments: One girl is welcomed back warmly, but Shannon asks what she needs to say to her teacher about her behavior the day before. She cheerily replies, "I'm sorry," and Shannon affirms that whatever happened yesterday has not diminished her in his eyes. ("That's not who you are.") He explains why it's important to take responsibility and they high-five; she is happy to make amends and be back to normal. Note also that the student's mother is aware of the incident—they've talked about it by phone—but Shannon reassures her that everything is okay.

Honestly, the whole arrival feels like a scene from a village in a bygone era, when community courtesy and connection were stronger, more prevalent, more central to people's lives.

There are a thousand ways a school could use arrival to shape culture, set expectations, and build belonging. Recently, for example, we watched Dan Cosgrove, principal of Uncommon's Roxbury Prep Middle School, greeting students as they arrived. He stood at the school's front door and welcomed students by name. He showed students several positive self-talk phrases reinforcing resilience he'd printed on a card and asked them to choose one of the phrases and think about a time when they could use it.

Arrival, in other words, is an ideal time for building community and shaping healthy mindsets—it's a mechanism. It allows staff members to connect and build relationships and set the tone for the day. (Note the handshakes and eye contact; notice that as Shannon and Anneliese greet students, they greet them back.) It's just the sort of social skills students didn't practice during the pandemic and don't practice when their lives migrate online.

Meals

Meals are another ideal time to shape culture. Eating together is a time of meaning and importance in almost every culture and faith. We tend to pray at meals. We invite people to eat with us as one of the deepest signs of welcome. We celebrate by feasting.

And in fact, we've seen several examples so far of how schools have harnessed meals to express culture.

Earlier we saw how London's Michaela School used the end of lunch to create a public setting where students could express gratitude. There were more details to the meal that built culture, though. Students rotated responsibilities like clearing plates, bringing over the meals, and pouring drinks out of plastic pitchers. The meal was family style, and students and teachers chatted meaningfully while they ate. And the school also often wraps up a lunch with communal recitation of poetry. It's a powerful moment intellectually. (Student are proud to know the poems by heart and prouder yet to be able to quote them to you.) To hear and to join with a hundred booming voices reciting in unison is a powerful experience.

In Chapter 2 we saw how Cardiff High School used the informal time after lunch to allow students to engage informally in a variety of ways to build atrophied social skills: chess and table tennis and cards.

Marine Academy also used family-style meals. It's worth noting that if it seems expensive or logistically challenging for schools in the US, communal meals don't have to happen every day. They could be on Fridays, or the days before vacations. Or there could be a "principal's table," where students were invited on a rotating basis or could earn the right to join based on the exemplification of character.

Breakfast also has the potential to serve as a culture builder. Stacey Shells Harvey, CEO of ReGeneration Schools in Chicago and Cincinnati, quickly recognized this need post-pandemic. During the first days of return, students were required to sit six feet apart, as in so many other places. They were masked. Only so many students could be in any given space at a time, so breakfast moved to classrooms. There was a lot of logistical talk about getting and returning trays and milk cartons. In such an environment, informal conversation withered. Perhaps this sounds familiar.

But the odd silence remained, even when masks came off and desks moved (slightly) closer. Stacey noticed an awkwardness during breakfast; there was still almost no morning chatter. And she noticed that some kids would be searching the room with their eyes for a connection they didn't know how to start. So she implemented an idea called "Breakfast Questions," written by teachers on a rotating basis and approved and reviewed by administration. They're posted each morning in the classroom, three per day, for students to discuss. The questions are engaging and interesting, a combination of playful and slightly more serious:

- Which make better pets, cats or dogs?
- Agree or disagree: the book is always better than the movie.
- Who would be the best celebrity to hang out with and why?
- Agree or disagree: the world today is better than when your parents were kids.
- Should schools be able to punish students for mean posts on social media?
- Would you rather be the worst player on a team that always wins or the best player on a team that always loses? Discuss.

In Stacey's case, students discuss these questions as a whole class, but students could just as easily discuss them in smaller groups at cafeteria tables. The idea is to foster conversation and build social skills through daily practice. Her school also uses the Habits of Discussion technique discussed in Chapter 3, and the approach to discussion here works in synergy with that even if the topics are much more informal. Students look at each other, rephrase, and try to connect ideas. "It has to be volleyball, not ping-pong," Stacey told us. "We tell the teachers, 'Its kid, kid, kid and then back to you to ask another question—often in lieu of giving your answer. You want to keep them talking to each other.'"

Even games can be useful in fostering connection and building social skills. Elisha Roberts, chief academic officer of Strive Prep in Denver, Colorado, shared an experience she witnessed during the meeting of the school's speech and debate club. In the activity, sometimes described as *group counting*, students had to count out loud from 1 to 25 (or higher) as a group without an assigned order, without two people talking over each other. If two people said "eighteen" at the same time, they had to start over. The purpose of this activity was to heighten students' consciousness of their peers, develop patience, and work as a group to complete a challenging task. Success required reading nonverbal cues, establishing eye contact, and learning patience and cooperation. Elisha noted that students became aware of the social cues in the room, and that it helped students to build trust with their peers by cooperating and achieving something. They happily played it at the beginning of each meeting and it became a kind of tradition. Although this sort of game could be played anywhere, it seems ideal for something like breakfast or lunch.

Hallways

Impromptu meeting places can also be wired for connection. Hallways are a great example. One of the unusual features of Rochester Prep, a school Doug helped found, was tables in the hallway. The idea was that on a rotating schedule, teachers would sit at the tables during free periods, preparing lessons and grading papers. But part of their job was what was called "passive supervision" ("passive" for short).

The adults were just there quietly working most of the time, but it turned out that having them in the hallway changed middle schooler behavior. A student coming out of a classroom into an empty hallway behaves (or is tempted to behave) differently from one coming out into a hallway where his or her math teacher is sitting at a table 20 yards away, glancing up from the laptop to say, "Morning, Alex." Being seen changes decisions about behavior. It is a subtle reminder that causes people to choose to do what is right.

Usually the teacher on passive would ask a student a question ("How are you, Alex?") but also, "Where are you going?" or "Do you have a hall pass?" or something similar as well. And even though the tone was warm, these interactions still felt a bit off, like the first thing teachers thought of when they saw a student was whether they had a hall pass. It felt like a missed opportunity.

This raised a question for the staff: What should be the first thing teachers said to a student they saw and why? The answer was that the best response was for teachers to ask questions about the things students were learning. Message: I see you and I see a scholar. So teachers on passive (and those merely seeing students in the hallway at non-passing times) would try to do something like this:

> *Hi, Alex. What class are you in?*
>
> *Oh, history? Love it. What are you guys talking about today?*
>
> *Oh, the Civil War? Cool. Have you talked about the Battle of Gettysburg yet?*
>
> *No? A lot of historians think it was the turning point of the war. I'm sure you'll hear all about it.*
>
> Or: *You have? Cool. Such bravery, right? Question for you then: Why do historians say it was so important in shaping the outcome of the war?*
>
> *Ok, one more question because I know you gotta go* [pointing to bathroom pass] *and get back to class, but let's see how*

you do. Within ten years either way, when did the Civil War start? Not bad! 1861! Look at you, you showoff!

Ok, good chatting. Get things done and get back to class quickly so you don't miss anything. And be ready for the Battle of Gettysburg. I'm sure Mr. Hassell will talk about it.

Okay, yeah. Let me know when he does. I might ask him to let me join class that day.

Or

Hey, there. You on your way to the bathroom?

Okay. Remind me of your name?

Oh, Alex. Of course! I'm getting older, Alex. You have no idea how many things I forget.

So listen, I'm quizzing people on their math facts today. You gotta get at least two to pass my table.

Yeah, I know, otherwise you'll be stuck here with me! Yuk, right?

Okay, let's start with some two-digit multiplication. Think you can do 15 times 11 in your head?

No? Okay, we'll start easier. First do 15 times 10. Okay, great, 150.

Wanna take a shot at 15 times 11 now? Yessiree, 165.

What about 15 times 12?

Okay. No more math problems for you, no matter how much you ask!

See you soon, Alex.

Oh wait . . . Alex!

What's 15 times 11?

165. Great job!

There were so many benefits to the arrangement. Fewer things went wrong in hallways between classes and the unspoken message throughout the school was this: When a member of the school staff sees me, their first thought is to treat me as a scholar. Students felt known and seen and teachers got to choose things to talk about that were an expression of themselves. ("I'm getting ready to teach this poem to my seventh graders. See if you can guess the title!"). One teacher posted a map on the wall so he could ask geography questions more easily. The result, to paraphrase educational consultant Adeyemi Stembridge, was kids connecting to adults through content. Young people found that learning things was a great way to build relationships with people around them.

The idea for worktables in hallways came from a reference in John McPhee's book *The Headmaster: Frank L. Boyden of Deerfield*. "In his first year," McPhee writes of the book's subject, "he set up a card table beside a radiator just inside the front door of the school building. This was his office . . . because he wanted nothing to go on in the school without his being in the middle of it."

The idea, in other words, started with the school leadership setting out to increase its own understanding of the daily life of the school—to be connected. First, they started working in hallways. (We spend a bit of time in this book criticizing the tech sector; here we pause to praise the rapid increase in laptop battery life they have achieved and the clear benefits to educators!) They found that they quickly came to understand the school a lot better. And they found that pausing every 50 minutes or so at passing times to greet or redirect or wave to or remind students in the hallway was beneficial in building relationships too. The idea worked so well that teachers were added to the rotation. It also helped establish a fair amount of mutualism among staff. It's harder to be the teacher who ignores students behaving poorly or being rude to a classmate in the hallway when you have shared responsibility for spaces beyond your own classroom.

The point here is that hallways, and the time students spend there, pose an opportunity for schools: it's overlooked time that could be used purposefully. The first step, we'd argue, is ensuring orderly hallways where respect among students is the norm. If that doesn't exist—if students fear the hallways or brace themselves for the negativity they will endure or dish out there—it's hard to feel a strong sense of community. One small trick that can help—at least in middle school when classes are almost all single-grade—is staggered passing times. The sixth graders from 10:31 to 10:37 and the seventh graders from 10:39 to 10:45. This gives you a smaller number of students to manage and so it's easier to shape the culture of interactions. Asking teachers merely to stand by their doors and "keep an eye on things" during passing time also helps in many of the ways "passive supervision" did.

What else could you do with your hallways? Could a teacher circulate with a daily quiz offering, a prize for the student who can identify, say, three countries on a world map or three pictures of world leaders? Could there be a display where students could pause to write notes of gratitude or appreciation? Could there be music playing from a small speaker with students who had exemplified school virtues allowed to set the playlist for the day (subject to approval of the adults, of course)? We're sure there are far more brilliant ideas out there. The key is to see hallways as a potential mechanism, a recurring moment that provides the opportunity to build character and positivity and belonging into the fabric of the day.

"Advisory," a daily or weekly meeting with a small group of fellow students (often from multiple grade levels) and a teacher, is another potential mechanism. Advisory might start the day and advisors could take attendance or at least sit somewhere in the school—a cafeteria table, their office, or a bench in a hallway or at a period just after lunch—where students could "check in" to start the day or linger and chat briefly. It's much nicer—and more welcoming—to check in with a small and welcoming group sitting around a table than in a typical classroom. Alternatively, advisory could happen at the end of the week: a brief check-in to make sure all homework assignments are complete or perhaps even step back and reflect, in a journal or via a gratitude exercise (i.e. three things I'm grateful for and why), in a small group.

STRATEGIC INTERVENTION

Students' social skills have in general almost certainly atrophied as a result of both pandemic and epidemic, but for some students the decline has been steep enough that they will struggle to build effective relationships. For these young people, conflicts will be more frequent or go unresolved. Potential connections will wither. They will be present in school but far less connected than their peers, possibly even alone in the crowd because they lack the skill to engage their peers. Schools will have to be even more prepared than before to teach certain students to socialize, especially those for whom merely providing an opportunity to connect is not enough.

At one school we know, the most adept connector on staff—a dean of students—invites certain students to lunch in the faculty conference room in the main office—a place that feels special and grown up. Kids are invited to come for lunch and sometimes allowed to bring along a friend if they want. Typically, most of the invitees are kids who are doing just fine—thriving even—it's a mix-and-match kind of thing, which has the benefit of causing students to connect with peers outside their social group. But a few of the invitees are carefully chosen because they struggle to connect. They are, without knowing it, the reason for the lunch. The conversation is mostly lighthearted. Sometimes he prepares a few questions in advance (they are a lot like Stacey Harvey's Breakfast Questions). Sometimes he reads a short article from the news and invites students to discuss. But he's always working and shaping the conversation, trying to draw in the kids who need drawing in, trying to subtly remind the kids who need to interrupt less not to interrupt. He's super-intentional to model eye contact and body language. Sometimes he'll offer a bit of feedback: "That's interesting, David, but maybe Shayna would like to finish the point she was making first." He's coaching social skills. Sometimes afterwards he'll pull a student or two aside and say, "You did a really nice job of showing your appreciation for Iyana's story," or "I'm going to invite you back next week and I want you to try to see if you can join the conversation without interrupting."

If students can benefit from guidance and instruction on the how-tos of face-to-face conversation, the same is true for online interaction.

In fact, we think it's a productive move for schools to consider offering students simply useful guidance on how to use social media in a way that's least damaging to their emotional well-being. (This could be schoolwide or for students who struggle with it or are involved in situations caused by it.)

One of the reasons some researchers think social media can be so destructive to young people, for example, is the constant feeling of comparison it evokes. There's a friend at a basketball game. There's another at the beach. There's a friend in a carefully presented photo to make it look like she's having the time of her life at a concert. All that comparison to a selective sample of other people's lives can wear you down.

It's also hard to find out through social media all the things people are enjoying (or appear to be enjoying) that you were not invited to.

Might it be useful to be aware that the version of other people's lives you see online is distorted? That you should avoid using social media most when you are feeling down and therefore most vulnerable to feelings of exclusion? It probably can't hurt.

To state the obvious, the tone and potential negativity (or positivity) of social media environments can vary widely among students and groups. We can probably help students to make their more positive support and build mutuality. Achor advises a small habit change to help shift the tone of one's social media engagements. Users should set a goal for themselves when they get on social media that they will seek out 5 or 10 nice things happening to people they know. The goal is to make a positive and supportive comment about them right away. This is another "scanning" exercise. That is, you see what you look for, so if you can make yourself look actively for happy things, if you frame them for as a good thing—"Congratulations, Chelsea! So happy for you"—it changes your perception of social media. You see more good news—or more "good" in the same news—because you are looking for it. This also makes it more likely that people will respond in kind, building a warmer social media environment.

Another useful piece of advice we have shared with our own children, students, and family members is not to respond to online meanness and snarkery if you can help it, even if it's directed at you, even if it hurts and you are dying to do so. It only draws you in further psychologically and signals to people that they can get a rise out of you by attacking you. It's also useful to avoid piling on when you see one person attacking another. It's the worst time to be insensitive and it too usually comes back to bite you. People remember betrayal for a long time. It's hard to do, but learning user skills like these for social media can be valuable for young people, doubly so for those who are most isolated or sensitive.

It's also probably worth considering social media training for parents. Not allowing students to sleep with their phones in their rooms is one of the simplest and most important things parents can do. Checking your children's phones periodically and maintaining an up-to-date list of accounts and passwords is also critical. "Most parents are totally unaware of much of their students' online lives," ReGeneration Schools CEO Stacey Shells Harvey told us. "They'll say: *No, no, no, she doesn't have any accounts on social media. She doesn't do any of that.* But because we end up dealing with so much of it I often know they're wrong. "Well, she's got an account called "wildgirl2026" and you should definitely be aware of the photos she's been sharing."

We're aware as we suggest this that one of the themes of this book is to seek butterflies—ways to make a difference without a massive investment of time and resources—because there is so much that schools have to do presently. We think social media education can be done this way, and in fact that it can be a labor saver when you factor in the conflicts that are avoided because they don't bubble up in school. "We've had such a rash of fights in our schools this year," one high-level administrator told us. "So many that I had my staff start tracking data on them. They were mostly happening just after school. They were almost always flare-ups in response to a comment on social media. And the flames were almost always fanned by other kids chiming in on social media: *they're going to have it out this afternoon at this corner after school.* Once that's happened, there's very little way for a student to back down."

Notes

1. Region 10, April 2022.
2. https://casel.org/cdi-ten-year-report/
3. Jubilee Centre for Character and Virtues.
4. We're indebted to the Jubilee Centre for Character Education for this framing.
5. A Framework for Character Education in Schools, Jubilee Centre for Character and Virtues.
6. To us, diligence implies everyday self-discipline about doing useful things proactively; perseverance is very similar but it implies continuing to do something worthwhile in the face of difficulty or tiredness.
7. We're adapting and adding to the Jubilee center's caught, taught, and sought framework.
8. This may be one of the most important aspects of character education. If the adults in the building are teaching about the value of respect, but then can be seen gossiping about one another or subtly rolling their eyes at the suggestion of a leader, this will obviously undermine the character education at your school. We may have neglected to mention the power of modeling in the technology chapter as well—a school that doesn't allow cell phones but then has teachers attached to their phones communicating via Slack, for example, needs to take a careful look at its adult culture.
9. https://www.health.harvard.edu/healthbeat/giving-thanks-can-make-you-happier
10. https://www.mindful.org/the-science-of-gratitude/
11. Bonnie Benard, Fostering Resiliency in Kids: Protective Factors in the Family, School, and Community, 1991, https://files.eric.ed.gov/fulltext/ED335781.pdf
12. SmugMug, USI https://uncommonschools.smugmug.com/New YorkCity/EGC/EGCSEA-Fall-2018/i-zGMDHdj/A

Chapter 5

Case Studies in the Process of Rewiring

In this chapter we'll discuss how we think a few key aspects of the way schools are designed might be adapted to better respond to students' needs, given the challenges we discussed in Chapter 1. Obviously, not every action we discuss will be relevant for every school and the word *adapt* could imply anything from a slight tweak of the current emphasis to a complete overhaul. We'll start with a story a colleague told us about rethinking extracurriculars through a belonging lens. In part we'll share it because some of his specific adaptations will be relevant for other schools and in part because we think the broader reflective process—assembling a group to rethink long-established components of what a school does in light of new and changed context—is a critical tool for schools in their current context. Our goal, in other words, is to jumpstart a process of strategic reflection. While we suggest a few key areas where we think that kind of reflection is especially critical—how extracurricular activities are designed, how school leadership spends its time, and how schools could think differently about what happens when student behaviors harm school culture—we hope that's just the beginning and the examples we discuss here will be easily applied to other relevant topics.

Let us begin at the beginning. We noted that the activities Jean Twenge described that appeared to have the strongest effect in mitigating loneliness, depression, and anxiety in young people were things like sports or religious services—group activities that implied steady involvement, shared purpose, cooperation, and active engagement. They are settings in which Martin Seligman's components of happiness would be present: students take pleasure in such activities, of course, but also feel engagement and find meaning. They're activities that build a sense of identity. And they're places where it would be odd to have one's phone out. We want more of that—or at least more high-quality provision of that—for our young people. And obviously schools play a big role in that.

But the calculus of running extracurriculars has changed. With students spending more of their time on their phones, they are less likely to join things at school. One principal described walking by the classroom where the once-vibrant debate club was meeting. It was just after school. There were five or six kids in the room—not enough of them to really do what they normally did—so they were waiting in hopes that others would show up. Several students were on their phones; perhaps they were texting friends to encourage them to come but perhaps they were just doing what all of us do nowadays when we're required to wait—scrolling. And this had the effect of making the room seem even more lifeless. There weren't enough people and those who were there seemed only half present.

Those five or six kids loved the club let's assume. It filled a role in their lives—they hung out with the other kids from the club. A few might have even thought of themselves as "debate kids." But how many of them would come back next Tuesday after an experience of waiting in a half-empty room for an activity that would never happen? The club was dying, in other words. The principal had walked by to witness one of its last meetings, ironically at exactly the time students needed it most.

Extracurricular activities offered in schools are incredibly important. They fill young people's lives with meaning, provide new experiences, and most of all offer connections, cooperation, and rich interaction with peers. But creating more engagement in activities is no longer quite as simple as throwing open the doors to classrooms and letting the Model United Nations and the Spanish Club file in.

This brings us to Charlie Friedman, who runs Nashville Classical Charter School in Nashville, Tennessee, and whom we discussed briefly in Chapter 2. Charlie was not the school leader we described above, walking through his building to see the debate club's last breaths. But he did feel his students' isolation strongly and he believed that extracurricular activities in his school could be better, so he assembled a group of seven colleagues in his office. The seven played a diverse range of roles in the school: one ran the choir, one was a coach, one or two were simply "connectors," teachers whom kids seemed to take to readily and who seemed to read them well.[1] Charlie asked them to help him think about how to make extracurricular activities really sing. And he wanted to start with the *why*. "When the pandemic hit we had sixth graders [as our oldest students] and when they came back they were eighth graders," Freidman told us. Not only had they missed most of their middle school years but the school, which was new and growing, was suddenly much larger. "And that provided a unique opportunity to step back and think about what the *purpose* was for extracurricular programs." They basically landed on three things:

- One: To provide students with a sense of identity, to give them a chance to say, "I'm in the choir." "I'm on the basketball team." "I'm a cheerleader." Charlie and his colleagues thought that was a powerful thing for a middle schooler to be able to do.

- Two: To give students an opportunity to build an informal relationship with a trusted adult.

- Three: To give students a chance to perform. Not every kid would be able to participate, but Charlie wanted to really try to incentivize and encourage people to watch performances and events so they felt more special.

Having laid out key principles to guide decisions, they asked themselves in a series of meetings: If those three things were true, what did that mean for their extracurriculars? They started to rethink them one by one, beginning with who led them.

> "We put a little bit more money into the stipends for coaching and leading those programs than we normally would have and really tried to steer some of our strongest teachers and connectors to lead them, sometimes at the expense of their coaching ability but with the belief that this was about trusted mentors more than anything else."

Ideally your tennis coach would be able to make you feel like you were a part of a team and make you look forward to practice, *and* be able to talk backhand grip and serve and volley tactics. But, the argument went, if you had to choose, the former was more important than the latter.

They also started to think about audience quite a bit, on two levels. First, if the purpose was to give kids a chance to perform, there had to be someone to perform for. If you spent all semester preparing for a play and 15 people showed up and they were all parents, that was different from how it felt if the parents showed up and so did a bunch of classmates, some whom you knew pretty well and maybe some you didn't. The next day they might say, "Hey, I didn't know you acted," or you could say, "Thanks for coming to the play," and suddenly you'd be connected.

Similarly if the gym seemed half empty rather than bursting at the seams, the game was a very different experience. The crowd needed to feel supportive and vibrant, both in numbers and in how they behaved. And as they thought about that, the group in Friedman's office started to talk about the idea that while not everyone could play, everyone could feel a part of the event *as an audience member* if they designed it right. They all knew people who'd chosen the college they attended in part for their big-time sports programs—not to play but to be a fan, to delight in flags flying and drums pounding, in dressing up or even painting your face, in chanting with the group. People chose a college for that. The experience of being in the audience was important. If they could engineer the audience experience, they would make each event more inclusive for those who watched and more meaningful for those who performed. As Friedman told us:

> "We're a school that utilizes choral response and class cheers and chanting. We have a really strong music program. And I saw something in a book I read over break about the research around music and chanting and dance being sort of this fundamental human connection and why lots of religions use these things. It's just a chance to do things with lots of other people and your heart beats a little bit faster. And so we came out of winter break saying those things are really important and it is really important for kids to cheer and chant together and for a school to sing together and we should find ways to do that at all costs because I think that's actually part of what being in a community means."

As a result, they spent a lot of time orchestrating what was happening in the stands during an event like a basketball game. This is to say, they redesigned the event by starting with the audience, and it's fascinating to think of how many ways you could take that idea and run with it. At college and professional sporting events, there's not only singing but often a section where, instead of sitting in clusters and haphazard groups, students can sit together and cheer as one. (Nashville Classical did that.) There are T-shirts being launched into the crowd, and competitions at half-time for the fans. (We're not sure if Nashville Classical has a T-shirt launcher but we're going to send them one.)

At college and professional sporting events, people ham it up for the camera on the jumbo screen. The camera is pointing at them in the first place to make them feel a part of the show. And it works. The camera points at people in a typical stadium and they stand up and cheer or dance. There really isn't any reason a school couldn't, in a simpler but still meaningful way, have cameras on the audience to make them part of the show. You might not have a jumbo screen to project on, but you could walk around interviewing and filming the crowd on your phone and post the video (or pictures) on Facebook afterwards. The "you" behind the camera could be school staff, of course, or it could be students, which would give more kids a way to have a meaningful role in the event.

To attend could be to join, and if it was, it would mean a vibrant crowd to support the performers and a vibrant crowd to belong to for the audience. Could you do the same or some version of it at the school play? Could you sell popcorn and give away a few T-shirts and walk around interviewing and filming so that people felt it was an "event" and they were part of it? *School spirit* is what they called that in a bygone era. Some of us might scoff at that phrase now. But then again, people felt far more connected to their school as a community then too.

The school also went all in on the idea of identity. To do that they did a lot of things that are characteristic of sports programs at bigger schools. (Nashville Classical is small.) "We planned a kickoff/spirit day to launch the season. Everyone got a T-shirt they wore to school. We had a teacher dress as the mascot, and so on. For kids on the team, we decorated their lockers. Kids on the team also got a 'warmup' shirt they wore to school on game days," Friedman recalled. "Our first home game was the Tuesday before Thanksgiving, and we went out of our way to advertise it to our community. Because so many people had family in town or were about to be on a holiday, attendance ended up far surpassing expectations."

At the last game of the season they held an "eighth grader" night for the girls' team, boys' team, and cheerleaders. "We announced the high school they planned to attend and each eighth grader gave a rose to a cherished teacher or family member [gratitude sighting!]. If you were a parent, a teacher, or another eighth grader, we wanted you to feel part of something bigger. Likewise, parents, families, and other students all wanted to attend to celebrate the students. We planned and hosted a banquet at the end of the season for all of the winter athletes and their families. We gave out awards, encouraged siblings to attend, and so on. Again, I think people did feel like they were part of something bigger."

All of those things are rites of passage for the sports kids. Couldn't the kids in the play and in the choir have them too? Why not have T-shirts for *them* to wear? Getting opportunities to wear your basketball uniform or your choir T-shirt around school established identity. Having a choir T-shirt like the athletes get builds identity. Why not a last event for the eighth graders with a moment for them to express their gratitude?

And while sports programs can share some ideas about audience with other activities, sports can also learn some things from them. As we noted in Chapter 2, extracurriculars can be divided into two groups: those that require significant accumulated expertise, and those that one can join based on interest and affinity alone. Schools have to invest in both and make both kinds valuable. For tenth graders who have not invested years of their life in mastering the sport, the basketball team may not be an option. But the debate club, the Spanish Club, and maybe the school play are. Students should have communities of interest they can join regardless of whether they have been involved in them since their first steps. Both kinds of programs need to thrive—the ones that reflect a long-term commitment and the ones that you can just decide to try.

But one challenge Friedman and his colleagues thought about was the "you can't just decide to play" problem in sports. Selectivity was both a good thing and a bad thing in sports. Could they balance the two—find a way to broaden access? "When the year began, we held 'open gym' tryouts for two months. As a result, there was a large group of students who didn't end up being on the team but felt like they were part of the team. They made connections; they had played with the varsity." Some of these students were younger and would be on the teams in a year or two, so there was a bit of "planting seeds for the future." But some kids had just spent a month playing—their season was a month long instead of three but it was still a season. They had felt what it was like to be on the team and built connections and camaraderie.

Nashville Classical's solution might not be the right one for your school. But the process is one of the core themes of this chapter: What are the things we believe about this part of our school? What questions does this force us to ask? What might be some solutions?

And we want to pause momentarily on one of the questions Friedman and his team caused us to consider: the fact that sports are by far the most popular single extracurricular activity, but what about all those kids dying to play a sport at most schools? What about the kids who are marginal? Think from a larger societal belonging, well-being, and mental health perspective about the kids who get cut and then, wanting nothing more than to participate in an activity that brings them not only joy but health and wellness, have to give it up. They are now caused to sit at home on their phones instead to going to practice where they'd rather be.

"My God, I remember that day," the parent of an athlete who was cut from the soccer team in tenth grade said. "All his life he'd been going to practice three or four days a week, watching on TV. He'd wear the jerseys of favorite players to school. It wasn't his only thing but it was a big part of his identity. And then one day it just ended. The coach said, 'You were really close,' but that didn't really change anything. He wouldn't wear his jerseys to school. There's no youth league to play in anymore when everyone else is playing school ball. Suddenly, he wasn't a soccer player anymore."

What if there was another team—a developmental team that practiced once or twice a week? What if the varsity coach came by for 20 minutes to run a drill or watch a scrimmage and tell the players there he or she thought they were doing well and hoped they'd all try out again next year? What if there were a few no-cut sports? (We know one school where the cross-country team does not cut from the JV.)

JV teams and freshman teams are disappearing, both at the K–12 and the collegiate level. Even when there are such teams, younger, more "promising," athletes often play up in age and the eleventh grader who has diligently come to practice every day for years and been a committed teammate and whose only crime is that she'd probably just warm the bench on varsity as a senior loses her spot. The message is this: *If you're just a committed and dedicated team member, there's not really a place for you.*

Winning in school sports is not irrelevant. We understand that. Seeking to win is a big part of what makes the experience of playing valuable. It's what causes us to have to cooperate and collaborate and subsume our own personal desire (I want to score) to the goals of the endeavor (but it's better to pass). That's a powerful learning experience. The lessons of striving to achieve a goal you care about are real and that's why young people love sports. We're not arguing "winning doesn't matter; it's all about participation." We are saying it's not always either/or.

Friedman and company doubled the length of tryouts so the kids who didn't make it got to be a part of things for much longer. And then they tried make "event" roles for them. "We built some committees to help sell concessions, take tickets, provide crowd control, and so on. They turned into a booster club/supporters of sorts. Organically, we ended up with a section of our gym reserved for them." That doesn't have to be everybody's solution. But given what we know about the immense benefits of being on a team in terms of well-being and belonging, maybe we should be thinking more intentionally about those last few kids we cut. There's surely space for more young people who want to be a part of something and are willing to do the work.

For their part, Nashville Classical's teams didn't win much. To be fair, they're a tiny school and it was their first year with eighth graders, but, Freidman notes, when they held tryouts recently, "twice as many students showed up to participate. So, I think we won where it counts."

LEADERSHIP FOR COMMUNITY AND BELONGING

Part of the story of the extracurricular redesign at Nashville Classical was the outcome and part of it was the process. The school decided that redesigning a key aspect of its programming through the lens of belonging and connection warranted a team of people from across levels and departments. The team "owned" the issue—one that doesn't ordinarily get a cross-functional administrative team—and had broad latitude to think about it in new ways. Not every idea they came up with was accepted but they were asked to do what you might call strategic design work. They planned out a vision carefully and intentionally in advance. And they met regularly to manage and prioritize it throughout the year.

Making things like connection and belonging—and culture more broadly—a focus of school life means engaging systematically in this kind of strategic design, often for topics that don't typically get that level of analysis. Doing that requires sustained reflection and focus. So it also requires different leadership decisions.

Start with a Clear Model

Charlie and company started with a conversation about what they believed to be true and important about extracurriculars, about why, as a school, they did those things in the first place. "When a group of people come together for a common cause they should start by thinking not about what they do, nor how they do it—but why," Simon Sinek writes in *Start with Why*. "We are drawn to leaders and organizations that are good at communicating what they believe. Their ability to make us feel like we belong, to make us feel special, safe and not alone is part of what gives them the ability to inspire us." Being clear about purpose is an effective tool to build belonging among staff as well, it turns out.

The team at Nashville Classical boiled down the *why* for extracurriculars into three core principles. They refined, discussed, and agreed to them. Then they mapped things out from there: If we truly believed these things, what would extracurriculars look like?

The work of most schools outside the classroom hasn't historically gotten this level of analysis. On the academic side, it would be expected for a school administrative team to meet to plan what assessments they would give, what grading would look like, and what curricula they'd choose. They'd meet to look at data on how things were going, drilling down to ask which kids in the fifth grade couldn't multiply fractions and whose reading words per minute was lagging. They'd discuss responses to data, both individual (tutoring for Sarah) and systematic (a tutoring system; more reading aloud in class). And then they'd circle back to assess the results. Were tutoring systems working? Why or why not?

But too often the cultural part of school-building gets far less of this sort of analysis. We leave the plan or its implementation to chance and good intentions. We don't constantly meet to ask how it's going and make small tweaks. Maybe we choose the virtues or values we want the school to instill, and we ask teachers to stress them whenever they can. Maybe there's an advisory when we ask teachers to talk about things like virtues but we leave them to plan (or not plan) for that as they wish. The procedures and expectations we want for public spaces—how we'll enter the building; how we'll sit in the auditorium for morning meeting—we leave to the mercy of whatever norm emerges.

Is it worth noting that the culture that exists in Denarius's math classroom began with him thinking through a series of granular, detailed questions about his own vision for the classroom? Something like: If my fundamental belief is that each young person in my classroom is capable of excellence; if I believe that caring involves not just pushing each of my students to give their individual best every day but also pushing them to do their part to build a mutual culture where they bring the best out of each other—if I truly believe those things, what should my classroom then look like? How should students sit? How should they talk to each other? What should they do when someone else is talking? What should they do when I ask them a question and they are not sure of the answer?

Is it worth noting that all of the answers and the systems he has subsequently built around them are subject to constant reflection and evolution?[2]

Arrival works the way it does at Shannon Benson's school because the school started with why. We want students to feel seen and known and welcomed individually and we want to gently remind them that they are entering a school where expectations are a little higher than in other places in the world.

Then they planned out the details of what that would look like: students would be expected to greet the adult at the door as they entered. They'd shake hands or perhaps high-five (generally at the discretion of the staff member) and have a brief moment of eye contact. There would be two staff members present so if one was drawn away (a student needing something; an opportunity to check in with a parent at their car), the ritual would remain intact. Some of these details they planned from the outset; some of them they figured out as they went along by having regular meetings to discuss aspects of the school's culture: How's arrival going? What's working well? What could be better? Where are the opportunities?

Breakfast at Stacey Shells Harvey's school works because there's a procedure for who will write the questions (rotating schedule), who will review them, and how discussion will be fostered. But again there was a constant feedback loop. A few questions teachers initially wrote were not ideal, so the school realized they needed to add an administrator review of questions just to be sure. And though teachers had been trained to use Habits of Discussion (they used it in their academic classes), there were reminders and tweaks for the new setting that emerged from asking, How's breakfast going? What's working well? What could be better? Where are the opportunities?

The themes here are:

1. A culture needs a blueprint, a clear description of what we want it to be and why. Building culture can't just be about ensuring that certain counterproductive things don't happen; there needs to be a detailed vision of what should happen.

2. Even once it's planned and installed, it will need a feedback loop of regular discussion and reflection.

3. To do that you need a consistent team and a regular time to meet and ask, over and over, how's it going?

Charlie's extracurricular team met regularly. They planned the changes they wanted and then once implementation started, they suggested adaptations—tweaks for this year, notes on bigger changes for next year. In *Switch: How to Change Things When Change Is Hard*, Chip and Dan Heath describe a common logical fallacy: we assume the size of a solution must match the size of the problem. But in fact this is not true. I could have a big problem and solve it with a tiny solution. In fact this happens all the time in schools. In a complex environment, a small change can initiate a cascade of subsequent changes.

Jen Brimming and her colleagues found this at Marine Academy in Plymouth, England. The culture of classroom and the school overall felt too quiet, low energy. Teachers weren't sure students were enthusiastic about learning. But introduce two tiny tools, Turn and Talk and Call and Response and, as you saw in the videos, suddenly everything changes. Students are engaged and enthusiastic and the classrooms come to life.

"Big problems are rarely solved with commensurately big solutions," the Heaths write. "Instead they are most often solved by a sequence of small solutions, sometimes over weeks, sometimes over decades."

From our point of view, that's the trick. Map a plan and then keep meeting to examine discuss and assess. Constantly seek small improvement every week. And that may sound simple but what it implies is that organizations' structures need to be different.

A CULTURE OF CONNECTION AND BELONGING WILL REQUIRE CONSTANT ATTENTION

Before Stacey Shells Harvey led ReGeneration Schools, she was a principal at Rochester Prep in Rochester, New York, and one of the things she took very seriously was culture. She was intensely focused on ensuring academic excellence for her students but also wanted a vibrant culture that fostered belonging. So she had two learnership groups that she met with weekly. One focused on academics. It was made up of the heads of each subject, who met weekly to discuss curriculum, instruction, and assessment. They looked at data and discussed tutoring or extra support for some students. It was a team. They shared the work of implementation and held one another accountable.

But she did the same with a culture team, which included a different group of staff: grade-level leads for each of the four grades in the school (fifth through eighth) as well as the dean of students. They met weekly too, to discuss all the things that build culture: the general feel of classrooms or the lunchroom from a cultural point of view, which students might be struggling and acting out, what visual culture in the hallways should look like, and especially what they would talk about at all-school "meeting" that week. This required planning because Harvey's standards were high! There had to be sharp-looking slides, and if there was music, it had to be right. The presentation had to be rehearsed. These things required collaborative leadership, constant teamwork, focus, and follow-through.

A "culture team" of dedicated people responsible for different aspects of the school but who consistently met to talk about things like belonging and connection and community would be an ideal setting to talk one week about arrival and the next about breakfast and the next about hallways—all of the mechanisms we describe in Chapter 4, plus others of your own devising.

PREPARING FOR WHEN IT BREAKS DOWN

No matter how well we design culture, no matter how strong the group norms, there will be breakdowns in the behavior of individual students. There will be students who engage in negative behavior or break the rules, particularly when they are teenagers, because teenagers are especially prone to testing limits and especially likely not to fully consider the consequences of their actions.

This is not a judgment about any particular group of young people—most of us broke rules at times when we were young. It does not express a lack of faith, belief, or trust in them. It expresses an understanding of the world they (and we) live in, where on one hand some people will be kind, thoughtful, and helpful and other people will be careless, thoughtless, or even cruel, and the institutions we build try to help more people do the former and fewer people do the latter. The fact that every society on earth has both norms for how people should aspire to behave and laws defining what happens when they don't is not the result of arbitrary convention but the outcome of vast accrued experience with human nature.

In schools, our job is to create a climate where the rules are fair, and their benefits are significant and evident to as many people as possible. Our job is to create a climate where shared norms of positive and constructive behavior are so well established that people want to give their best and are less likely to consider negative behavior. And then, despite that, we have to be ready for *breakdowns*—times when norms or rules are broken with adverse consequences for both rule-breakers and others in the community. When that happens we have to be prepared to teach young people alternatives to thoughtless, cruel, or selfish behaviors, ready to help them glimpse the best version of themselves and to understand how much they have to gain from moving closer to that version.

If we know this will be required of us, we should be prepared for it, but our strong sense is that this is often not the case. Having a plan to respond effectively to breakdowns (counterproductive behavior that disrupts the learning environment and erodes culture) is a critical aspect of building an environment where students feel safe, supported, and connected. It is hard to feel a strong sense of belonging in a place where you feel anxiety in the hallways and the bathrooms, where you sense that some number of your peers are snickering at your struggle or scoffing at your aspirations.

Schools, this is to say, owe it to students—both those who can do better and those who suffer the consequences—to have a clear plan around behavior breakdowns: Whose job is it to respond? What's the plan for how they'll do that?

We think that like any complex and challenging work, it needs both a champion and a team—a lead person to own it and a group of people who meet regularly to assess the process and ask how it's going, what's working well, what could be better, and where are the opportunities.

We call the role of leading the work of addressing disruptive behavior in schools the 'dean of students' role. Other people call it other things. In the UK it's often called pastoral. In many schools in the US there is no name for it, and this can sometimes reflect a lack of clarity about what should happen when a student significantly disrupts the learning environment or breaks a rule that protects the safety or learning of classmates. Sometimes that student is sent to an assistant principal or the principal herself, and sometimes to another teacher, or sometimes to a social worker. Sometimes the student isn't sent anywhere at all.

We'd argue the word "sometimes" isn't a very good one. If there isn't an "always"—a consistent process for how it's supposed to work—things will fall apart. The most challenging kids—the ones already pressing up against the systems in the school—will quickly exploit the ambiguity. We won't know what happened after this morning. We won't know that what happened in Mrs. J's class this morning also happened in Mr. P's class yesterday. And we won't be able to put resources in a consistent location so that when negative behavior happens we can ensure that the person who responds will have the resources to do what is supposed to be our core work: teach.

The dean's role is often the hardest role in the school (we have all done it so we speak from experience!) and a common problem is that when there *is* such a person they are often simply told to "deal with" behavior. They rarely get serious training and support. The result is an overreliance on consequences. Don't get us wrong; consequences for poor behavior are often part of the process of learning, especially if they are combined with teaching and behavior change. But they are also simpler to use and easier to deliver than teaching, and there's an attraction in that they create instant proof that a school has "done something."

And it's often important to do something. Censure and limit setting matter. Consequences can help with learning and behavior change. But we all know that they don't help automatically, and they can sometimes make behavior worse. We know that "doing something" can be a short-term fix and does not result in students learning how to change. And it is least likely to result in learning among the students who need to change most.

Consequences are an important tool for schools to design and use wisely—that's also technical and demanding work—but they are not teaching. And teaching is, in the end, what schools are tasked with. So the question is, what tools are available beyond (or in addition to) consequences to shift responses to student behavioral breakdowns so they focus more on teaching?

Before we discuss that, let us pause for a moment to answer the question: Is this really that big a deal? Is failure to plan for and design systems of response to behavior breakdowns really a major problem in schools? Aren't there too many suspensions already? Isn't this why skeptics have invented the red herring term "carceral" to describe some schools?

Is Behavior Breakdown Really a Problem?

A survey from 2019 (i.e. before the pandemic) by the Fordham Institute captured the extent of behavior issues at a national scale. Authors David Griffith and Adam Tyner surveyed over 1,200 teachers from across every strata of public school and asked them questions about the behavioral environment in their schools as they experienced it. Crucially, Griffith and Tyner separated the data according to school—and teacher—characteristics.

They found that two-thirds of teachers worked in schools where discipline policies were "inconsistently enforced," and more than three-quarters (77%) believed that "most students suffered because of a few persistent trouble-makers."

But of course, school problems, like everything else, are not evenly distributed in society, and the authors disaggregated their results according to poverty rates in schools. In "high-poverty" schools—those with more than 75% of students eligible for free or reduced-price lunches—more than half of teachers surveyed reported that they dealt with verbal disrespect from students *daily or weekly*. More than half reported that physical fights occurred *more frequently than once a month*. Fifty-eight percent of teachers in high-poverty schools said that "student behavior problems contributed to a disorderly or unsafe environment that made it difficult for many students to learn." When you consider that effective schools are perhaps the single most important vehicle in society for ensuring equality of opportunity and social mobility, these data represent a massive and regressive tax on families of poverty.

And again these data were gathered before the pandemic and before the groundswell of reports that behavior had significantly degraded as a result.

For those who might be wondering, the authors also disaggregated the results by race of teacher and found few differences: on the question of whether student behavior "contributed to a disorderly or unsafe environment that made it difficult for many students to learn," for example, Black teachers said yes at roughly the same rate as White teachers: 60% for Black teachers to 57% for White teachers. The issue, in other words, is not likely White teachers seeing harmless high spirits among kids of color and reading danger and defiance where none exists.

The issue is that almost every student assigned to a school where poverty is the norm is consigned to spend a significant portion of their school years in classrooms where disorder is the norm, where behavior makes it difficult for them to learn, and where anxiety and stress make the idea of loving school and feeling profoundly connected to it a distant dream.

The adults close to the problem see this clearly and consistently. As one teacher put it about her school the previous year, "Students understood that there would be no consequences for their actions. The classrooms were often disrupted by . . . behavior, and many students would communicate their safety concerns, but to no avail."

The idea that students themselves feel unsafe much of the time in school was shown in a recent study by the United Negro College Fund, which reported that fewer than half of African American students (43%) feel safe at school[3]— (those numbers are not disaggregated to show the disparate impact on low-income Black students specifically). Think for a moment about the significance of that finding: feeling unsafe is *normal* and it is how the average Black student feels in school. And this survey too was conducted before the pandemic.

Not surprisingly, there are secondary effects in schools like this. Just under one in seven teachers in the Fordham Institute survey reported having been assaulted by a student. Teachers leave schools that are unruly and disorderly and those schools—the ones that need the best teachers the most—invariably get last choice and constant turnover. But it's not just that teachers leave a specific school in which they cannot do their job or do not feel safe. They leave the profession. A recent report by the education research organization TNTP found that half of the new teachers in high-poverty schools had left the profession after three years. We sometimes talk about the problem of recruiting enough teachers; the bigger problem is keeping them and perhaps allocating their expertise to where it is most urgently needed, but poor working conditions mean that teacher mobility patterns accelerated the effect of poor school climate and amount to yet another regressive tax on the lives and opportunities of people who live in poverty.

The above findings are echoed in a recent national survey of public school parents and teachers by *Phi Delta Kappan*. In it, 60% percent of teachers thought discipline in their school wasn't strict enough as did 51% of parents, compared to 4% who said it was too strict. That said, the findings were also complex; for example, most parents and teachers don't trust their schools to handle discipline even while they want them to do more of it. This suggests that schools are generally not building the sorts of carefully designed intact systems to address breakdowns.

And while the data also show that it's hard to "speak for teachers" or for parents—their views are a polyglot of complex and disparate opinions, even within a single school—a consistent signal emerges that schools have failed to build the climate necessary to support learning and a sense of belonging. This has had disparate impact on the students who rely on them most.

The argument of this section so far has been that culture needs intentional planning and management of the sort that Charlie Friedman and company brought to their study of extracurricular programs, and that this gap is most glaring in the plan for behavior breakdowns. The general lack of clarity about the process of what happens and why, based on a set of core beliefs, planned out in detail and constantly reflected on, is a major contributor to an environment in which the conditions necessary to learning and socioemotional flourishing do not exist for a large number of students.

PREPARING FOR BREAKDOWN, PART ONE: TO TEACH WELL YOU NEED A CURRICULUM

Our belief about the dean's role, and about responding to breakdowns, is that the school's primary response should be to teach. This does not preclude consequences, but it would ideally both supplement them and improve them by making them more effective in changing behavior. A deep and profound reflection where you write extensively about the ways to use social media positively, study examples and then use the resulting insights to reflect on your own actions can supplement a consequence for injurious online behavior. Done well it can serve as the consequence in and of itself in some cases.

This points us to a key observation. If we expect people in the dean's role to teach in response to breakdowns, one of the first things they will need is a curriculum, a set of carefully designed and planned lessons to structure and enrich what they teach. Having a curriculum not only increases lesson quality but it saves labor. It means not having to invent a "lesson" in response to each new situation on the spur of the moment (and while managing an often emotional young person).

If the choice is between teaching by the seat of your pants when you are busy and not prepared on one hand, and giving a consequence that requires little reflection but probably results in little learning on the other, the rational person will often choose the latter. And even if the latter is an appropriate response, it will be far more successful if combined with the former.

In looking at the role of the "dean of students" (or whatever name you give it), what we are describing is a job that is "predictably unpredictable." A dean knows that some young person in the building will make a poor decision on social media, or will behave in a way that is rude and demeaning to peers or a teacher, or will copy someone else's work. They know these things will happen because they are the sorts of things that always happen when a large group of young people learn to make their way in the world and test a variety of strategies to figure out who they want to be in different contexts. That part is entirely predictable. The dean just doesn't know which students, when, and where. That part is unpredictable.

But if much of the behavior deans seek to address is predictable, the opportunity is in advance preparation.

Consider something as simple as writing a letter of apology to another student—let's say after having deliberately thrown a basketball at them during a game of knockout gone wrong. What would you get if you asked a representative sample of students to write such a letter?

You would get immense variety. Some young people would write sincere letters using direct and accountable language. You'd notice sentences that began with the word I to describe what they'd done. ("I apologize for throwing the basketball at you." Or "I threw a basketball at you today and I want to apologize for that.")

They'd demonstrate their awareness of how their behavior made the other person feel. ("I know it must have hurt, and it was probably embarrassing too, with everyone watching.") Some might affirm their appreciation and respect for the other person. ("I want you to know that I think of you as my friend.") Some might express a desire to make amends. ("Maybe we could play knockout again at recess tomorrow.")

The four of us have all read a version of a letter like that, where a student's ability to own their actions and rebuild trust with a peer has earned our respect such that they leave our office having raised our appreciation of their character and maturity despite the initial mistake.

More important than our own esteem, though, is that such a young person is far more likely to build successful and meaningful relationships as a result of the integrity, compassion, and empathy they are able to express. For this reason, we wish that every young person had the skill of writing a genuine apology.

But of course they don't.

In addition to the ideal apology letter, you would get, in your representative sample, letters from young people that were vague and merely "apologized" without apologizing *for* something. ("Jason, I am sorry about what happened on the playground. David.")

You would get letters that failed to take responsibility ("I'm sorry you got hit by the basketball"). You would get letters that subtly (or not so subtly) blamed the recipient. ("Sometimes you act like you think you're better than me, but that's no excuse for throwing a basketball.") You would get letters that suggested the writer was unlikely to rebuild the relationship with the recipient going forward. ("Next time I will just try harder to ignore you.")

If you are the one who deals with the young person who has thrown the basketball—and maybe the thrower's erstwhile friend has been sent to you as well—you have a lot of work in front of you if your goal is to teach the art of apology and the reflection and emotional self-regulation that come with it.

You are going to be spending a lot of time talking about what makes a good apology and why those things are important. You are going to be spending some time drafting and redrafting the letters in question. Or you are going to be signing off on some poor apology letters that don't accomplish much and tacitly send the message that making amends is a process easily sidestepped after having done someone wrong.

You will probably be engaged in this task of teaching two potentially emotional young people how to make a proper apology while you are doing other things. Perhaps there are other students in your office. Perhaps one of them is crying. Perhaps you have to go check on a student to make sure she's doing okay today. Perhaps a parent has just shown up to ask for his daughter's cell phone, which you confiscated yesterday. (Good job, by the way; see Chapter 2.)

Having a curriculum would mean having a lesson plan, or a series of lesson plans, about apologizing at the ready. You'd walk to your file cabinet and pull it out. It would be rigorous and challenging but also interesting. Maybe it would start with a general reflection on apologies, something like this:

> *We all make mistakes, but how you respond to mistakes can make a huge difference in how others perceive you and the situation you were in together. Simply apologizing by saying "I'm sorry" is often a helpful first step in those moments.*
>
> *When you apologize, you're telling someone that you're sorry for the hurt you caused, even if you didn't do it on purpose. You are showing that you have the maturity to understand their point of view. Apologizing also often makes you feel better because you are clearly trying to put things right. That again is a sign of maturity.*
>
> *When you say, "I'm sorry," it helps people refocus their attention away from identifying who was to blame. Now you can be working together to make things better. It can help you maintain—and even strengthen—your rapport with others.*
>
> *Stop and Jot: What are some of the benefits of apologizing when you've done something wrong?*

———————————————————

———————————————————

———————————————————

———————————————————

———————————————————

Then maybe it would ask students to look at some samples. Like this:

> *An effective apology should be honest, direct, and acknowledge that you did something that negatively impacted others.*

It should not cast blame on someone else or try to provide justification for your actions.

"I'm sorry about what I said to you."

"I'm sorry I lost your book."

"I shouldn't have called you a name. I'm sorry."

"I'm sorry I hurt your feelings."

"I'm sorry I yelled at you."

"I'm really sorry I hit you when I was mad. That was wrong. I won't do it anymore."

Stop and Jot: Why are these apologies effective? What are some things they share in common?

_____

_____

_____

_____

_____

_____

Then perhaps it would ask them to reflect in writing on apologies they've experienced in their own lives, like this:

Answer the following questions in complete sentences.

1. Describe a time when someone apologized to you. How did it make you feel? Why?

2. When was the last time you apologized to someone else? Why did you apologize, and how did you feel afterward?

3. When do you find it hardest to apologize to others? Using what you learned from the first reflection, what could you say to motivate yourself to apologize?

Then perhaps they'd be asked to apply their growing knowledge of apologies to situations they might face in the future. Like this:

Explain what you might do and say to apologize in these situations:

- You accidently bump into a classmate in the hallway when you are not watching where you're going. They drop all their things, which scatter in the crowded hallway. You mutter, "Oh, sorry," but you don't stop to help. You see him in class that afternoon.

- You promised your mom you would be home on time, but you did not make it home on time because you were talking with a friend and missed the first bus. She'd made dinner for you and it was cold. Now she is watching TV by herself on the couch.

- You were mad about something and were sulking in class. You didn't participate at all and were looking out the window. Then you put your head down on your desk and said, "This is so boring." You said it to a friend, but you know the teacher heard you. You're in the hallway just before dismissal and see her standing outside her classroom talking to another teacher.

Then perhaps your student would write their letter of apology. Perhaps you'd provide them with a list of do's and don'ts as a helpful reminder. If they were struggling, you'd have a sample letter they could read and annotate.

As with any good lesson, you'd want to end with an assessment, an Exit Ticket that would allow you to see what your students understood differently now and maybe even how they might use it to respond differently to the situation they'd initially struggled with.

You could use some or all of these tools depending on the situation. Maybe your student who has thrown the basketball gets it immediately and is sincere and ready to write and doesn't need a lot of further analysis. But maybe that student is just going through the motions and doesn't really think he or she should apologize. In that case the student would then get *different* activities from the sequence of possible learning tasks you had available. Or maybe both participants in the incident have been sent to you and each owes the other an apology, but they are in different states of readiness and reflection. In that case there would ideally be different tasks for each of the young people involved.

Ideally they'd work hard at the tasks—so hard, in fact, that further consequences wouldn't really be necessary. You'd simply make a copy to send home to their parents so they were aware of the situation and the work their child has done in self-reflection. Perhaps you'd ask the child to have the parents sign and return the letter. Then you'd put the student's work in a file. You'd never see one of them in your office again, but the other one would be involved in a similar incident two weeks later. You begin then by taking out what the student wrote the first time around and asking them to reflect on how the two times are connected and why they were in your office again.

Really *teaching* about behavior requires content and preparation, this is to say. If we're serious about responding to breakdowns with teaching, this is a gap we'll have to close. Teaching in any setting won't happen without meaningful things to teach, organized in a useful way. That means a curriculum, which in turn means planning and resources: perhaps a team of people, perhaps a few weeks of paid time during the summer to prepare lessons, perhaps the addition of a team member on staff whose job is to develop activities in response to incidents and then organize and file them so they can be reused and adapted.

It might seem like a lot, but with young people more and more likely to struggle at the skills required in challenging social situations, it is more important than ever to do the work in advance that allows us to teach in response to misbehavior.

LESSONS FROM THE FIELD

As it happens our team recognized the need for a dean of students' curriculum in 2018[4] and have developed a pilot version[5] with 70 or so lessons targeted to middle school students[6] and focused on a wide range of topics that cause students to show up at the dean of students' door. We've been piloting it for a few years and think the results are promising.

Here, for example, is a student's response during our version of the apology exercise described above:

> **Stop and Jot: Why are these apologies effective? What do they share in common?**
>
> these people are making up so' they can prevent any further harm. They both prevent further harmful actions

And here is a typical piece of student work a young woman did before reflecting on her own poor choice on social media. (Lessons typically end with a series of reflections along the theme of "In retrospect what could you have done differently in this situation?" and "What are you going to do differently next time?")

Cyberbullying, Social Media and the Community

Directions: Imagine you have been asked by your community to give a 5-minute speech about using social media responsibly. Draft your three core arguments then draft your speech. Use at least two pieces of supporting evidence for each of your arguments.

Argument #1	Argument #2	Argument #3
You can use social media responsibly by minding what you post	Watching what you say to other people online	Not using your page to spread negativity

Your Speech:

Using social media responsibly is very important, and there are many ways to use social media such as, minding what you post, watching what you say to other people online, and not using your page to spread negativity. minding what you post is showing responsibility on social media because your being responsible with what you post and watching what you say to other people online is being responsible because it the opposite of saying mean stuff which is unresponsible.

As we've piloted our version, we've found in fact that it can be used in three ways. First, it can be used to teach values and virtues in advance in an advisory setting or a homeroom, as described in Chapter 4.

Here's an excerpt from our lesson on gratitude, for example. It's as effective in proactive teaching of virtues as it is in reacting to specific situations where students struggle with behaviors.

Application of Terms
1. Name a person at school who did something for you that you're grateful for. Explain why.
_____
_____
2. Is it possible to feel entitled to *and* grateful for something at the same time? Why?
_____
_____
3. Can a person ever feel gratitude towards themselves for something they did? Why?
_____
_____

Second, it can be used in what we'd describe as therapeutic settings—small group pullouts for students who have specific skill gaps such as managing anger or responding to peer pressure. Like proactive teaching, it is designed to build skill and head off potential incidents. The difference is that it would be used with individuals or targeted groups of students who might be especially likely to have issues.

Finally, we've found it useful in the setting we've described here: responding to breakdowns. Users have noted that the written work students have done is also useful in sharing with teachers whose classes their behavior may have disrupted. In many cases a challenge schools face is demonstrating to that teacher that "something" has happened and "steps have been taken." A student may have been working hard reflecting on an incident but a teacher may not know that. Their perception may be, "She waltzed back into class an hour later as if nothing had happened." This is a recipe for further tension. Now a dean (or the student herself) can share the work she's done with relevant teachers so they understand and appreciate the level of response.

Schools have also appreciated one of the themes of the curriculum: its emphasis on replacement behaviors. It's not enough to tell a young person not to do something. Effective intervention means helping them identify and develop the ability to use an alternative, what we mean by a replacement behavior. It's hard to think of a replacement behavior on the spur of the moment, which is another benefit of a curriculum.

We also added an Exit Ticket to all of our lessons. This ensured that deans would be able to assess what students understood differently as a result of their work together. Making Exit Tickets separate from the lessons allowed them to serve both responsive and proactive purposes. That is, if we were using a lesson therapeutically with a group of students we were trying to keep from having incidents because we knew them to be high risk, we wouldn't want to ask, "How does all of this apply to what brought you to my office today?" But we would also want to ask that if we were reacting to such an incident.

Name: _____   **Date:** _____

Exit Ticket

Directions: Answer the following questions based on what you just learned.

1. What is one thing you learned from the lesson you just completed?

_____
_____
_____

2. How does this help you become the person you aspire to be?

_____
_____
_____

3. ☐ If your Dean has checked this box please discuss how this lesson relates to the reasons you have been asked to discuss your actions with him or her today.

_____
_____
_____

Student signature: _____
Parent signature (if required) _____

We mention these things not to trumpet our own work—it's a work in progress and will require constant attention and improvement—but so you have a model in mapping your course if you develop materials, lessons, and what ultimately becomes a curriculum designed to address breakdowns. (That said, if you'd like to know more about ours, you can check it out here: https://teachlikeachampion.com/dean-of-students-curriculum/.)

PREPARING FOR BREAKDOWN, PART 2: TEACHERS NEED TRAINING

If we expect people in the dean's role to teach in response to breakdowns, the second thing they will need is a clear model for what teaching in that setting should look like, ideally one that draws on our knowledge of effective teaching in the classroom.

We'd want to have a high Ratio during lessons, for example. For those not familiar with that terminology,[7] it means we'd want students to do the lion's share of the cognitive work. "Memory is the residue of thought," the cognitive psychologist Daniel Willingham says. Thinking hard results in learning. Being in the dean's office should mean doing a lot of thinking, reading and writing, just like anywhere else in school where we want to maximize learning.

And at the end of a learning cycle, we'd want to check for understanding—that is, make sure of what the learner learned.

We set out to build a model by taking the video cameras we usually train on teachers and training them on deans instead. We followed them around all day and made note of what they did. We then identified principles for what the teaching parts of the work should look like, one set for Private Deaning and one for Public Deaning.

Private Deaning refers to one-on-one conversations and interactions with students in which we discuss their behavioral choices and their outcomes and attempt to teach them the most productive responses or strongest robust skills.

Public Deaning is the equally important role that deans play of circulating throughout the building and interacting with students and others to reinforce positive values and set strong norms.

PRIVATE DEANING IN SIX STEPS

Here are the principles for successful teaching that we discuss with deans during our training workshops, expressed in six steps.

Private Deaning, Step One: Assess readiness. Any conversation starts with a viable connection. Make sure a student is able to listen and discuss behavioral choices in a mutually respectful and productive manner. Remaining calm and using a slow, quiet voice can help. So can stressing purpose over power, something like "I want to hear what you say happened and I promise I will listen carefully," or "I want to hear what you say happened and I promise I will listen carefully but you will have to listen as well and speak to me in the same calm voice I am using with you." If you don't have those things, don't proceed.

Private Deaning, Step Two: Gather information. Make sure you know the details of what happened from the teacher, from other adults, and other students. Get it calmly and clearly and ask follow-up questions if necessary. "I know you said she was teasing Michaela. Can you just be a bit more specific so I can be specific with her and, if necessary, with her parents? What exactly did she do and say?" Ideally, ask them to write down their version of events so you can refer to it carefully. This will also slow them down and give them a way to process potential frustration.

Private Deaning, Step Three: Teach. Try to build students' knowledge. "We're going to talk about your impulse control in the classroom. I want to first make sure you know what an impulse is and what it means to control your impulses. I might even tell you a bit about a region of the brain called the amygdala."

Writing is a powerful tool for thinking and reflecting. If there's any doubt, have the student write to describe the incident. This will cause them to have to reflect on it, think more deeply, and articulate a response in writing. Ask clarifying questions and potentially ask them to revise what they've written so they get things down in a version of events that you can refer back to later. Ask follow-up questions to try to get very specific answers. "What do you mean by 'she was rude'? When you say she was disrespectful to you, what did she do exactly? How do you know she meant it that way?"

You could also ask them to write in response: "Now I'm going to tell you the story from another perspective. I want you to take notes on what Mrs. Hopkins said because I'm going to ask you to respond."

If there's no debate about what happened, have the student focus on writing and thinking about what they can learn from the situation. If possible, help them identify a replacement behavior and how they might have used it: "David, the science here is pretty clear. If you can slow yourself down by even a second, you increase the chances that you won't do something impulsive. That means if you can simply make yourself take a deep breath when you find yourself getting upset, it can make a big difference."

Check for understanding at the end. Consider an apology or give a consequence to make amends.

Responsibility: **That's an Important Word**

In the video clip *Responsibility,* you can hear a few minutes of an exchange between Student Support Specialist Rosilyn Currie and a student at Believe Memphis Academy. The exchange is based on a lesson in the curriculum we described previously. The student, a fifth grader, had repeatedly failed to do his work and was attempting to distract classmates instead.

Notice that the session starts with a definition of two key terms: *responsibility* and *negligence.* Next Rosilyn asks the student to reflect on those terms in his own life, both in and out of school. They discuss his responsibility for his dog. They share the fact that they are both occasionally negligent about taking out the trash. Notice also how much reading and writing the student does (we trimmed the intervals some when he was writing silently), and how tirelessly and adeptly Rosilyn supports the student in his reading.

Notice her calm demeanor as well. Her purpose is to help her student learn so she wants him focused on thinking, not on intense emotions—his or hers. It's easy to presume that making a student feel bad is part of the learning process after a behavior breakdown, but our purpose, as her work reminds us, is behavior change. She wants her student to understand the importance of responsibility and his responsibilities in school, including working hard.

Speaking of working hard, notice that that's exactly what he is doing. Writing constantly. Reading. Learning new words and applying them. Though we weren't lucky enough to tape it, the session ended with the student writing a reminder to himself about changing his own behavior and apologizing to his teacher, who welcomed him back to class. The school noted the behavior change they'd been seeing from students who had been completing these sorts of lessons. We hope it has something to do with the benefits of having a real curriculum; we're sure it has something to do with the dedicated work of staff members like the one you heard working here.

Private Deaning, Step Four: Build them up. Remind students that while you do not approve of their behavior in this instance, you believe in *them*, and that making mistakes is common as people learn and grow. Talk aspirations to connect the behavior to goals. "I know you said you want to be a fire fighter. I want you to think for a minute why you will be a better fire fighter someday if you are able to control your impulses." One purpose of a consequence is to make amends, so adults should not hold a grudge. You should make it clear to a student that they are back in good stead with you.

Private Deaning, Step Five: Close the loop. Inform the teacher, the parent, and other staff (if appropriate) of what the students worked on. If the incident involved being removed from a classroom, transfer authority back to the teacher by allowing the teacher to accept the student back and facilitating that conversation. "David has worked really hard for almost an hour now at reflecting on his behavior toward his peers and he's written an apology to Whitney. Are you ready to have him return? (Have a conversation ahead of time with the teacher wherein you address any lingering issues so that conversation with the student does not take unexpected turns.)

Private Deaning, Step Six: Follow up. Ask the student how things went at the end of the day. Ask the teacher as well. Make sure the student knows you asked the teacher! Let the family know you followed up and let them know how things went, especially if there was an improvement! This demonstrates that your interest is in the student and their long-term success, as opposed to merely having a narrow interest in resolving a single event. It also helps the student succeed by making it clear that you are looking for and will follow up to see long-term behavior change.

Ensuring a Smooth Transition Back to Class

One commonly overlooked aspect of processing a behavior breakdown is ensuring a smooth and successful transition back to class for the student in question. Sometimes the student will return to class and the conditions of their return make further incidents more likely! Perhaps the teacher is still angry, or is not expecting the student back. Perhaps the student is now lost academically. Perhaps classmates snicker at the student or egg the student on. Perhaps the student takes the moment to do something foolish to earn credibility with peers. These are all things that can undercut an effective intervention in the aftermath.

One of the best moves we think a dean can do is to walk a student back to class and ensure they are settled effectively there. You can watch Jami Dean, former dean of students at Williamsburg Collegiate Charter School in Brooklyn, New York, in the video *Jami Dean: Back to Class.*

Notice that, just before they enter the classroom together, Jami gives her student a reminder of the things he needs to do to be successful: "Walking in, straight to your seat.

Super-professional (a school value), getting started on work." Jami strives to be clear and emotionally constant. She wants him focused not on her feelings but on what will cause him to transition successfully.

As the door opens, Jami follows the student in. Notice that the teacher does not appear surprised at all. Jami's been in touch and she is expecting them.

Her student does as reminded and goes straight to his seat. Notice that Jami is not walking with him at this point. She is giving him a little space and trying to avoid calling too much attention to herself. She begins to glance around the classroom and interact with other students—fans of Props in Chapter 3 will note that she sends one student a bit of "shine" and a big smile just after she enters the room. This is important too. Her presence is positive and supportive. She's not marching in and looking around scowling.

The student sits down and gets to work with the materials his teacher provides. That seamless exchange, from dean to teacher, is important and reflects outstanding teamwork. Again it's facilitated by the fact that Jami's let her colleague know they'd be coming so she can be ready. And of course it shows the teacher trusts Jami and perceives that she's there to support the teacher as well. A smooth transition is a win for everyone!

Now Jami stands near the student but a few steps back. She wants to be able to see him get started successfully and help him if he needs it, but she's trying to respect his privacy. She glances around the room as if she might be there for some other reason. She lingers a few paces away for a moment, making sure he gets started on his work right away. When it's clear he has, she gives him positive reinforcement.

With things off to a good start, Jami now walks away a bit to check in on other students—she's Public Deaning here—encouraging a group of students who are positively engaged, reminding one student to tuck in his shirt. This communicates her trust to the student she's helped transition back to class and provides him with a bit more privacy—creating the feeling that maybe she's just dropping in to check on things. Of course, that sense is much more convincing if she does occasionally walk through.

It's a tiny moment from Jami's day—it takes about two minutes. But imagine how much better the day will go for the student, his teacher, and herself, now that a rocky return has been avoided.

As the video of Jami Dean shows, it's critical that individuals who deal with students after behavior breakdowns not be tied to their desks. The job should be to shape and speak for the culture in the school and to build right and multi-acted relationships with students. It's important not to act like a B-movie villain, whose entry into the room causes everyone to know something bad is about to happen. Deans should celebrate positive culture too. In so doing they make themselves more able to connect with and teach students when they err. We call this part of the work Public Deaning and it too requires clarity around purpose, careful planning, and constant reflection.

Here are the principles:

Be visible: Cycle through classrooms, and every part of the school, constantly interacting with students, showing appreciation for positive engagement, and building connections. This is also an opportunity to teach students how to be productive and positive in class before things go wrong.

Gather data: One of the best reasons to be a constant presence in classrooms is to gather data. You might look for such information as: Which classrooms' culture seems strongest and most vibrant? These classrooms are a great place to bring a struggling teacher. You might stand in the back and observe, perhaps guiding the teacher's eyes: see how crisp and clear the teacher's directions are (no extraneous words). See how the teacher smiles when reminding students of the expectations? That's a great way to remind our kiddos that the rules are there because we care about them. You could also spot the teachers whose classrooms are a bit rocky. Perhaps you could model a few things for them. If you don't feel comfortable with that, you can always learn about which kids seem to struggle to focus, which ones seem hugely engaged in one class but not another, and which seem to look at you as you enter as if they are hoping for a connection with an adult.

Embody values: Everywhere you go, you have the opportunity to speak for the school's values. This can mean looking out for moments when virtues are exemplified and calling them out. "Thank you for helping James wipe down the table after lunch. You're always helping out, Jordan." It means you can make small corrections and find opportunities to teach social skills. "You're really shouting at Josefa right now. I know you're friends; there's no reason you couldn't tell her to pick up her stuff with a bit more warmth in your voice. Like this . . ." You can also model yourself. Even small things, like always saying *please, thank you*, and *good morning*. Small courtesies, as we learned in Chapter 1, are key belonging signals. In fact, you could literally be a walking, talking, belonging signal.

Build relationships: That's critical to all of the principles we've described. But to make it easier, we've got a list of simple actions and **phrases to help students feel seen, valued, safe, and connected:**

- **Nonverbals**
  - Smile, point, wink, send magic.
  - Use high five/fist bumps/warm hand on shoulder.
- **Make Students Feel Known**
  - "What are you reading?"
  - Leave notes or smiley face on desk or seatwork.
  - Follow up to ask about something they did or told you about previously. "How'd that science project turn out?"
  - Shout out students at community meetings or with their teacher. "Ms. Jenkins, you should see Jabari's notes back here!"

- Talk to students at lunch/dismissal, especially about academics.
- Use or even invent names/nicknames.
- **Stress Values and Virtues**
  - "I'm proud of the fact that you . . ."
  - "Thank you for your hard work on. . . ."
  - "Nice job on _____. Keep it up."
  - "That was impressive when . . ."
  - Recognize student work.
  - Positive calls and texts home—with a picture is great!

CLOSING: DEANING FOR CONNECTION AND BELONGING

In this series of images, we see Jamal McCullough, dean of students at North Star Academy Downtown Middle School in Newark, New Jersey, illustrating a point that we've made multiple times—the classroom is the primary place where a culture of connection and belonging is cultivated. As such, schools must organize their personnel and resources to align with this truth.

In his role as dean of students, Jamal is responsible for designing, embodying, and upholding all aspects of his school's culture. Anyone who's held this role or a similar one knows how complex it is, encompassing everything from teaching replacement behaviors, to data collection, communicating with parents and other stakeholders, filing reports, and monitoring schoolwide transitions. Jamal can usually be doing all of those things, but he tries to prioritize time in classrooms above all else because there is no more important space for a school to cultivate a culture of connection and belonging.

On this particular day Jamal is observing classrooms, partly as a matter of habit and partly to follow up with a student who was sent to his office the day before. Each of these images tells a story of connection and belonging.

In the first image, we see Jamal sitting *with* students. He's been listening intently as a student explains how he arrived at an answer. He's very much in role here, pretending to be a sort of senior, most experienced, role model student.

Now the teacher has sent students into a Turn and Talk, and with an odd number of students Jamal has eagerly grabbed the opportunity to be partners with the student in the foreground. Consider the message this student is receiving: The dean sees me and cares about my work. In fact, think about how many students never get to interact with the dean until they've been sent to his or her office. This student gets to spend time with the dean when all is going well, as opposed to when they might have made a poor choice. This matters for establishing a school community where students feel connection and belonging.

Dean McCullough knows. Ellanise knows.

In the second image, Jamal is sitting with a group of students and the teacher has just asked a question. Jamal's hand shoots right up, modeling how to show positive engagement in class in the way one raises one's hand. The teacher playfully acknowledges Jamal in this moment saying, "I see Dean McCullough knows the answer." It's a delightful moment, one full of belonging and connection cues, for both adults and students. The teacher receives signals of support, alliance, and trust. There's a partnership here and Jamal wants her to know he's there to support her, not to check and see if she can manage her classroom. Students can feel this too. The partnership they see between dean and teacher is a mirror for how people work together within the community, and communicates how invested they are in the success of students.

In the final image, we see Jamal crouching down and holding a quiet conversation with a student who was sent to his office the day before. To encourage him, he says, "You're a student and this is where the magic is happening, right in this classroom, alright?" Then he asks, "Do you need anything?". Message: Jamal's goal yesterday was not to give a consequence or "process" him in the dean's office. It was to help him learn. The follow-up visit communicates that this— successful engagement in class—is his purpose.

The cues for connection and belonging in this short exchange are also important. The message the student receives is: there are high expectations here but I'm going to support you in meeting them. There's nothing more important than you being here and I'm here to make sure you receive the education you deserve.

Observing Jamal's work in the classroom affords us an opportunity to close by observing that deans of students are not always a priority in schools. Some don't have them. Some have just one who struggles to leave his or her office. If schools are serious about building purposeful cultures grounded in connection and belonging, they must align resources, especially key personnel to make that a reality. Building connection and belonging means recognizing that schools are first and foremost cultures. If that's true, then they need a person—a team of people—who are its champions, who wake up every day thinking about building and sustaining it to ensure that something real and meaningful and rigorous exists for all students and to make sure that all students get the support they need to connect to it.

Notes

1. The group consisted of Marisa Frank, Xavier Shackelford, Hasan Clayton, Trent Carlson, Kristin Barnhart, Marina Carlucci, and Jasmine Parker. Charlie wishes to thank them deeply and note for the record that "the work and wisdom was all theirs."

2. In one of the last edits of the book, Denarius observed how his preferred language to cue tracking had evolved so that he was using the phrase "Let's put our eyes on . . ." more and more.

3. https://www.uncf.org/wp-content/uploads/reports/Advocacy_ASATTBro_4-18F_Digital.pdf

4. Thank you to the Kern Family Foundation for supporting the development of this curriculum.

5. You can read more about it here: https://teachlikeachampion.com/dean-of-students-curriculum/

6. We hope to add high school and perhaps elementary school as soon as possible.

7. See *Teach Like a Champion 3.0.*

8. Out of respect for the student's privacy, we have shared only audio instead of video and not named the school or the staff member. We are nonetheless grateful to them for sharing and appreciative of their thoughtful work with young people.

Afterword: How We Choose

In May 2022, Tom Kane, an education professor, economist, and director of Harvard's Center for Education Policy Research, wrote in *Atlantic* magazine to describe the findings of a study he'd helped lead. He and his colleagues had studied test results of 2.1 million students from 10,000 schools in 49 states, comparing their yearly pre-pandemic progress to their progress on the same assessments during the pandemic.

The results were consistent with almost every other serious study: the pandemic had been devastating for student learning, and its disparate impact on students already living in poverty was a double injustice. On net, students had lost 13 weeks of learning in low-poverty schools and 22 weeks of learning in high-poverty schools.

But if the conclusions in Kane's study were in keeping with research, one thing that was different was Kane's ability to put those numbers into context, to explain what they meant relative to interventions schools might take to try to fix the problem.

Twenty-two (or 13) weeks of lost learning was just a number until one understood what it took to catch up from that. Given his position, Kane had about as good a sense of that as anyone.

Assigning students to double math classes for an entire school year had yielded gains equivalent to about 10 weeks of in-person instruction, Kane observed. That would still leave you shy of being halfway to closing the gap the pandemic had created in math (based on what was in many cases insufficient progress anyway, we note). And that was the good news. The data on double reading classes was far less encouraging.[1]

High-dosage tutoring is another commonly proposed solution. Generally speaking it's the most aggressive response that's been proposed, but its downside is that it is very expensive and complex to implement.

A year of high-dosage, small-group tutoring, Kane noted, is "one of the few interventions with a demonstrated benefit that comes close" to producing a gain of 22 weeks. It offers a benefit of about 19 weeks of instruction.

This is to say that a trained tutor working with students in groups of one to four at a time, meeting three times a week for a whole year, only partially gets you to the equivalent of 22 weeks of learning.

But, Kane goes on, "The obvious challenge with tutoring is how to offer it to students on an enormous scale." Even the most ambitious plan so far, Tennessee's, would serve just one out of 12 students in the state in targeted grades. It would require hiring and training thousands of qualified tutors. It's an impressive and ambitious proposal, but at that scale it's logistically daunting. We want to be clear, *we are not arguing against high-dosage tutoring.* Our point is that the complexity of the endeavor, and the fact that even if everything went well it would still probably leave us short of closing the full gap, puts the size of the problem in context. As Kane noted, "Very few remedial interventions have ever been shown to produce benefits equivalent to 22 weeks of additional in-person instruction." He concluded, "Given the magnitude and breadth of the losses, educators should not see tutoring as the sole answer to the problem."

There isn't a single intervention we know of that's robust enough.

We're going to need a bunch of them.

And, as we have tried to point out in this book, among the most productive interventions is much greater effectiveness in the classrooms we're already running. Better teaching with better curriculum in every classroom plus tutoring plus other potential interventions might just work.

But of course "better teaching and better curriculum" is a simple phrase that quickly runs up against reality. It requires a hundred good decisions and well-executed initiatives: better professional development, more flexibility in hiring decisions, and so on, all done quickly and done best in schools that often struggle most to hire and implement effectively.

As a society we've been working on that for a while with marginal results so it's ambitious to think we could make dramatically better progress unless we removed every possible barrier. That applies to every solution we discuss in this book and every solution we don't discuss but which you are perhaps thinking of. Every minute we spend highly focused on better implementation of the core work of schooling helps, and every minute we spend distracted hurts.

Which brings us to the story of a colleague, the principal of a suburban elementary school. She was recently struck by how much bus behavior needed fixing. It wasn't just that otherwise delightful students were often mean or hurtful on the buses that setting or that older students spoke in language (or about topics) that was just not okay for six- and seven-year-olds to hear. The issue in the end was also academic. The time she spent mopping up from bus behavior was time she could be spending on curriculum and instruction, on developing her young teachers. "I just kept thinking, 'I am not doing what's most important because I am spending time every morning on mundane bus-related things.' I will never tolerate bullying, so I knew I couldn't just ignore the buses, but I was pretty sure I could fix them in a way that let me spend my time more productively."

Her first step was assigning seats. She announced the change to parents and the response was…outrage. Or perhaps better put, acquiescence from the great majority of parents and extremely vocal dissent from a small group of outliers. But that was enough. "My whole afternoon was taken up with phone calls with them. First it was about the fact that I had no right to tell their child where to sit on the bus. I was overstepping my authority. Then they wanted me to tell their children they didn't have to follow the rules I'd made for everybody else. Then they announced they were going to tell their children not to obey the rules despite me. The most difficult of them (they were lawyers) threatened to sue me and the district and so then I had to call my superintendent. There were a series of meetings with our lawyers about what I could and could not say to the parents."

She ended up spending the time she was hoping to spend improving teaching and learning on the phone with her least aligned parents. She didn't get much time back to do what she thought was most important for the overwhelming majority of families. She rapidly came to realize that wrestling with unaligned parents could be immensely time consuming.

On net she wondered whether she had gained anything at all. The capacity of the few to take her time away from the needs of the many was no small thing. A generation ago, maybe fewer parents would have presumed to make such a big issue out of the buses. Those who did would have been more likely to call, register their disagreement, and then accept the principal's decision if it went against them. "Part of being in school is accepting the rules," they might have told their kids. Nowadays almost everything is an issue for somebody, and in the echo chamber of social media it is easy for people to whip themselves and a small group of peers into a state of high dudgeon. People trust their schools to decide appropriately far less and—reflecting the rise of individualism—feel less obliged to accept what is in the group's interest if they don't agree. That's tricky calculus for running schools.

We want to be clear, lest our comments be read as a criticism of one side or the other of the political spectrum. We're not referring to any specific group or ideology. Frankly, it's a broader change. *All parts* of the political spectrum are more likely to dissent more vocally at more cost to schools, and so are a lot of other people who aren't especially political but who have issues of overwhelming importance to them and who don't think they should have to compromise on them. And of course we're not immune either. If you scratched the surface with the four of us, we'd each have our own (probably different) issues that we'd be willing to call the principal over.

In other words, we are describing a larger societal trend that we have not yet addressed as a sector. Disagreement in and about schools is expensive, far more frequent, and far more pronounced. It is increasingly unlikely to be resolved quickly. It distracts schools from focusing on the core work—reading, science, math, music—which is already plenty hard. And the bottom line is this: time spent arguing is time not spent on other tasks. A bit consensus building is fine—a good thing—but too much of it makes schools far less effective for everybody.

Again, please don't misunderstand us. Schools are democratic institutions. They must listen and respond to the citizens and the society they serve. The process of listening can often make them better and more responsive. It's a question of degree in a fractious society—in all likelihood one that is not temporarily fractious but will likely remain that way as social media polarizes and emboldens us. How much dissent is worth having, and what do we do when there's so much of it that it becomes even more difficult to accomplish the institution's social purpose?

There are a lot of circles to square in running a school, and for some of them the price of squaring can be prohibitive. The era of social media and the culture of outrage it fosters have created a new layer of collective action problems for schools to deal with at exactly the time they need to be thinking about things like reading, science, orderly and productive learning environments, and inclusive cultures of belonging.

For this reason we think expanded school choice deserves to be part of the conversation.

The importance of allowing parents to choose schools based on their quality is something the four of us all believe in. Though we work with schools in every sector—district, charter, private, public, rural, urban, and suburban, in the US and in other countries—and though our goal is to help every teacher succeed and every student thrive, no matter the school, many readers will know that we all have worked in the charter school sector, where choice is implicit.[2]

We have done that because we believe that every American family deserves access not just to good schools but to great ones: safe and happy and radically better academically.[3]

But we have come to see the potential benefits to the idea that parents (and teachers) should also be able to choose schools based on *beliefs*. We hadn't seen that as clearly before. Of course we can't have choice on every single issue but there are big ones to be made where we simply aren't all going to agree. Or where the benefits of letting us agree to disagree (in reasonable ways) can let us focus on *doing* rather than *arguing*.

Would it help us to get to more important decisions if, say, each school shared its core instructional principles and its core principles for school culture and values, and then parents and teachers chose?

School A might say: We stress gratitude, consideration, and civility in a high-text, low-tech atmosphere.

School B might say: We stress student autonomy and prefer limited rules so that students make their own decisions about their behavior and their use of technology.

It's no secret which school we would choose, but we know other parents would choose differently. We respect that. It's their children they are deciding for. And if lack of choice hurts everyone because more time spent negotiating and stake building and less time spent implementing means overall school quality is lower, then greater choice potentially provides parents, teachers, schools, and just maybe society, with broader benefits.

First, parents would be more likely to get a school more aligned with what they wanted. A bit of the social contract we agree to has been made more explicit. An agreement on purpose and methods at the highest level mean a big step forward in fixing the "trust in institutions" issue. It will still have to build consensus—we can't have a school for every micro issue; people will still disagree and compromise—but we've reduced the proportion of time all schools spend convincing stakeholders that their chosen direction is valid.

When a school's leadership has made a promise, it's public and transparent. When the least aligned parent calls and says, "You have no right to take away my child's phone," the answer is simple—or at least simpler. "I understand your concerns. But we have tried to be clear that we offer a screen-reduced learning environment. We perceive this to be in keeping with what we have promised other parents in the school and so this has to be our decision."

It is easier to defend decisions when you can refer back to an agreement it serves. It's also easier for families to hold the school accountable for doing what it has promised. They can cite the promise too. "You said you were about student autonomy; why are there all these mandates?" If it comes down to it, they can vote with their feet.

This is also true for staff. One of the biggest benefits of school choice is that it allows—and just maybe requires—teachers to choose.

Imagine our colleague striving to bring order to the buses. Let's say she no longer has to argue with her least aligned parents. They've either chosen to send their children to a school that reflects their vision or they understand that her decision is in keeping with what the school has committed to and have accepted it. Now at last, with time to focus on improving teaching and learning, she chooses to make the school writing-intensive.

In each class, every day, she believes, students should put pencil to paper and write at least one well-crafted sentence to explain a core idea from the lesson. She announces this to the staff, but not everyone likes it. Mr. J thinks this writing-across-the-curriculum business is another fad. He's been teaching math for 20 years and doesn't like fads. In the professional development sessions, he folds his arms and is barely engaged. He creatively non-complies with efforts to get him to use writing in his classroom. "Oh, yeah, I'm doing my own version of that," he says. He knows he can wait it out.

As he says this, he winks at his colleague, Ms. K, who's in her second year as a teacher and wasn't sure of what to make of the writing idea at first. Mr. J will explain after faculty meeting that most of the stuff they tell you in professional development is a waste of time, that she doesn't really need to do it. Suddenly the school is struggling to implement even this simple idea with fidelity and consistency.

Everyone is losing in this scenario.

Imagine if, when Mr. J applied, the school had said, "There are three foundational things we believe in and one of them is writing. Please only take this job if you agree." In that case Mr. J would have seen his disagreement with the school coming and could teach somewhere where he'd be left alone to do what he loves.

Who, in the end, wants to spend their time working for an organization they are at odds with, folding their arms in meetings and passively resisting initiatives? That does not sound like a recipe for connection and belonging among teachers. As discussed in Chapter 1, feeling a clear sense of mission, Martin Seligman found, is critical to happiness.

Much better to know at the outset. Yes, much easier and fairer for the school to hold Mr. J accountable, but also perhaps far less necessary. With a room full of teachers who are down for writing, the norms in the staff room—as important as those in the classroom—will be all about action, about shared purpose.

When we don't allow (and encourage) teachers to make informed choice on principles, we risk getting a culture of crossed arms and waited-out initiatives. We get schools that soon enough realize that under those conditions they can't really implement any idea with fidelity. They will always be pushing a rock up a slope. And so in many cases they stop trying.

The result is a great many schools that are a muddy mix of poorly implemented ideas. And one cost of *that* is that we never learn much.

If two educators disagreed about whether schools should be writing-intensive, they could wage a running ideological battle. They could write and argue and post on Twitter about who was right and who was wrong. They could wage that battle for years. In fact they have, on a thousand topics, and now years later we still don't know much more about either idea, and under what conditions they are likely to work.

But if one could run a writing-intensive school and the other could run a not-so-writing-intensive school that focuses on something else, and a hundred other people did the same, in five years we'd have a pretty good idea of who was right in what circumstances and what caused that success. We'd learn a lot.

When organizations don't explicitly choose, in other words, it is hard to implement and then test and learn from ideas. This detracts from the larger endeavor of learning.

Let's choose instead, we say, and both implement with fidelity and intention and see what it teaches us. If it turns out you were right and we were wrong, so be it—all the better, in fact. If it turns out we're both right for certain kids under certain conditions, also great. Now we're smarter.

Any outcome that makes us smarter about how to serve our young people, especially in a time of need, is better than fighting, which is what we spend a lot of time doing in education. That, often, is a waste of time for everybody. And right now, we have no time to waste.

Notes

1. This is probably because reading is so complex and most schools, in our estimation, continue to teach it in a way that does not align to what science tells us about the critical role of systematic, synthetic phonics among younger students and background knowledge, fluency, vocabulary instruction, and writing among older students. But that is a story for another day.

2. We note that we have also worked in other sectors of education and Darryl, for one, was a senior administrator in one of the country's largest school districts. We do not think of ourselves as "charter people." We think of ourselves as "more great schools for kids people."

3. We think it's unjust to require a parent to send their child to a school that is not safe and does not prepare them to succeed academically, and we don't know a single person who would accept that for their own child. And we note that everyone who can choose does choose. The residential real estate market is the most common way parents choose schools—they move to areas with better schools—but private schools and magnet schools are other examples.

Index